"Hunter and Robinson offer an itera.... .. how black life—as song and tune, as fight and struggle—is necessarily geographic life. Here, threads of black geographies emerge across and underneath prevailing cartographies—within the United States while also reaching out to touch other global diasporic sites—to show that the black imagination is tied to place-making practices. Powerfully, the authors write black geographies and chocolate cities as 'living geographies'—sites shaped by brutal and unforgiving racial economies that engender creative praxis and freedom struggle."

—Katherine McKittrick, author of *Demonic Grounds: Black Women and the Cartographies of Struggle*

"Rarely does a book disrupt existing paradigms and displace dominant narratives. This is exactly what Hunter and Robinson achieve in *Chocolate Cities*. This book changes the ways we understand Black and White Americans in profound ways, especially how they experience and define themselves according to geographic regions throughout the United States. This book creatively weaves together data from rich and untapped sources to tell a unique American story. A must-read for all who wish to rethink current racial dynamics in America and unravel them in fresh new ways."

—Aldon Morris, author of *The Scholar Denied: W. E. B. Du Bois and the Birth of Modern Sociology*

"A significant, timely, and provocative race-based social mapping of the United States, reflecting a sense of the everyday lives of African Americans. These masterful sketches, rooted in oral history and illuminated by poetry, music, fiction, and film, make it an extraordinary book that needs to be read and considered far beyond the academy."

—Elijah Anderson, Yale University, author of *The Cosmopolitan Canopy* and "The White Space"

THE GEORGE GUND FOUNDATION
IMPRINT IN AFRICAN AMERICAN STUDIES

The George Gund Foundation has endowed
this imprint to advance understanding of
the history, culture, and current issues
of African Americans.

The publisher and the University of California Press Foundation gratefully acknowledge the generous support of the George Gund Foundation Imprint in African American Studies.

Chocolate Cities

A NAOMI SCHNEIDER BOOK

Highlighting the lives and experiences of marginalized communities, the select titles of this imprint draw from sociology, anthropology, law, and history, as well as from the traditions of journalism and advocacy, to reassess mainstream history and promote unconventional thinking about contemporary social and political issues. Their authors share the passion, commitment, and creativity of Executive Editor Naomi Schneider.

Chocolate Cities

THE BLACK MAP OF AMERICAN LIFE

Marcus Anthony Hunter
and Zandria F. Robinson

UNIVERSITY OF CALIFORNIA PRESS

University of California Press, one of the most distinguished university presses in the United States, enriches lives around the world by advancing scholarship in the humanities, social sciences, and natural sciences. Its activities are supported by the UC Press Foundation and by philanthropic contributions from individuals and institutions. For more information, visit www.ucpress.edu.

University of California Press
Oakland, California

Library of Congress Cataloging-in-Publication Data

Names: Hunter, Marcus Anthony, author. | Robinson, Zandria F., author.
Title: Chocolate cities : the black map of American life / Marcus Anthony Hunter and Zandria F. Robinson.
Description: Oakland, California : University of California Press, [2018] | Includes bibliographical references and index.
Identifiers: LCCN 2017028630 (print) | LCCN 2017033913 (ebook) | ISBN 978-0-520-96617-8 (ebook) | ISBN 978-0-520-29282-6 (cloth : alk. paper) | ISBN 978-0-520-29283-3 (pbk. : alk. paper)
Subjects: LCSH: African Americans—History.
Classification: LCC E185 (ebook) | LCC E185 .H86 2018 (print) | DDC 973/.0496073—dc23
LC record available at http://lccn.loc.gov/2017028630

Manufactured in the United States of America

26 25 24 23 22 21 20 19 18
10 9 8 7 6 5 4 3

For Black people here, there, and everywhere

Contents

Preface

"We didn't get our forty acres and a mule, but we got you C[hocolate] C[ity],"
George Clinton declares victoriously on the title track of Parliament
Funkadelic's 1975 *Chocolate City* album. Rather than wait for unfulfilled
political promises, Black Americans were occupying urban and previously
White space in massive numbers, their movement and increasing political
power embodied on the track by multiple yet complementary melodies. Bass
and piano take turns keeping the beat and beginning new melodies, saxo-
phones speak, a synthesizer marks a new era, and a steady high hat ensures
the funk stays in rhythm. The Parliament, its own kind of funky democratic
government, chants "gainin' on ya!" as Clinton announces the cities that
Black Americans have turned or will soon turn into "CC's": Newark, Gary,
Los Angeles, Atlanta, and New York. Parliament's "Mothership Connection"
public-service announcement is broadcast live from the capitol, in the capital of chocolate cities, Washington, DC, where "they still call it the White
House, but that's a temporary condition."

Spurred on by postwar suburbanization, by 1975 the chocolate city and
its concomitant "vanilla suburbs" were a familiar racialized organization
of space and place. The triumphant takeover tenor of *Chocolate City* may
seem paradoxical in retrospect, as Black people inherited neglected space,

were systematically denied resources afforded to Whites, and were entering an era of mass incarceration. Still, for Parliament, like for many other Black Americans, chocolate cities were a form of reparations and were and had been an opportunity to make something out of nothing. For generations these chocolate cities—Black neighborhoods, places on the other side of the tracks, the bottoms—had been the primary locations of the freedom struggle, the sights and sounds of Black art and Black oppression, and the container for the combined ingredients of pain, play, pleasure, and protest that comprise the Black experience.

Four decades after *Chocolate City*, including eight years of the first African American president, what is the status of Clinton's Afrofuturist vision of the chocolate city? Did Barack Obama turn the White House Black? Which cities became chocolate cities?[1] How have the connections between cities expanded and shifted? And what does it mean when the CC capital is no longer, in fact, a CC? How have Black Americans mobilized space, place, geography, and movement to resist and repair the conditions in which they find themselves?

Inspired by a collection of Black intellectuals, adventurers, explorers, culture producers, and everyday folk, the goal of this book is to expand and extend the idea of the chocolate city, tracing it from its antebellum origins to the Black Lives Matter era. We use and pluralize the funk-inflected sociopolitical concept, henceforth *chocolate cities*, to disrupt and replace existing language often used to describe and analyze Black American life. Though always present in Black artistic and intellectual endeavors, the idea of chocolate cities and this book are uniquely linked to the story of how we came to meet, know, understand, and care for one another.

The road to *Chocolate Cities* began more than ten years ago, thirty years after the Parliament Funkadelic manifesto, with two Black twenty-somethings heading to Chicago in search of ourselves. Although our earliest conversations revealed a fictive kinship of the highest order, it was in our graduate school classes that our imaginations began their dynamic collision. It was truly a straight-outta–South Memphis meets straight-outta–South Philly synergy.

We debated regions and music, celebrated our mutual feelings that our respective cities, Memphis and Philly, were always overlooked in favor of their first cousins, Atlanta and New York City. We compared the bass lines from Memphis Stax records like Isaac Hayes's *Shaft* and Philadelphia International's O'Jays *For the Love of Money*. We agreed that Black musicians were some of the greatest philosophers and sociologists: rapping, singing, playing, and chanting truths and insights about Black America on wax. Place mattered for these artists. We could hear it in Bessie Smith's and Anita Baker's vibrato, John Coltrane's and Sarah Vaughan's jazz riffs, Lil' Kim's "Lighters Up" and Queen Ifrica's "I Can't Breathe" anthems, Lauryn Hill's *Miseducation* and Outkast's *Aquemini*. We saw it in Erykah Badu's headwrap–turned-locks-turned-Chaka Khan–inspired Afrofuturism. Philly was the Memphis of the North and Memphis the Philly of the South. Or maybe it was all just the South—up, down, left, or right. As George Clinton predicted, our respective motherships, our hometowns, were indeed connected.

While we didn't immediately begin writing this book at the moment of revelation, early seeds of *Chocolate Cities* would make their way into both of our first books: *This Ain't Chicago* and *Black Citymakers*. Both books took aim at the intellectual, political, and scientific blindspots in our chosen vocation and discipline, sociology. *This Ain't Chicago*, through narrative, culture, and some savvy Black southerners, illustrated that not only had scholars and tastemakers purposefully and willfully ignored the South, especially the urban South, but that this tendency had also caused great gaps in our understanding of the intersections of race, place, space, and region. The Black South Matters.

At the same time, *Black Citymakers* sought to recenter the people, city, and author of the first major work of American sociology—Black urban residents, Philadelphia, W. E. B. Du Bois and *The Philadelphia Negro*, respectively. By ignoring and forgetting this 1899 classic, social science was advancing the pervasive and dangerous idea that Black citizens, especially in urban America, are only and always already reactive. Black residents were rarely ever leading actors in city making but instead its hapless, helpless victims. *Black Citymakers* offers an alternative reading of Black people as agents of place making, a guiding viewpoint reflected in *Chocolate Cities*.

Read together, both books provide a comprehensive way to understand and do asset-based social science on Black communities. We began to call this takeaway and connection across our work *chocolate city sociology*. We thought of ourselves as chocolate city sociologists, as young theorists in a long tradition of Black and brown scholars using Black lifeworlds to answer the riddle of the Sphinx and solve our most pressing problems.

This book, though, is based on more than hunches and two-way conversations. We traveled the country, going hither and thither, places large and small, rural and urban and suburban, in search of deeper insights. Despite our respective penchant for the importance of place, rather than enumerating distinctions across chocolate cities, we began to see, hear, feel, and capture the continuities and connections—pleasant and unpleasant, purposeful and inadvertent—across Black places.[2]

Without direct collaboration, Black people were doing and experiencing a lot of the same everywhere—block parties, unemployment, pan-African festivals, family reunions, Black faces in high places, shootouts and fistfights, resistance organizing, police brutality. Black folk were getting disappeared by systems, peoples, and policies. The waters of Hurricane Katrina baptized a new generation of involuntary Black migrants across the domestic diaspora.[3] Barack Obama's ascendancy reflected both the fulfillment and unfinished business of the civil rights movement.

Then Trayvon Martin was killed, and Emmett Till's face looked back at us. The chocolate city as one place, or "Black is a Country," came into sharp relief.[4] The Movement for Black Lives mobilized, galvanized, and connected communities on the ground as well as in the digital sphere. Baltimore was on fire, and Black folk in Flint couldn't drink or wash with the city's water. Whether shot in the back or gunned downed in their church pews, Black South Carolinians loomed large as memories of the "Old South" raged back. Sandra Bland and Sakia Gunn lost their lives, extinguished by the violence of anti-Black misogyny, patriarchy, and an emboldened police state. Black Americans were crying together, shouting, protesting, and disagreeing with these people and events across America's chocolate cities.

Chocolate Cities is our effort to draw out these connections and make them plain. Drawing on the Black intellectual tradition of situating geography as paramount to Black futures—pioneered by Marcus Garvey, Amiri Baraka, Huey Newton, Katherine McKittrick, and Clyde Woods—we provide a different way of seeing Blackness, Black places, geography, and the past, present, and future. This is a book about the enduring and overlapping connection that is Blackness and Black people here, there, and globally everywhere.

Our way, the chocolate cities approach, follows Black feminist Barbara Christian's insight that the wisdom of everyday Black folk is knowledge, scientific, and underutilized.[5] We know that intersectionality matters.[6] The matrix of domination is wherever the oppressed and marginalized are gathered.[7] Linked fate is not just a political perception and attitude; it is also manifested in place—chocolate cities to be exact.[8]

Chocolate cities are a perceptual, political, and geographic tool and shorthand to analyze, understand, and convey insights born from predominantly Black neighborhoods, communities, zones, towns, cities, districts, and wards; they capture the sites and sounds Black people make when they occupy place and form communities. Chocolate cities are also a metaphor for the relationships among history, politics, culture, inequality, knowledge, and Blackness.

Importantly, chocolate cities also function as an interpretative template, providing new glasses for those unable to see or blinded by the lenses of "ghetto," "slum," "hood," and "concrete jungle." We came to fix the prescription and adjust sight lines. *Chocolate Cities* is a sorely needed assets-based approach to capturing and examining the linked destinies of Black communities and the consequences of enduring patterns of disadvantage and inequality while surviving and thriving as Black in the United States since Emancipation.

1 Everywhere below Canada

Oppressive language does more than represent violence;
it is violence; does more than represent the limits
of knowledge; it limits knowledge.

Toni Morrison, Nobel Prize Lecture, 1993

A clamoring audience hustled and squeezed their way into the seats of
Detroit's King Solomon Baptist Church to "hear a speaker of and on civil
rights." More than two thousand people were in attendance on April 12,
1964, awaiting Malcolm X's "The Ballot or the Bullet" speech.[1] As he
approached the microphone, Malcolm X fixed his black tie and black-
rimmed glasses, the pleats of his cream suit swaying subtly as he began:
"Mr. Moderator, Reverend [Albert] Cleage, brothers and sisters and
friends, and I see some enemies." This easy latter recognition was met with
applause and laughter from the audience. He continued, acknowledging
directly what had become a familiar reality for Black activist communities: "In fact, I think we'd be fooling ourselves if we had an audience this
large and didn't realize that there were some enemies present."

From Detroit to Jackson, Mississippi, chocolate cities across the country were emerging as battle sites in the Black Freedom struggle.[2] A post-
pilgrimage Malcolm X, now renamed el-Hajj Malik el-Shabazz, spent
1964 traveling across Black America, articulating a diasporic Black political platform—one that linked America's urban grassroots civil rights
uprisings to struggles for independence from colonial rule across the global South and on the continent of Africa.[3] New civil rights legislation and

a critical election were on the horizon. As the concentration of African Americans living in cities increased, the future and fate of Black politics was becoming more linked to that of chocolate cities.

The prodigal son of Michigan race relations, Malcolm X had returned home to talk about the changes that had not come to pass. The audience that April afternoon was painfully aware of the absence of change. Frustrated that the Emancipation had come and gone and that the Great Migration had been in many ways a fool's errand, Black Detroit was living proof that escape from racism was a false promise of the so-called North. This was an audience on fire. This was an audience looking to hear and see racial diplomacy melded with the plain-talking truth telling that had distinguished Malcolm X from his peers and colleagues in the Black Freedom struggle.[4]

"If you black, you were born in jail, in the North as well as the South. Stop talking about the South," Malcolm X implored his audience. "As long as you South of the Canadian border, you South." Laughter and loud affirmations followed. He had declared an uncomfortable truth about Black life in the nation's Great Migration destinations. "The South" was everywhere that Black people called home—at least in the United States. "So we're trapped, trapped, double-trapped, triple-trapped. Any way we go, we find that we're trapped. And every kind of solution that someone comes up with is just another trap," Malcolm X said, peering out into the packed audience, his words echoing as they bounced from the church's stained glass to the ears of Black Detroit.[5]

Malcolm X's portrait of The South—an idea as much as it is a geographic location—runs contrary to dominant geographies of Black life. The accepted map of Black life in the United States is one drawn most prominently by the lines of the Great Migration, extending from the Mississippi Delta, the Georgia Piedmont, and the plains of Texas to the Midwest, Northeast, and West Coast. It imagines Black people moving en masse from the rural South directly to the urban Midwest, and East and West Coasts, remaking the landscape around them but moreover being remade by the bright lights of big city living. It is a modern narrative of progress, one in which "progress" is defined almost uniformly by increased urbanization. The Mason-Dixon Line, then, is a mythical and actual barrier between freedom and enslavement, North and South, progressive race relations and Old South mores.

Surely, the map of American life is also created by the aspirations and dreams—some realized, others not—of Black migrants. Not all Black migrants' journeys were as successful or promising as they had hoped, and migration hadn't always made Black Americans' dreams realities. As Gladys Knight and the Pips remind us in the classic "Midnight Train to Georgia," Los Angeles had "proved too much for" one migrant.[6] "He couldn't make it," and he had opted to return to Georgia. Still, Black Americans exercised their right to get on down, moving especially from rural to urban neighborhoods. As historians of the Great Migration Isabel Wilkerson and Nicolas Lehman have shown, the idea, stories, and lived injustices of the South loomed large in Black American experience and memory, motivating a popular push out of the region.[7]

Early twentieth-century advertisements and articles frequently called for Black folks to go west and north, to finally escape to the "Promised Land" and grab a bit of the freedom they were owed. Stories of successful migration north and gainful employment opportunities were commonly splattered across the front pages of Black publications such as the *Chicago Defender,* the *Baltimore Afro-American,* and the *Philadelphia Tribune.* Thus, a dominant geographic logic of equality, rooted in notions of the North as a promised land during slavery, emerged: when Black folks move from the tainted part of the map—the South—to somewhere above the Mason-Dixon Line, their lives change decidedly for the better. This is a flawed logic, one indicative of the manufactured distinctions between "The North" and "The South" in the United States.[8]

Chocolate Cities is built on a simple premise: *our current maps of Black life are wrong.* Instead of the neat if jarring linear progress of movement from the rural South to the urban North, we suggest that the history of Black life in modernity is a boomerang rather than a straight line of progress. Certainly, the deferred dreams of the Great Migration, including expanding poverty, hyperincarceration, extrajudicial and police violence, and diminishing opportunities urban Black Americans found within and outside of the geographic South, are undeniable evidence. As Malcolm X made clear in Detroit over half a century ago, the geography of the Black American experience is best understood as existing within and across varying versions of "The South"—regional areas with distinct yet overlapping and similar patterns of racism, White domination, and oppression alongside place-inspired Black strivings, customs, and aspirations for a better and more equal society.

This book is based on two social facts about Black American life. One, Black American social life is best understood as occurring wholly in "The South"—one large territory, governed by a historically rooted and politically inscribed set of practices of racial domination, with a series of subregions; one large geography that has the characteristics popularly ascribed to the Jim Crow South: racism,[9] residential segregation,[10] disparate incarceration rates,[11] poverty,[12] and violence.[13] Here the work of a range of scholars across a series of disciplines—such as Derrick Bell, Elijah Anderson, Joe Feagin, Michelle Alexander, Khalil Gibran Muhammad, Eric Foner, Darlene Clark Hine, Thomas Sugrue, and Jonathan Holloway—and their focus on the intersection of the South, history, race, and inequality are especially fruitful.[14]

Two, Black migrants brought and bring "The South"—Black regional customs, worldviews, and cultures—with them to their new homes in destinations across urban America. Taking cues from scholars such as Daphne Brooks, Aldon Morris, Manning Marable, Robin D.G. Kelley, Walter Rodney, Hortense Spillers, Gaye Johnson, and Mark Anthony Neal, we explore how Black southern cultural forms travel across the United States.[15] "The migration brought to the city," we learn in Alan Spear's *Black Chicago* (1967), for example, "thousands of Negroes accustomed to the informal, demonstrative, preacher-oriented churches of the rural South."[16] Black southern migrants sought to relieve themselves of the culture of White domination in the South, but they were invested in retaining customs and cultural traditions they had come to value.[17]

"The South" is not just shorthand for systematic inequality and racism but also a frame for understanding and analyzing the striking similarities across Black communities and neighborhoods. Black neighborhoods, meccas, towns, communities, and urban enclaves, or chocolate cities, across the United States, highlight new ways to map and analyze geography, inequality, and the Black American experience. Chocolate cities are windows into Black migration, urbanization, rural and suburban life, and racial inequality. Informed by a variety of sources, experiences, and data, we call this new geography and framework the *chocolate maps*—a per-

Map 1. The Black map, a race-conscious rendering of the United States.

spective that more accurately reflects the lived experiences and the future of Black life in America, and thus of the nation.[18]

Chocolate maps center the movement, politics, histories, and perspectives of Black Americans as consequential to patterns of change, inequality, and development throughout the twentieth century. We make use of national and regional health, educational, and economic data. Our resources also include decennial census data, Black arts and social sciences (e.g., music, literature, research, and visual arts) scholarship, news media, ethnography, and narratives and oral histories from Black Americans across the United States. Based also on the cultural and cognitive maps we collected, these Black geographies, as shown in maps 1–3, reflect the varying though consistent redefinition of America based on the perspectives of Black Americans.

Of all the configurations we discovered, time and again a regional restructuring of the United States like that reflected in map 1 was recurrent. Centered throughout the book here, this Black map of the United States is composed of six regions: Up South, Down South, Deep South, Mid South, Out South, and West South.[19] As the map demonstrates, these regions replace traditional designations of North, South, Midwest,

Map 2. Black map alternate 1.

Northwest, and West as indicated in existing maps of and census data for the United States. Chocolate cities have been crucial sites through which Black Americans have shaped and been shaped by the United States— from the Seattle that begot Jimi Hendrix, to the Dallas that shaped Erykah Badu, to the Detroit that welcomed Malcolm X in April 1964, to the Birmingham from which Martin Luther King Jr. penned his most famous call to action.

X MARKS THE SPOT

By February 1965 Malcolm X was back in Harlem, expanding his newly developed Black Nationalist platform. Standing before several hundred people at the Audubon Ballroom just north of Harlem in Washington Heights, X was in the midst of a protracted and increasingly bitter departure and break away from the Nation of Islam. Having spent much of 1964 traveling from chocolate city to chocolate city with his "The Ballot or the

Bullet" speech in tow, X's return to Harlem was its own sort of homecoming. Though he had lived in many places throughout his life, including Detroit and Boston, Harlem had become his chosen home.

Steeped in a rich Black history of its own, Harlem was its own kind of South, even as it lay in upper Manhattan. It was also a diasporic Black South, a multiethnic space with migrants from the Caribbean shaping the space in concert with migrants from the U.S. South, as well as with other racial and ethnic groups. On the same streets that had provided the fertile terrain on which Duke Ellington, Countee Cullen, and Madame C.J. Walker illustrated the power and beauty of Black life, Malcolm X had found refuge. Such refuge, however, had become fleeting by late 1964, as the animus surrounding his departure from the Nation of Islam increased to the point where X had become especially reliant on his own measures of self-protection, most prominently manifested in a photo published by *Ebony* magazine in September 1964. In the photograph we see Malcolm X, dressed in a suit, dark tie, and white dress shirt, peeking through the curtains with a rifle in his left hand, concerned that those who had been sending him death threats were watching and waiting for an opportunity to kill him.

Not one to shrink under the pressure of fear of death, Malcolm X continued on with his work and ensured that he had a staff that could provide added protection to him and his family. On February 19, 1965, things came to a head in the Audubon Ballroom less than a mile from his Harlem headquarters. Just as he was beginning his address, he was interrupted. "Nigger! Get your hand out of my pocket!" a man's voice yelled from within the audience. Distracted and caught off guard by the sudden outburst, Malcolm X looked closely into the audience as his team sought to protect their leader. As suddenly as the outburst had occurred, men with guns were unloading more than twenty bullets into X's body. Pronounced dead later that afternoon, Malcolm X was mourned the world over, but especially in his chosen chocolate city of Harlem. More than twenty-five thousand mourners wept and shared parting words at a public viewing lasting from February 23 to 26 at Harlem's Unity Funeral Home.[20]

Dapper Dan, the Harlem-bred influential tastemaker and stylist, was among the millions of Black people for whom the loss of Malcolm X was deeply felt. Reflecting on X's prominent role in organizing Black resistance

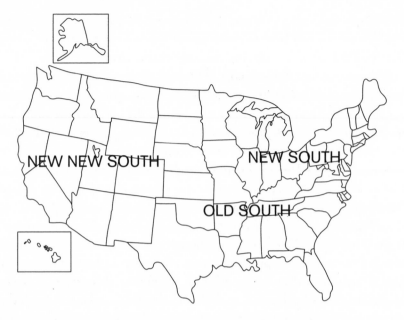

Map 3. Black map alternate 2.

after "a policeman got killed in the Mosque on 160th Street" in the 1960s, Dapper Dan recalled it as "the most powerful time in [his] life." By 1968 Dapper Dan was on the cover of the newspaper *40 Acres and a Mule,* standing in front of the spot where New York State had decided to build an office complex in Harlem holding a replica of the Trojan horse. "You know what happened in Troy? They built a Trojan horse, and the soldiers snuck in and took over," his comments forecasting the attempt by the state to surveil and change Harlem's racial makeup. "That state building was the first major state building that they put there as a part of the gentrification program."[21]

Then, as now, the bond between Harlem and Blackness and Malcolm X still resonates. Currently, Harlem is a chocolate city undergoing its own melting of sorts due to the massive dispossession triggered by gentrification and White migration to urban America. Even still, interviews with a range of Harlemites reveal the enduring importance of this Black city within a city and some of the key dynamics of and within chocolate cities. As Jai Hudson, a Black woman author and fashion stylist raised in Harlem during the 1980s, proclaimed, "Harlem is culture. Harlem is music.

Harlem is Black excellence. Harlem is style. Harlem is rich. . . . Harlem is the heartbeat of N[ew] Y[ork]. The heartbeat!"[22]

Echoing Hudson, prolific music producer and Harlem-raised entertainment-maestro Sean Combs (aka "Puffy" and "Diddy") was unapologetic about his pride in the chocolate city that reared him: "Harlem influenced America in the arts; it was the home of music, soul, and fashion. . . . It is the Black Mecca. To be able to have one place touch fashion, music is a tremendous amount of power. . . . You have Black people from everywhere. . . . Harlem was the first big African American borough. You had actors, doctors, lawyers, and literary cats. . . . It was the Mecca of Black culture and still is!" Combs suggested that "the presence of Malcolm X, the Cotton Club, the Renaissance period, the Apollo performances, [and] rooftop parties" were not only features of the real and symbolic importance of the chocolate city of Harlem but also a living example of how the neighborhood demonstrated that Black people had long been place makers and city makers whose efforts changed and influence the world. When asked what Harlem meant to him, Combs was heartfelt and matter-of-fact: "Home. The essence of who I am."[23]

Harlem is one of the most diverse chocolate cities, composed of a vibrant collection of Black people from across the African diaspora, including West Africa, the Caribbean, and South America. Janice Combs, Sean's mother, who raised him at 145th and Lennox Avenue, recalled such Black diversity while reminiscing over her wealth of experience and time in Harlem: "When I was coming up as a kid, I always wanted to be in the parade. They used to call it the West Indian Day Parade in Harlem. It started at 110th Street and ended at 155th Street. They had different groups that they had at the time. The parade was festive, and beautiful. . . . We would sit on the sidewalk on Seventh Avenue and watch the parade go by. We sat and watched and danced as kids." Illustrating how the range of Black people from a variety of places across the country and the globe was the essence of Harlem, Janice's insights highlight how Black cultural diversity was and is a core feature of the chocolate city. "Harlem is my heritage," Janice said. She expressed her deep appreciation for her hometown: "It's my home. I love Harlem and will always love Harlem. It raised me."[24]

As it turns out, the chocolate city of Harlem, like many of those discussed in the chapters that follow, does not enjoy the CC future that

Parliament Funkadelic might have predicted. Still, differences in time and composition do not necessarily shake away the attachments to and power of the chocolate city for its residents and creators. Along these lines, *Chocolate Cities* offers a new way of imagining and assessing race, place, and inequality in the United States, illustrating the powerful and lasting effects and lessons of Black migration throughout the twentieth century. To animate these connected Black geographic sensibilities, chocolate maps, and chocolate cities, we revisit the life and times of well-known and everyday Black American figures, our Black Lewises and Clarks. Guided by the expeditions, observations, and stories of these Black travelers and adventurers, in the chapters ahead we come to see how place, politics, race, and history are uniquely intertwined with the enduring South.

Our exploration of the social, economic, and political life of chocolate cities begins with an exploration and explanation of chocolate maps. Using a combination of census, archival, and ethnographic data, we put chocolate maps into contemporary and historical context. We then further detail and outline the multiple Souths encompassed in this new geography of the intersections of race, place, and enduring patterns of inequality.

Chocolate Cities is divided into four parts. In Part 1 we elaborate the concept of chocolate maps, following Zora Neale Hurston, James Baldwin, and Lou Rawls as they theorized the connections and similarities between Black people across place and space. We revise typical conceptions of regional difference by focusing on the many and multiplying Souths created across the United States as Black people moved and made new places. Instead of the Midwest, Northeast, Southeast, Pacific Northwest, and Southwest, we offer Up South, Out South, West South, Mid South, Deep South, and Down South. Through chocolate maps, we show the versatility of the chocolate city. No matter the size—whether a small town, a neighborhood, or an entire city that has become synonymous with Black culture, power, and place making—every place on the map is a chocolate city.

The next sections focus on three concepts central to the chocolate cities idea: the village, the soul, and the power. The *village* reflects the intricate, tight networks and strategies Black communities developed behind the veil of segregation to survive and thrive. It emphasizes the importance of place making in the most inhospitable and unequal circumstances in the cultivation of Black power and Black resistance. The *soul* highlights the range of cultural production that emerged from chocolate cities as a result of and in service of Black people's place-making efforts. *Chocolate Cities* is deeply invested in the voices of various culture workers who consistently describe and analyze the state of Black America, and this section travels with Aretha Franklin, Tupac Shakur, and Big Freedia to illustrate the movement of *soul* across the chocolate maps. Finally, we turn to the *power*—people power, economic power, political power—embedded in chocolate cities. We travel with Mary Ann Shadd Cary, Mary Sanders, Mos Def and W. E. B. Du Bois to examine how Black people have turned place making into political power at the local, state, national, and international level and how they have often been punished for their desire to move freely about the world. Together, these concepts form an assets-based analysis of Black life in America from the nineteenth century to the present.

We conclude with a discussion of what it means to be a chocolate city, and to see and think like a chocolate city, in the era of the multifaceted Movement for Black Lives. As Black spaces and places are continuously under siege and taken over through various state, municipal, and police practices, we ask how chocolate cities will continue to exist and thrive. We use what we know about chocolate cities and maps since Emancipation to help us understand how Black people will respond to these and other challenges in the twenty-first century. Moreover, we demonstrate that Black people, concentrated in places, have been central to the advocacy for and survival of democracy in America. Black people's exemplary creative place making is the light toward both true civilization and broad liberation.

PART I The Map

Blackness
is a title,
is a preoccupation,
is a commitment Blacks
are to comprehend—
and in which you are
to perceive your Glory.
. . .
The word Black
has geographic power,
pulls everybody in:
Blacks here—
Blacks there—
Blacks wherever they may be.

Gwendolyn Brooks, "Primer for Blacks," 1980

2 Dust Tracks on the Chocolate Map

I hate to see de evenin' sun go down
Hate to see de evenin' sun go down
'Cause ma baby, he done lef' dis town
Feelin' like tomorrow like I feel today
Feel tomorrow like I feel today
I'll pack my trunk, make ma gitaway

Bessie Smith, "St. Louis Blues," *Bessie Smith*, 1925

A young Zora Neale Hurston dropped her bags in Harlem in early January 1925. Her trek up through the South had revealed the powerful draw of urban America for Black people. Still, she realized quickly that her experiences coming of age in a village town, Eatonville, were different than the Black life she had encountered on the way to Harlem. Nearly twenty years after she first arrived in Harlem, she wrote in her autobiography, "I was born in a Negro town. I do not mean by that the black back-side of an average town. Eatonville, Florida, is, and was at the time of my birth, a pure Negro town—charter, mayor, council, town marshal and all. It was not the first Negro community in America, but it was the first to be incorporated, the first attempt at organized self-government on the part of Negroes in America."[1] Hurston draws a sharp distinction between the "black back-side of an average town" and a "pure Negro town" like the Eatonville, Florida, village paradise in which she proudly claims to have been born.

Zora Neale Hurston, though, had not born in the town of Eatonville but in the Black back side of Notasulga, Alabama, near where her father, John Hurston, had been born.[2] This personal fiction of Hurston's is easy to understand, given the violence most Black people were subjected to at the hands of Whites in such spaces. Of course, she preferred to have been born in this relatively free and freeing place, a veritable country and southern Harlem. Hurston conjured many tales about her life, omitted large swaths of her personal history, and wrote herself into and out of her memoir and fiction work. Even still, her work on Eatonville, fiction and anthropological, remains some of the most important work on early twentieth-century Black life in the South.

Eatonville's status as a "pure Negro town" was undoubtedly connected to its incorporation, a legal, political, and place-making step that ensured residents the most autonomy possible. Like many other independent Black towns, it had been made possible because White benefactors, for benevolent, economic, and racist reasons, purchased land for its existence. It was nonetheless Black people and Black leadership agitating for space that made Eatonville into the glorious town Hurston remembered and created.

Wealthy Black people and Black Civil War veterans also purchased land that would become Black village spaces. As the tensions of Reconstruction and the post-Reconstruction era mounted, White land speculators capitalized on increasing White violence and racism, recruiting for and advertising these towns widely, and sometimes falsely, as ready-made havens for Black people looking to determine their own lives and space. Black folks were longing for Liberia, an elusive diasporic chocolate city nation-space, and the Back to Africa sentiment had resurged in response to invidious post-Reconstruction American racism.[3]

Still, many Black Americans nonetheless cast their hopes onto the cities of the South and the new Black towns being established in the rural South and on the frontier. Historian Norman Crockett counts at least sixty such towns between the Civil War and World War I, after which their establishment and existence declined.[4] This short-lived golden period, during which these towns functioned fairly independently as self-governing municipalities separate from their White counterparts, would be interrupted by war, interwar racial violence against Black people, and the Great Depression. In these towns, in this short time, residents cultivated a robust Black civic and social life beyond the White gaze.

Eatonville is especially extraordinary because it still persists. Most incorporated Black towns either no longer exist as independent towns or no longer exist at all, destroyed by harsh physical conditions, White violence, and state disinvestment. Later, desegregation, declining populations, and shrinking work opportunities in postindustrial America further threatened Black towns. In Eatonville's mythical afterlife, Hurston's work resonates as a rare archive of everyday Black life away from the daily drone of the commonplace uncomfortable racial interactions Black people have with Whites in city space.

Completing her long journey from Florida to New York, Hurston realized that most Black people did not live life in an Eatonville. In Eatonville, Hurston grew up "on a big piece of ground with two big chinaberry trees shading the front gate and Cape jasmine bushes with hundreds of blooms on either side of the walks." Harlem, with its densely populated close quarters, buzzed with possibility and, like Eatonville, was a predominantly Black place. Hurston was struck by the differences and similarities between Harlem and Eatonville. "When I got to New York," she reflected, "and found out that the people called them gardenias, and that the flowers cost a dollar each, I was impressed. The home folks laughed when I went back down there and told them."[5]

Hurston frequently found herself moving between Black life in "The North" and "The South," especially after she had earned a fellowship from famed anthropologist Franz Boas to collect folklore. During her return to the South—traveling down to the Carolinas and to Florida, and then over to Alabama and Louisiana—Hurston documented Black life, gathered oral histories, and developed a sophisticated grasp of the various Black dialects, rituals, and cultures of the residents she encountered. In her North-South research and travels, Hurston discovered that Black Americans "had whole treasures of material just seeping through their pores." Moreover, she extended this finding and work to the global Black South, connecting her folklife research in Florida, Alabama, and Louisiana to Haiti. In the end, from Haiti to Harlem, she came to the same conclusion: "Differences in geography and language" were merely just "differences in sounds, that's all" because "the sentiment [was] the same."[6]

Hurston's findings use notions of language and folk sentiment to suggest a Black geography of the United States, a way Black people map their American experience. Where others saw tremendous differences, Hurston had observed critical similarities across Black places. We follow Hurston's findings to their logical end, examining the ways that, nearly a century after she conducted this research, Black geographies of America have both shifted and remained remarkably consistent.

To be sure, current maps of the United States are varied and distinctive. From textured maps that feature the mountainous regions, major cities, waterways, and borders, ways to map the United States are many. These maps commonly feature regional notations for the U.S. landscape such as North, Northwest, South, Southwest, East, and Midwest. Yet despite differences in the emphasis on certain details about these maps, they share the same foundation. Based on the territorial arrangements following the Lewis and Clark Expedition, the Louisiana Purchase, the Oregon Trail, the Mexican-American War, and British colonization, the current U.S. maps are organized by the mindset that the actions and attitudes of Whites are most important for place making and for establishing and creating national, local, and regional boundaries. These maps, and their implicit logics, are then taught in schools and universities, near and far, informing everyday understandings of and scholarly research on change, immigration, migration, and urbanization across the United States and within its regions.

The current maps are wrong. They require adjustment, one informed by non-White perspectives that indicate other viable and valuable American geographies. Inspired by the call by critical geographers and social scientists such as David Harvey, Katherine McKittrick, Paul Gilroy, Neil Smith, and Rinaldo Walcott to question and transform fundamental tools for measuring space, place, and time like maps, we call into question existing American geographic common sense.[7] Using different philosophies, geographic points, narratives, and events, many other maps of the United States could be drawn. For example, Native Americans' experience has within it its own mapping of the United States, starting with their lands as they existed before they were ravaged by European settlement and then winding across the country as the Trail of Tears, forced reservation settlement lands to which they were pushed, and their enduring resistance to encroachment, as exemplified in their leadership of the resistance against the Dakota Access pipeline.[8]

The Japanese American map of the United States might mark their remaking of the West Coast of the United States, as well as White westward expansion and brutal internment.[9] The Mexican American map would refigure the existing national borders and reclaim Mexican land, offering a very different picture of migration, immigration, and border politics across the Southwest and now the Nueva South more broadly.[10] In short, the maps people of color draw of the United States include features overlooked in the traditional maps, which include racial and ethnic inequities. Though we do not focus on them in *Chocolate Cities*, multiethnic cooperation, tension, and organizing is central to the ebb and flow of chocolate cities, even in the context of the hypersegregation that often characterizes Black life.

Where are these maps, and why are they not a part of our shared understanding of U.S. geography? Across many disciplines, the experiences of people of color have not often been a central inquiry site. When social scientists have examined these experiences, especially within Black communities, they have been most concerned with how Black residents have been shaped by social structures or other external forces. Our approach, instead, is to look at how Black people made and live within their own maps, whether in response to or in spite of institutional discrimination. Following cues from Malcolm X's critical Black geography of the United States, we provide chocolate maps—a living geography, whose areas and regions are always actively being constructed, mirroring and defined by the movement of Black Americans across the United States over time.[11] As maps 4–14 show, we not only center the Black American experience and migration but also use it to redefine the geography of the United States.

Decennial census records mapped in this way indicate persistent Black migratory flows.[12] Over the twentieth century, as our maps demonstrate, Black migration has persisted through 2010 and is not easily defined using common Great Migration and "return South" migration explanations. Where the Great Migration is thought to have the common bookends of 1910 and 1970, our maps show that this conventional wisdom is incorrect. Our maps reveal the Great Migration (1) was not strictly South-to-North or North-to-South, (2) featured cyclical movement of people over the standard accepted period, and (3), perhaps most important, never ended.[13] Therefore, recent trends of Black migration being described as "reverse migration" or "return South" migration are better understood as a *long migration*—the continual reshuffling of the U.S. Black population, whose pursuit of equality of life, happiness, and opportunity affects the spatial location of non-Blacks in America.[14]

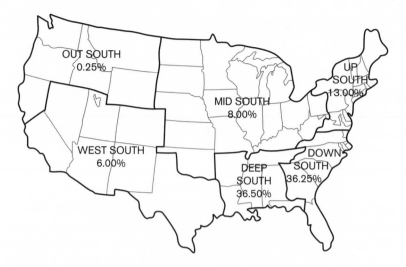

Map 4. U.S. census Black population percentage by region, 1900.

Map 5. U.S. census Black population percentage by region, 1910.

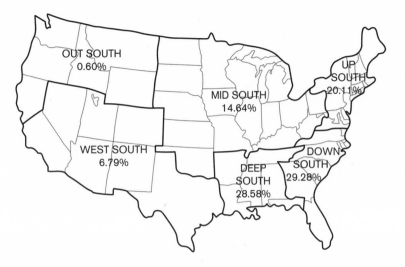

Map 6. U.S. census Black population percentage by region, 1920.

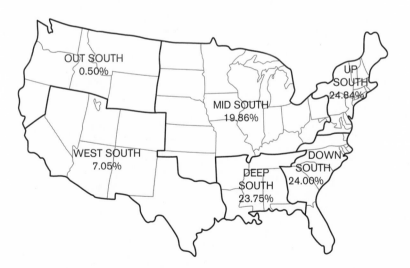

Map 7. U.S. census Black population percentage by region, 1930.

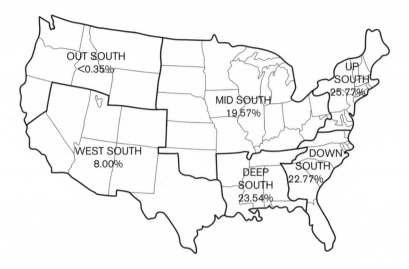

Map 8. U.S. census Black population percentage by region, 1940.

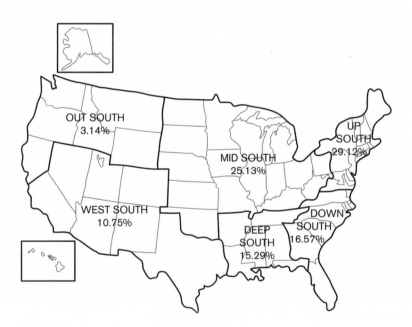

Map 9. U.S. census Black population percentage by region, 1960.

NEW MAPS, NEW VIEWS

Said, I heard it through the Grapevine
Oh, I heard it through the Grapevine
Not much longer would you be mine
Don't ya know I heard it
Heard It
Yes, I Heard it

Gladys Knight and Pips, "I Heard It
through the Grapevine," 1966

Maps are guided with an accompanying compass for large and sometimes unknown terrain. They are formed by experience and perception. Christopher Columbus and Amerigo Vespucci cemented firm places in world history for famously mapping the Americas, using a combination of existing writings and maps of places along with their own adventures and misadventures across the globe. These maps, and their hegemony in global geography, have in turn made others invisible, leaving many other geographic perspectives on the cutting-room floor.

When we look across the globe through the lens of the Black diaspora, we can retrieve some of these invisible geographies like those Hurston discovered and documented in the early twentieth century. Consider, for instance, the following lyrics to "Every Ghetto, Every City," from Lauryn Hill's critically acclaimed album *The Miseducation of Lauryn Hill* (1998). "Story starts at Hootaville, grew up next to Ivy Hill, when kids were stealin' quartervilles for fun," Hill reflects. "Kill the guy in Carter Park, rode a mongoose 'til it's dark." Hill's voice riffs with sharp confidence: "watchin' kids show off the stolen ones."

From her travels across the country and the globe, Hill sings her epiphany in unison with the hip-hop–inflected percussion: *"Every ghetto, every city and suburban place I've been / Make me recall my days in the New Jerusalem."* With joy and pride Hill travels even deeper into her formative years, connecting a variety of cities, towns, and sounds: "Bag of Bontons, twenty cents, and a nickel, Springfield Ave. had the best popsicles. . . . Drill teams on Munn Street, remember when Hawthorne and Chancellor had beef? Movin' Records was on Central Ave. I was there at dancing school South Orange Ave. at Borlin' Pool, writin' my friends' names on my jeans with a marker. . . . July Fourth races outside of Parker Fireworks at Martin Stadium. The Untouchable P. S. P., where all them crazy niggas be and car thieves got away through Irvington. Hillside brings beef with the cops, Self-Destruction record drops and everybody's name was Muslim."[15]

In "Every Ghetto, Every City," we learn from Hill that Black geography is linked across space and time. Whereas Brooks's center of gravity is Chicago's South Side, northern New Jersey is the urban Black landscape on which Hill's map is built. It is a Black geography motivated by a childhood and daily life that required her to move within and across a Black region. We are presented with a Black map of north Jersey, Essex County (the state's third most populous), reflecting a *county within a county.*

This Black county within Essex County, dubbed "The New Jerusalem," has its own geography, based on an existing Black residential savoir faire— the knowledge of Black areas that are the context where Black residents watch fireworks on July Fourth, fight and experience police brutality and gang crimes, and attend funerals and birthday and block parties. This Black Belt through and around Essex County borders is defined by the Ivy Hill neighborhood of Newark to the working-class Black city of Irvington to the Black Hootaville (Hill's childhood) neighborhood adjacent to South Orange (a predominantly White suburb of Newark) to the long blocks of Central Avenue, a major thruway in East Orange (a predominantly Black suburb of Newark). In the song Hill gives us the sounds and rhythms of a recurrent and important urban Black coming-of-age story, one where Black residents traverse many Black neighborhoods across a series of cities as a part of their daily lives. It is a Black geography based on a cultural and visual map springing from the lives and neighborhoods of Black residents.

The world described by Hill is one that is predominantly Black, surviving and thriving. Similar to scholarly and literary narratives of Black life, "Every Ghetto, Every City" illustrates that Black residents must frequently move between administrative, local, county, and state lines to survive and thrive. This process generates a Black map of a broader area. That map is navigated using a compass informed by a variety of social, economic, and political contexts. These distant yet close Black enclaves are connected socially and culturally and are strikingly similar. This is in striking harmony with sociologist Mary Pattillo's argument that the "Black middle class," for example, "has not abandoned the Black poor, either ideologically or geographically."[16]

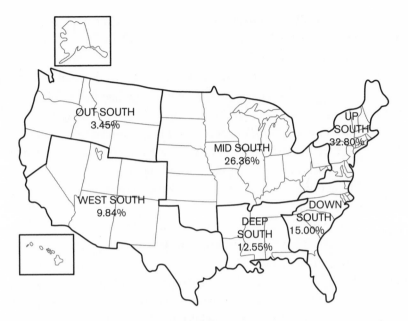

Map 10. U.S. census Black population percentage by region, 1970.

Hill's lyrics echo this social fact, reflecting journeys through the Black diaspora: "every ghetto, every city and suburban place I've been / Make me recall my days in the New Jerusalem." These invisible geographies represent the perceptions and movements of Black people, greatly influencing how, where, and why spaces and places change over time. This type of geography provides a template for better measuring and examining the diversity of Black experiences, as well as strategies of resistance and resilience—from the advent of the transatlantic slave trade through two terms of the first African American president of the United States.

Where one begins on the chocolate map yields pathways as different and varied as the histories of the Black diaspora and slave trade indicate. Black folks in the chocolate cities of western Europe, for instance, might forge pathways that begin on the continent of Africa, then may pass through the Caribbean (because of the slave trade), and then end in London, Paris, or Hamburg, as a result of colonization and African independence movements. For Black Africans, geographies likely traverse the continent and move across western Europe and to the metropolises of the United States. Yet wherever one begins on the chocolate map, Black folks share a critical epistemology of space and place born of language, culture, experience, and resistance.

Caribbean revolutionist C. L. R. James recounts the colonial history of Hispaniola (now the nations of the Dominican Republic and Haiti), under-lining key shared experiences of Black peoples across the diaspora. "Many slaves," writes James in *The Black Jacobins* (1963), "could never be got to stir at all unless they were whipped. Suicide was a common habit, and such was their disregard for life that they often killed themselves, not for personal reasons, but in order to spite their owner." James narrates the sobering and consequential reality: "Life was hard and death, many [slaves] believed, meant not only release but a return to Africa."[17] Making plain the histories and impacts of slavery, colonization, and African independence, each of these scholars demonstrates that "there are some similarities and some important differences in the ways that slavery affected the development" of life within the Black diaspora. No matter where Black folks are on the map, they are subject to oppression that yields remarkably similar outcomes.[18]

The enslavement and forced transportation of Africans to the Americas is the defining moment for our creation of Black maps of the United States as they exist today.[19] While more Africans remained on the continent than were transported to the West, the trauma of the transatlantic slave trade, and the alteration of lives on both sides of the ocean, is a focal point of Black American identity. Scholars, including Mary Waters, Christina Greer, and Richard Iton, show that this can be true even for Black ethnics who do not share an American history of enslavement.[20] The experiences of Black people across the diaspora provide an "alternative culture of loca-tion to the state," illustrating that Blackness is shared yet diverse "and [suggesting] different and dissident maps and geographies."[21]

In the United States, African groups were located from New York to Florida to westernmost Texas, often brought to locations because of their expertise in certain kinds of agriculture. They were compelled to trade their "country marks," the distinguishing features of their varying ethnici-ties, for tenuous membership in newly created categories—that of enslaved, Black, and Negro.[22] The diversity of origins of enslaved Africans, from Angolans on the Sea Islands of South Carolina to the Bamana and Wolof groups in New Orleans, brought a rich variety of African experience

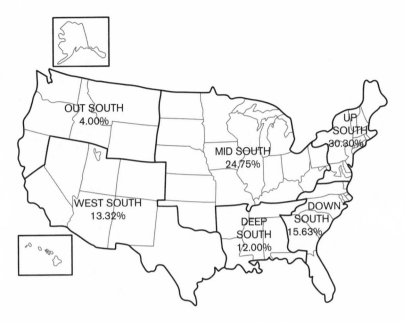

Map 11. U.S. census Black population percentage by region, 1980.

to the United States. These practices were exchanged, reimagined, and combined intergenerationally over the course of enslavement and following Emancipation, folding into one diverse but shared experience.

Through the American grapevine, a Black resource and information network, word of the nature of other Black places and opportunities therein traveled distances as short as one plantation to the next to stretches as far as one country to another. Through the grapevine Africans in America learned the cultural, economic, and political geography of their new homeland. Political scientists such as Michael C. Dawson and Cathy J. Cohen have found that Black political behavior is influenced greatly by assumed and real links within and across Black America. This research has also shown that shared Black media and experiences can generate informational links among Black Americans that traverse the political landscape, zigzagging across urban America. These links have informed a Black political sensibility that relies on a working assumption of intertwined Black fates and destinies within the American socioeconomic and political context.[23]

Map 12. U.S. census Black population percentage by region, 1990.

Whether investigating the whereabouts of kin and friends sold away, "sold down the river," or sold abroad, Black Americans gained an innovative sense of U.S. geography shaped by their experiences across generations and movements. "The North" loomed in the consciousness and imagination of the enslaved as a space for freedom, even as Black Americans living in the North recognized their second-class freedom above the Mason-Dixon Line. Even before Malcolm X's provocation in his "The Ballot or the Bullet" speech, the Canadian border was a *real* marker of freedom.

American slave policies, like the Fugitive Slave Act of 1850 and racialized laws and discrimination that emerged in tandem with these policies, made the Canadian border a freedom land.[24] Although Canada was no paradise, given its own history of racial exclusion and violence, it nonetheless emerged as a relative site of northern freedom, a place into which U.S. fugitive slave laws did not extend. Enslaved Black Americans developed a sense of the geographies of freedom, even as they were painfully aware of the distance of that freedom from their homes and communities in the United States.

After Emancipation Canada's symbolism as the "freedom destination" receded, as in the post-Emancipation era, Black Americans were "set flowin'" across the United States in search of opportunity, work, kin, love, and a fresh start.[25] They left the plantations and rural towns of the South for the urban South, moving up to the nearest big southern city. They left smaller southern cities for bigger southern cities. And they left southern cities for large urban and near-urban areas of the eastern seaboard, the Midwest, the West, and stops in between.[26]

Black migration fundamentally altered the American landscape; Chicago, Detroit, Philadelphia, Memphis, Los Angeles, Atlanta, Charlotte, Charleston, Saint Louis, and Dallas are but a few examples of the cities and towns whose Black populations swelled to historic numbers as a result of the Great Migration. These migrants were drawn to promises of labor opportunities in America's growing metropolises and pushed to flee a defeated, economically depressed, and increasingly vengeful post-Reconstruction White South.[27] Following public lynchings many Black migrants would commonly take leave in the dark of night. Such was the case for the remaining Carter family of Van Vleet, Mississippi, in 1926. After witnessing their relatives, the Carter brothers, hanged for saying "something to [a] white lady," after the funeral "the surviving Carters packed up and left Mississippi. They went to a place called Milwaukee and never came back."[28]

Rivers (e.g., the Mississippi, Missouri, Ohio, Colorado, Hudson, and Delaware) and the seaboard served as natural guides for Black migrants out of the South to the midwestern, western and northeastern United States. As literary scholar Farrah Griffin reminds us, although trains were segregated, they also proved important modes of northward transportation and were "a symbol of escape to freedom in African-American oral culture from the spirituals to the blues."[29] In their new locations Black migrants made new homes and neighborhoods built on the aspirations that compelled their journey out of the Old South.

But as anecdotal and scholarly accounts indicate, the North was not the imagined North that had been conveyed in intergenerational lore and newspapers and other media. "It wasn't all it was cracked up to be," Great Migrant Elise Watson confessed from her row house in South Philadelphia. Her sister Lorraine Wilson had called Watson to Philadelphia from Savannah, Georgia. In the summer of 1954 Watson traveled "by train and did a lot of bus riding and a whole lot more walking." The "amount of travel I did to get to Philly was enough to keep me right on here," Watson revealed, eyes shining with self-pride, recalling the sheer stamina her journey required. Her pride faded as she confessed, "Even though Philly is still the South. New York, too! For a long time I was sad but maybe there's no escaping it anyhow."[30] Like many Black Americans during the Great Migration, Elise Watson discovered at the end of her journey northward that she had only found a new version of the South—an Up South or an Out South, but a South nonetheless.[31]

During Jim Crow two forms of segregation developed in the North and South, de facto and de jure, respectively. As Black Americans moved from the South, they were crowded into small isolated sections of the city, cut off from access to resources despite the absence of de jure segregation. In the South the sheer numbers of Black folks created the separate city, autonomously operating socially and economically but nonetheless subject to a regime of White supremacy.[32] "White people were everywhere around her, but they were separate from her, in a separate schoolhouse, on separate land on the other side of a firewall that kept white and colored from occupying the same sidewalk," Great Migrant Ida Mae recalled in *Warmth of Other Suns* from the segregated Mississippi she left.[33]

Although scores of Black migrants left the South and never returned, the boundaries between North and South are porous. Consider W. E. B. Du Bois's key observations in *The Philadelphia Negro* (1899). After examining Philadelphia's history from 1630 to 1898, Du Bois found that growth in its physical size, the "increase in foreign population," the "development of large industry and increase of wealth," and the large influx of southern Black migrants made it resemble migration destination cities such as Baltimore, Washington, DC, and Boston. A "natural gateway between the North and the South," the Black population of Philadelphia was the product of the gradual process of Black migration. Strikingly, Du Bois finds that the racial geography of Philadelphia was influenced by frequent within-region migration. Though some Black residents had been born in Philadelphia, most had southern roots. Black migration to the Philadelphia region was fragmented and frequent, as migrants would commonly "come from country districts to small towns; then go to larger towns, eventually . . . drift[ing] to Norfolk, Va, or Richmond . . . next . . . to Washington, and finally . . . settl[ing] in . . . Philadelphia."[34]

As Black people left "The South" for "The North," some returned to care for relatives and tend to other business in their home regions. As a result, North-South exchange was significant and, as our maps show, persisted within and beyond the typical temporal boundaries of the Great Migration. However, the South remained a "closed society," wherein Black migrants moved from rural to urban spaces and between southern cities. In the process, remarkably similar neighborhood patterns developed, evolving into a notable and persistent phenomenon of chocolate cities—the Black bottoms, Black back sides, Black quarters, Black sections, and hoods that were creations of structure (i.e., institutional racism and segregation) and agency (the Black mapping of American space since Emancipation).

By the time Parliament Funkadelic paid homage to chocolate cities, Black neighborhoods across America were being devastated by an expansion of the prison industrial complex, the contraction of the welfare state, and sharp declines in manufacturing jobs that had traditionally aided Black upward mobility. The rapid industrialization of the Rustbelt that had brought many African Americans north, especially after World War II, was being almost just as rapidly dismantled by globalization and deindustrialization. Jobs were moving back down South, back to states with fewer union allowances and cheaper land, before they moved to the global South, disappearing forever to much cheaper labor and, later, to automation. This left even the most robust chocolate cities economically devastated, as primary sources of income simply vanished as a result of the convergence of corporate and government interests in an emergent era of neoliberalism. Sociologist William Julius Wilson notes, "From 1967 to 1987, Philadelphia lost 64 percent of its manufacturing jobs; Chicago lost 60 percent; New York, 58 percent; [and] Detroit 51 percent."[35]

Taken together "these percentages represent the loss of 160,000 jobs in Philadelphia, 326,000 in Chicago, 520,000—over half a million—in New York, and 108,000 in Detroit."[36] These broad shifts increased other disparities, including employment discrimination, the wage and achievement gaps, and housing inequality.[37] Although Jim Crow had been legally eradicated, its effects reverberated throughout the nation, leaving the map of Black America looking very much like the South's enduring principle of "separate and unequal," much like the global chocolate cities like London's Brixton, the *banlieues* (or suburbs) of Paris's Saint-Denis, and the shantytowns of Soweto.[38]

Map 13. U.S. census Black population percentage by region, 2000.

Social scientists have recognized the similarities across these Black neighborhoods and communities. This research often emphasizes the effects of structural top-down policies and procedures that shape neighborhood outcomes. The study of Black neighborhoods and communities, in particular, has consistently shown the detrimental impact of flawed federal policies, large-scale economic shifts, and segregation.[39]

Sociologists Douglas Massey, Nancy Denton, and Camille Zubrinsky Charles, for instance, have shown how racial practices impact residential patterns and Black mobility. They have found that practices such as race-based neighborhood preferences and policies (e.g., restrictive covenants, suburbanization, and redlining by real estate agents, corporations, and White residents) have adverse effects on Black upward mobility and Black neighborhoods. We learn from this line of research that "barriers to spatial mobility are barriers to social mobility."[40] This research indicates that the U.S. map is one where racial residential segregation is prominent. These patterns of segregation leave visible geographic marks across the

Map 14. U.S. census Black population percentage by region, 2010.

United States—ones strongly correlated with Black-White disparities in wealth, mortality, poverty, and health outcomes.

Acutely felt by the "truly disadvantaged" such as urban Black Americans, each economic shift has resulted in massive urban disinvestment, White flight, and (to some extent) the shrinking Black middle class. These urban population shifts later result in gentrification as White flight reverses, and White residents seek urban neighborhoods that have usually become neighborhoods predominated by racial minorities. Gentrification has also shifted and often devastated Black neighborhoods across urban America, and Black mapping provides a framework for understanding how Black people make place in response and critique these gentrification processes.[41]

Here Toni Morrison's opening in the novel *Sula* is quite instructive. Emphasizing the recovery of spaces and places lost, Morrison offers a literary and ethnographic revisit of the life history of Lorraine County, one of Ohio's chocolate cities. "In that place," Morrison writes, "where they tore the nightshade and blackberry patches from their roots to make room for the Medallion City Golf Course, there was once a neighborhood."

Morrison's tale reveals the shifts brought about by changing White residential interests: "It is called the suburbs now, but when Black people lived there it was called the Bottom. . . . Generous funds have been allotted to level the stripped and faded buildings that clutter the road from Medallion up to the golf course. They are going to raze the Time and a Half Pool Hall. . . . A steel ball will knock to dust Irene's Palace of Cosmetology. . . . There will be nothing left of the Bottom."[42] The racial turnovers caused by gentrification have ripple effects because displaced Black residents migrate to find refuge in new cities, towns, and neighborhoods in search of "home."[43] This persistent cycle shapes the geography of Black America.[44]

The influential link between Black mobility and migration remains. We know, for instance, that Black residents, especially those who are poor, tend to move frequently, leaving their neighborhoods for other neighborhoods with better resources.[45] Add to this that research continues to indicate that White migration, notably White flight, is shaped by Black migration, and we come closer to a fuller picture of how race, place, and politics shape the U.S. map. As Black Americans migrate, other demographic groups take cues from that movement and adjust their neighborhoods, migrations, immigrations, and broader residential patterns accordingly.[46]

To build the chocolate maps, we heed cultural theorist Stuart Hall's advice to look not only to original and existing research but also to Black public and popular culture, a "site of strategic contestation" and information.[47] Chocolate maps are in some ways visible only through popular culture, as artists and other Black people in the public sphere talk about and make place through their work. We mine this popular data to provide a more comprehensive assessment of Black American life in the twentieth century.

For a closer look at Black mapping, we turn to prolific fiction writer, essayist, and activist James Baldwin, whose writings also indicate a distinct Black geography of the United States.[48] We then develop the idea of a critical Black regionalism to account for how Black actions and attitudes have shaped the United States, shifting the border, as Malcolm X did, from the Mason-Dixon Line to the Canadian-American line. We begin by identifying the regions within a common Black map, providing a series of tables using U.S. census data for the Black population from 1900 to 2010.[49]

3 Multiplying the South

I pick up my life
And take it on the train
To Los Angeles, Bakersfield,
Seattle, Oakland, Salt Lake,
Any place that is
North and West—
And not South.

Langston Hughes, "One Way Ticket," 1949

Drug abuse and domestic violence had compelled Emma Berdis Jones to migrate from Down South to the Up South chocolate city of Harlem in the early 1930s. Drawn to the spirit of the Holy Ghost swelling in local preacher David Baldwin, Jones married him and took his last name. Her son James would also take the preacher's name. And, thus, James Jones was reborn James Baldwin.

Raised in Harlem, James Baldwin "began plotting novels at about the time [he] learned to read." After exploring the possibilities of life through Black religion and early play and fiction writing, Baldwin began to experience America and its racial problems as limits on his possibilities. As he reveals, "By the time I was twenty-four I had decided to stop reviewing books about the negro problem—which, by this time, was only slightly less horrible in print than it was in life—and I packed my bags and went to France, where I finished, God knows how, *Go Tell It on the Mountain*."[1]

His first major novel, *Go Tell It on the Mountain,* is a semiautobiographical coming-of-age tale of a young Black boy in Harlem seeking the blessings and gifts the elders told him the sweet blood of Jesus would bring. Sexually attracted to the same gender and somewhat skeptical about the ability of religion to save his soul, by the novel's end the protagonist is fluent in the apostolic tradition of speaking in tongues. Though he is only a teenager, the novel ends with a gesture toward the new possibilities of a young Black boy in Harlem who had been selected by God to be one of the chosen saved believers.

Although the book was critically acclaimed, Baldwin still felt different, a feeling that was of great consequence to his life thereafter. While Paris and Europe more generally proved to be avenues to new opportunities he couldn't find in the United States, Baldwin came to observe how his American citizenship altered his experiences with White Europeans, making parts of his experience markedly different from his Black European counterparts. "I know," Baldwin professes, "that the most crucial time in my own development came when I was forced to recognize that I was a kind of bastard of the West; when I followed the line of my past I did not find myself in Europe but in Africa." This revelation led Baldwin to the conclusion that, like other Black people, he "brought to Shakespeare, Bach, Rembrandt, to the stones of Paris, to the cathedral at Chartres, and the Empire State Building, a *special attitude.*"[2]

The buildings, art products, place, and literary works "were not really my creations," Baldwin writes. "They did not contain my history; I might search in them in vain forever for any reflection of myself." "I was an interloper," Baldwin surmises. Surveying popular and critical culture, Baldwin finds that it is through Black music, "which Americans are able to admire because a protective sentimentality limits their understanding of it, . . . that the Negro in America has been able to tell his story."[3] Black "music is our witness," Baldwin attests, "and our ally. The beat is the confession [that] changes and conquers time. Then, history becomes a garment we can wear and share" and not hide, and "time becomes a friend."[4]

Indeed, Paris had proven to be full of racial animus. In December 1949, when Baldwin had been in Paris for a year, he was imprisoned for eight days after being arrested for receiving stolen goods. The circumstances were murky at best, and Baldwin felt set up after a random encounter with another American led to police checking his bedroom and his person on the suspicion that he may have stolen something. What it was that was stolen was never quite clear, but the hotel staff and French police seemed convinced that Baldwin was capable of having stolen something. The freedoms he had found in Paris had been a fleeting illusion, and by the time he returned to the United States, Baldwin possessed a critical racial geographic consciousness that would appear prominently in his subsequent autobiography.

Baldwin outlines his own Black map in his autobiographical collection, *Nobody Knows My Name* (1961), one informed by his travels through the American South in the late 1950s. He had found racial fears about the region to be paradoxically compelling, and, though he could have been anywhere in the world, he left Paris and returned to America to tour the South. Though his family had southern roots, Baldwin himself had never spent any substantial time in the South. Baldwin was admittedly apprehensive about the trip but nonetheless moved through the American South, inspired by what Black southern culture had produced, from the bluesy coos of Bessie Smith to the emergent jazz genius of John Coltrane.[5]

In the book Baldwin offers a sharp comment on the hypocrisy and immorality of segregation. Unlike so many autobiographical notes of that era, Baldwin's evaluation is not one that purely indicts and criticizes the South. Rather, Baldwin writes of his tour as bringing about a needed awareness of the vast similarities between "The North" and the "The South," two American regions previously thought of as night and day.

In Charlotte and Atlanta, two bustling southern metropolises, Baldwin is instantly struck by how similar each city was to those in "The North." In both cities Baldwin finds that "the racial setup in the South is not, for a Negro, very different from the racial setup in the North. . . . Segregation is unofficial in the North and official in the South, a crucial difference that does nothing, nevertheless, to alleviate the lot of most Northern Negros." Surprised by the diversity of Souths within the region too often considered as a monolith, Baldwin disabuses himself of cultural and racial assumptions of North-South differences.[6]

Baldwin observes, "the South is not the monolithic structure which, from the North, it appears to be, but a most various and divided region." Time and again Black Charlotteans repeated to him, "Charlotte is not the South. You haven't seen the South yet."[7] These residents were likely referring to spaces beyond Charlotte, the rural hinterland where Black-White relations still very much mirrored the power and spatial arrangements of the early twentieth-century South. For these Charlotte residents, the

South was something geographically and culturally more southern than Charlotte, the Queen City. Indeed, just as the northern cities of Chicago, Detroit, and New York had lured Black migrants from the South with promises of escape and opportunity, southern metropolises like Charlotte and Atlanta had also been relative bastions of freedom for people leaving the rural and small-town South.

Cities such as Memphis, New Orleans, Nashville, Jackson, and Birmingham were more progressive in some ways than their rural surroundings. By maintaining and enacting racial and housing restrictions, though, such cities were less attractive to some Black migrants than cities like Charlotte and Atlanta, which attempted a set of more neutral racial policies that privileged middle-class sensibilities and buying power across race. Distinctions between rural and urban communities, between neighborhoods, and between cities created multi-Souths—a varied and diverse Black South and experiences even as the region was unified under the general principle of Jim Crow. Cities like Atlanta, with its mantra of "too busy to hate," and Charlotte, with its aspirations toward being a leading metropolis in postwar America, balanced racist policies with the fact that Black populations were economically significant.

As Baldwin discovered during his interviews and ethnographic exploration, Black southerners were well aware of and living with the varied Souths—sharing real and oral maps of the American South indicating racial hotspots, predominantly Black areas, and which towns to avoid during travel and migration. Baldwin witnessed and came to the conclusion that distinctions between "The North" and "The South" were arbitrary and not nearly as clear-cut as conventional wisdom and media often suggested. Consider Baldwin's reflections after spending significant time among Black Charlotteans:

> Northerners proffer their indignation about the South as a kind of badge, as proof of good intentions; never suspecting that they can thus increase, in the heart of the Negro they are speaking to, a kind of helpless pain and rage— and pity. Negroes know how little most white people are prepared to implement their words with deeds, how little, when the chips are down, they are prepared to risk. And this long history of moral evasion has had an unhealthy effect on the total life of the country, and has eroded whatever respect Negroes may once have felt for white people.[8]

Though Jim Crow was not official or explicit in the North, Baldwin's time in Charlotte demonstrated that the North's informal racial structure mirrored and mimicked the South's formal one.

Black southerners and White southerners influenced Baldwin's racial takeaways about the South. One key exchange at a Charlotte public school especially affected Baldwin, forever shaping his perspective on race, the United States, and "The North versus The South" paradigm. Steeped in the fight over the desegregation of schools, Charlotte was fertile ground for exploring "the race question" in the South; schools were a key battleground space where Whites wanted explicit control.

During an "awkward" and telling conversation "with a local white principal," Baldwin leaves Charlotte, disavowing the myth of real differences between "The North" and "The South":

> "What do you think," I asked him, "will happen? What do you think the future holds?" He strained a laugh and said he didn't know. "I don't want to think about it." Then, "I'm a religious man," he said, "and I believe the Creator will always help us find a way to solve our problems. If a man loses that, he's lost everything he had." I agreed, struck by the look in his eyes. "You're from the North?" he asked me, abruptly. "Yes," I said. "Well," he said "you've got your troubles too." "Ah, yes, we certainly do," I admitted, and shook hands and left him. I did not say what I was thinking, that our troubles were the same trouble and that, unless we were very swift and honest, what is happening in the South today will be happening in the North tomorrow.[9]

Baldwin finds clear and binding links between the North and South. Not only are the two regions socioeconomically and politically linked, but also their racial dilemmas and problems reverberate within and across both regions. This ripple effect means that Black life is connected beyond administrative boundaries of North and South. While place and regional histories certainly matter, similarities abound for Black people in Black areas across the nation.

After his time in Charlotte, Baldwin immediately heads farther "down South," visiting the burgeoning Black Mecca of Atlanta. There, he finds that, while Black home ownership and other signs of upward mobility were a reality, the trappings of racial segregation and White domination were ever present. From this social, economic, and political atmosphere,

Baldwin surmises that "as far as the color problem is concerned, there is but one great difference between the Southern white and the Northerner: the Southerner remembers, historically and in his own psyche, a kind of Eden in which he loved Black people and they loved him. Historically, the flaming sword laid across this Eden is the Civil War." "None of this is true for the Northerner," Baldwin quips. "Negroes represent nothing to him personally, except, perhaps, the dangers of carnality. He never sees Negroes. Southerners see them all the time. Northerners never think about them whereas Southerners are never really thinking of anything else."

"Negroes are, therefore, ignored in the North and under surveillance in the South, and suffer hideously in both places," Baldwin notes. "Neither the Southerner nor the Northerner is able to look on the Negro simply as a man." No longer invested in the relative differences between North and South, Baldwin adds, "It seems to be indispensable to the national self-esteem that the Negro be considered either as a kind of ward (in which case we are told how many Negroes, comparatively, bought Cadillacs last year and how few, comparatively, were lynched), or as a victim (in which case we are promised . . . he will never vote in our assemblies or go to school with our kids)." Baldwin concludes his tour of the American South with a new perspective on Black life, North and South, making the calculation: "They are two sides of the same coin and the South will not change—*cannot* change—until the North changes."[10]

Just a few years later, during an early Sunday morning on September 15, 1963, four little Black girls were killed in a Ku Klux Klan bombing of Birmingham's Sixteenth Street Baptist Church, making the front page of newspapers across the country. In the weeks following the church bombing, Baldwin found, especially among White liberals, that the horror of the event exemplified the distance between Black life in "The North" and Black life in "The South." Compelled to action and further investigation of American race relations, in the wake of the Birmingham bombing, Baldwin decided to visit San Francisco to explore the quality of Black life in the West. This time, however, Baldwin would be accompanied by a mobile camera crew, as his time in San Francisco would serve as the focus of *Take This Hammer*—a documentary nationally televised in early 1964 for National Educational Television and on local Bay Area station KQED.[11]

Arriving in late 1963, Baldwin was escorted by Orville Huster, executive director of the Youth for Services—a local Black community organization focused on developing opportunities for youth in Black communities in Bayview and Hunter's Point in San Francisco. Standing among a group of Black folk of varying ages, just before the cameras began to roll, a member of the production crew appears to have asked one of the young men, "How is San Francisco?" The young Black man answered, "San Francisco?! . . . Aw, man, let me tell you about San Francisco. Ever since I got out of high school, I had a couple of jobs. I worked at a couple of hat companies, warehouses. I mean, after a while they say, 'Well, I guess we gon' lay you off for a couple of weeks, you know.'" The Birmingham church bombing still fresh in his mind, he offered a searing take on race in the West versus the South: "All right, they talk about the South. The South is not half as bad as San Francisco. You want me to tell you about San Francisco? I'll tell you about San Francisco! The White man, he's not taking advantage of you out in public like they do down in Birmingham, but he's killing you with that pencil and paper, brother." Looking around at the nodding heads of the Black men surrounding him, he concluded by asking a rhetorical question: "When you go to look for a job, can you get a job?"

Many of the Black members of Bayview and Hunter's Point had migrated west from areas of the Delta just a few years, months, or decades earlier. So, for them, the South was not merely a myth. Rather, the South was and had been home for them and their relatives. In many cases the advertising of opportunity and mobility promised in the West had caused their migration from states such as Alabama, Mississippi, Louisiana, and Texas, making a comparison between the West and the South much like that between the North and the South. The West was the New North, or at least had been advertised explicitly and implicitly as such. Indeed, Baldwin determined that San Francisco was fertile soil in which to extend his earlier considerations of the American South, as it often advertised its "liberal and cosmopolitan traditions" and was a place where "a white person would look . . . and see everything as at peace."

While in San Francisco, Baldwin met with Black residents, leaders, and youth and discussed everything from police brutality to unemployment to integration to Black life across the United States. Time and again Baldwin was told of one racial injury after another. Racially integrated high schools

were not producing equal outcomes, leaving many Black women gradu-
ates searching for domestic employment from the very same White families whose children they learned alongside in high school. A Black mother
from Texas remarked to Baldwin at a community meeting at the Bayview
Community Center that "Hunter's Point is just like being in Alabama right
now!" Another woman followed up with a sentiment reflecting a broader
sense of linked fate, reminiscent of what Baldwin encountered in other
Black communities: "The Black people in Alabama are my people. I'm
from Texas but the Black people in the South are my people."

This extended visit and interviews with Black San Franciscans led
Baldwin to a powerful conclusion. Adorned in a striped short-sleeved dress
shirt and bright white ascot, Baldwin turned to the camera, eyes wide open,
with a matter-of-fact tone: "Birmingham is just an incident. . . . What is
very crucial is that the citizenry are able to recognize there is no moral distance, *no moral distance*—which is to say no distance—between the facts
of life in San Francisco and the facts of life in Birmingham."[12] Having heard
and lived similar tales of racial injury and racism elsewhere, Baldwin found
that, while race relations may have appeared differently in San Francisco,
it is not because they do not exist. Despite this fact, Baldwin found a pervasive White ignorance and resistance to the idea that race relations were
awry everywhere, including within the conventional South: "Everywhere I
have been in this country, you talk to a White person who says race relations are excellent, and I cannot find any Negro who agrees with that."

Instead, "San Francisco is just another incident," he exclaimed, an
example of the enduring continuity in the Black experience, modified by a
tendency in the West to place race relations "under the rug [because they]
haven't hit the headlines yet."[13] Further collapsing the boundaries between
the South and everywhere else in the United States, like *Nobody Knows
My Name* before it, Baldwin's *Take This Hammer* demonstrates that practices of White supremacy and domination travel, imbuing every State in
the Union. "This is the San Francisco America pretends does not exist,"
Baldwin surmises. "They think I am making it up."[14]

Baldwin's observations provide clear and compelling evidence defying
conventional wisdom about the relative differences between the North
and the South, and the West and the South. His observations and experience further illustrate a key principle of Black mapping: *Black American*

life across the United States varies little from dominant ideas about Black American life in the South. The South is not merely the common geographic location below the Mason-Dixon Line. It is, rather, America—the broader cultural, economic, and political soil on which Black communities and neighborhoods have been planted and supplanted, the soil on which they have grown, persisted, and evolved. The notion that there is no "North" is one that runs throughout Black political culture, even as it coexists alongside narratives that still situate the North as the Promised Land. From Malcolm X to Lou Rawls to Gwendolyn Brooks, Black Americans have long provided critical examinations of the realities of race in America, West, North or South, revealing their overarching similarities and differences.

To be sure, repression in the South, and in the rural South in particular, marked the region with the scourge of lynching and rape. These twin racial terrors—enabled and encouraged by the Supreme Court's 1896 *Plessy v. Ferguson* decision authorizing Jim Crow laws, a legal "separate but equal" racial policy—created real political and local boundaries. Yet histories of incidents of racialized violence abound at every location on Black maps, then and now.

4 Super Lou's Chitlin' Circuit

> And, in one sense, popular culture always has its base in the
> experiences, the pleasures, the memories, [and] the tradi-
> tions of the people.
>
> Stuart Hall, "What Is This 'Black' in Black Popular
> Culture?," 1993

In 1966 soul singer and native Chicagoan Lou Rawls took his show on the
road, touring Chitlin' Circuit cities and towns and narrating his life, travels, and aspirations before belting out his classic renditions of "Southside
Blues" and "Tobacco Road."[1] Affectionately known as "Super Lou" for his
incredible baritonal prowess, Rawls grew up as a poor Black kid from
Chicago's notorious South Side.

Having cut his teeth in the music industry as a background singer for
the legendary Sam Cooke, Rawls was familiar with the roundabouts,
theaters, and Black audiences that characterized what became popularly
known as the Chitlin' Circuit. A network of Black performance spaces,
Black audiences, and Black popular culture, the Chitlin' Circuit flowed
from Boston to Detroit, Philadelphia, Baltimore, Charlotte, Memphis,
Chicago, Atlanta, and Cleveland.

Over the year 1966 Rawls had a successful music run with several R&B
hits, helping him forge his way into the hearts and radios of Black residents across the United States. He decided it was time to be personal. He
had sung a lot and had seen a lot. During the set Rawls told audiences his
life story over a spare, staccato musical arrangement. "Soon as I was big

enough to get a job, save me some money, and buy me a ticket and catch the first thing smokin', I left [Chicago]."[2]

Rawls's baritone echoed as he continued, "And I made a promise that if they could just keep the thought out of my mind, I'd keep my feet outta the city limits." Rawls continued his narrative, punctuated by drum cadences and audience claps, and revealed his own "Black Map":

> In Detroit we call it Black Bottom; in Cleveland they call it Euclid Ave., 55th Street, 105th, Central Ave; in Philadelphia they call it South Street; in New York City they call it Harlem. Drop down below the Cotton Curtain, as they call it; in Atlanta they call it Buttermilk Bottom. But then you come out West, where it's the best. In San Francisco they call it the Fillmore District; in Los Angeles they used to call it Watts; they changed the name though. I speak about this place because I'm quite familiar with it. Everyone is in some sense or other.[3]

Rawls, like many musicians of the time, traveled across the United States from Black rural areas in Mississippi to Black urban neighborhoods like New York City's Harlem, New Orleans's Tremé, and Los Angeles's Watts and Compton; these travels informed his perspective about Black space and experience and how race impacted the map of the United States. This geographic roll call transported the audience, who responded with a variety of cheers, laughter, and vocal affirmation to a universal and shared Black urban space.

Black people everywhere in the United States were connected by the geography and character of the places they created, from Detroit to Cleveland, Atlanta, Philadelphia, Fillmore and Bayview (San Francisco), and Watts (Los Angeles). These places were similar yet different, striving but often economically constrained, full of life and possibility yet plagued by common problems.[4] As Rawls's portrait asserts, Black America is both geography and an experience with interconnected Black enclaves differing in regional location but existing under shared conditions of inequality.

Malcolm X, Lou Rawls, and a host of other culture producers in music, literature, and scholarship are chocolate city theorists, and scholars of Black life more broadly. Offering a new perspective, we look to Black scholarship and writings alongside a range of original and archival data. Drawing inspiration from W. E. B. Du Bois's handmade maps of Black Philadelphia in

1899, Cheikh Anta Diop's corrective world histories centering Africa instead of western Europe, and Paul Gilroy's retracing of Black life in and across the Atlantic Ocean, we put forward Black mapping as a concept and analytic framework for understanding change and life in the United States over the twentieth century.[5] "Black matters are spatial matters," as Black feminist geographer Katherine McKittrick reminds us.[6] Therefore, we bring to the fore a variety of chocolate cities and the histories, dynamics, and trends therein to explain and animate the chocolate maps.

Prior to the civil rights movement, chocolate cities such as Memphis, Atlanta, and Washington, DC, existed as what political scientists Christopher Silver and John V. Moeser aptly call a *separate city*—a "self-contained, racially-identifiable community separated from the larger white city."[7] Within these separate spaces, Black folks developed a life, economy, and culture that existed in some ways outside of the White gaze. Still, even within these Black and White spaces, competing interests and pursuits among Black residents impacted patterns of migration and urban development.[8]

Although existing scholarship has made clear the connection between competing interest groups and the growth of cities and places, too much attention is given to the decisions of White stakeholders and officials and not that of their Black counterparts.[9] Addressing this gap, our analysis focuses on Black actors, perspectives, stakeholders, and residents across the United States during the twentieth century. Political disenfranchisement certainly limited the impact of Black agency.[10] However, choices Black residents made about a range of issues—including public space, employment, politics, and popular culture—helped to create and consolidate emergent Black areas across the United States (often prompting White residents to leave such areas).[11]

Even though Black migrants fled the South during the Great Migration, "The South" followed them, awaiting them in their new destinations; issues of discrimination, police brutality, and White domination did not disappear.[12] Raced-based oppression awaited Black migrants and residents wherever they made their homes and persists across many key measures, such as the achievement and mortality gaps.[13]

Black Americans also created and recreated "The South," especially within Great Migration destinations such as Central District (Seattle), Greenwood (Tulsa, OK), Memphis, Chicago, Houston, and Los Angeles.

Through cultural practices and products Black Americans have sought to represent their ambivalent and enduring links with the imagined, lived, and real South. These consistent racial and historical truths serve as the cornerstone and inspiration for our analysis.

What would a U.S. map look like if it were drawn with attention to Black actions and attitudes? What would that map look like if everything below Canada were the South? *Chocolate Cities* uses critical Black regionalism to offer a new view and a new map of Black experiences and urban change in America.[14] Using our data and resources we sketch a series of Black regions, aligning them with U.S. census data. Tables 1–6 illustrate the raw numbers and persistence of Black migration within and across the regions from 1900 to 2010. Alongside our maps, these tables also set forth the critical and porous boundaries within the chocolate maps.

DOWN SOUTH

The keys to navigating these regions on the chocolate map already exist in Black popular and public culture. In Spike Lee's *Crooklyn*, for instance, protagonist Troy Carmichael is sent "down South" to be with relatives after economic troubles make it difficult for the family to support the children in the summer. In Maryland Troy encounters a place she finds strange, with people who "talk funny," plush lawns, privilege, and pressing combs. This storyline is not unlike that of scores of children sent home every summer from the South Side of Chicago, Detroit, or New York to be with relatives and perhaps to stay out of trouble.[15]

There are a number of existing configurations of Down South. In its designation of American regions, the U.S. census breaks the "South" region into three areas: (1) west of the Mississippi River to Arkansas, Louisiana, Oklahoma, and Texas are in the "West South Central" portion of the South; (2) Alabama, Kentucky, Mississippi, and Tennessee constitute the "East South Central" South; and (3) the Carolinas, Delaware, Florida, Georgia, Maryland, the Virginias, and Washington, DC, make up the "South Atlantic" South. These designations reflect distinctions born of topographical differences—the West South Central region is characterized by its location west of the Mississippi; the East South

Central region by its location east of the Mississippi; and the South Atlantic region by its proximity to the Atlantic Ocean. These useful distinctions attend to how topographical features shape economic and social realities in places.

Yet there are many other ways to divide the South as a region, reflective of long traditions that attempt to draw distinctions between "better" and "worse" Souths as well as differences in agricultural practices, spatial practices, and geographies of movement. By some estimations Down South consists of the seven original Confederate states—Alabama, Florida, Georgia, Louisiana, Mississippi, South Carolina, and Texas. In these records, for example, these states and the cities within them are often referred to as the Lower South or Deep South and sometimes include western Tennessee and eastern Arkansas as part of this designation because of their contribution to the production and selling of cotton. Others include everything below the Mason-Dixon Line, save for the border states of Delaware, Kansas, Kentucky, and Oklahoma. Still others include all slaveholding states.

To think about how Black people experience the region thought of as the South, we offer a revision and different configuration than that imagined by the census. First, we look to Down South, the region created by the movement of Black folks along the eastern seaboard. This space includes the Carolinas, Florida (along the eastern seaboard), Georgia, and southern Virginia. We consider the contemporary and historical Black enclaves within the regions typically referred to as the East Coast, Southeast, and the South (i.e., Atlanta, Charleston, Charlotte, Columbia, Durham, Greensboro, Hilton Head Island, Jacksonville, Miami, Norfolk, Raleigh, Richmond, and Savannah). As Table 1 indicates, Black movement has been persistent Down South, beginning with nearly a 50 percent Black population in 1900 to slightly over a quarter of the Black population in 2010.

UP SOUTH

Recognizing that there were fewer distinctions between South and North than had been advertised, Black migrants from the South to the North began referring to their journeys as "Up South," a terminology that most

Table 1 Down South Black population: U.S. census, 1900–2010

Year	Total population	Black population	Black population (%)
1900	853,239	407,991	47.82
1910	2,675,587	1,093,584	40.87
1920	3,251,584	1,205,873	37.09
1930	3,800,280	1,247,660	32.83
1940	4,418,779	1,372,588	31.06
1960	7,838,081	1,907,116	24.33
1970	9,900,132	2,177,797	22.00
1980	12,320,629	2,773,360	22.51
1990	15,101,747	3,486,163	23.08
2000	18,813,871	4,625,427	24.59
2010	22,264,963	5,806,584	26.08

NOTE: Based on Census Metropolitan Area estimates. 1950 data incomplete.

Table 2 Up South Black population: U.S. census, 1900–2010

Year	Total population	Black population	Black population (%)
1900	6,495,653	145,556	2.26
1910	13,621,928	653,083	4.79
1920	16,117,767	828,340	5.14
1930	19,547,200	1,266,359	6.48
1940	20,962,198	1,555,115	7.42
1960	28,127,322	3,350,703	11.91
1970	31,995,182	4,762,969	14.89
1980	31,673,001	5,361,966	16.93
1990	33,522,017	6,163,177	18.39
2000	36,413,432	6,758,076	18.56
2010	38,431,876	7,228,156	18.81

NOTE: Based on Census Metropolitan Area estimates. 1950 data incomplete.

likely began with part of the area's original distinction as "Upper South," as opposed to the "Lower South." The Upper South included the border states of Kentucky and Missouri as well as Arkansas, North Carolina, Tennessee, Virginia, and West Virginia.

However, for Black migrants, Up South included a wider range of spaces along the eastern seaboard that began with the nation's capitol in the south and ended with the Canadian border. Thus, the Up South includes Delaware, Maryland, New Jersey, New York, eastern Pennsylvania, and northern Virginia, as well as the New England states of Connecticut, Maine, Massachusetts, New Hampshire, Rhode Island, and Vermont. Up South includes contemporary and historical Black enclaves within the East Coast, Mid-Atlantic, and the Northeast, including Baltimore, Boston, Bridgeport, New Haven, Philadelphia, Harlem, Brooklyn, Newark, and Washington, DC.

MID SOUTH

When Ida B. Wells's friend Thomas B. Moss was lynched along with two other Black grocers in 1892 by a White mob jealous of their economic success, Moss's final words were reportedly, "Tell my people to go west; there is no justice for them here." Angered by the murders of her friends, Wells used her paper, the *Free Speech and Headlight of Memphis,* to carry on Moss's message, encouraging Memphians to boycott the streetcar line and to "go west" to escape the tyranny of White supremacy. From Memphis, west would have been across the Mississippi River but beyond Arkansas and the confines of the Deep South. It would have meant the border states of Kansas, Missouri, or Oklahoma, the relative welcome of Iowa and Nebraska, the vast possibilities of Texas, or even California.

Depending on one's position on the chocolate map, then, the Mid South could have been west, north, or northwest. The Mid South includes a majority of what we think of as the Midwest, including the Dakotas, Illinois, Indiana, Iowa, Kansas, Kentucky, Michigan, Minnesota, Missouri, Nebraska, Oklahoma, Ohio, western Pennsylvania, and Wisconsin, as well as West Virginia. The Mid South is far less densely populated than the Atlantic South, although it contains several chocolate cities, including

Table 3   Mid South Black population: U.S. census, 1900–2010

Year	Total population	Black population	Black population (%)
1900	3,007,864	89,084	2.96
1910	11,620,523	368,508	3.17
1920	14,467,086	603,065	4.17
1930	18,232,198	1,031,727	5.66
1940	19,104,229	1,180,174	6.18
1960	26,895,508	2,889,763	10.74
1970	29,985,647	3,823,924	12.75
1980	30,274,965	4,391,217	14.50
1990	30,863,385	4,618,179	14.96
2000	33,393,729	5,168,719	15.48
2010	34,724,152	5,379,923	15.49

NOTE: Based on Census Metropolitan Area estimates. 1950 data incomplete.

Black communities within the North and Midwest (i.e., Chicago, Cincinnati, Cleveland, Detroit, Flint, Gary, Indianapolis, Kansas City, Lincoln, Louisville, Milwaukee, Minneapolis, Omaha, Pittsburgh, and Saint Louis).

OUT SOUTH

Stax recording artist Otis Redding's last song, "(Sitting on) The Dock of the Bay," was inspired by the musician's time in the San Francisco Bay Area, where he was performing at the Fillmore before his tragic death in a plane crash, which also killed most of the members of fellow label mates The Barkays. Whereas Los Angeles was a place where Black Americans could make it, or it could prove too much for them, the Bay Area offered a different space, worlds away from other Souths, to make it. The Bay Area was a geographic reality and metaphor for the Out South destinations to which Black folks migrated as they followed pathways west and began new lives and new communities in northern California, Colorado, the Dakotas, Oregon, Utah, Washington, and neighboring

Table 4   Out South Black population: U.S. census, 1900–2010

Year	Total population	Black population	Black population (%)
1900	499,320	2,933	0.59
1910	2,762,619	19,370	0.80
1920	3,448,107	25,387	0.74
1930	3,636,966	25,485	0.70
1940	4,908,525	20,669	0.42
1960	9,044,244	361,634	4.00
1970	9,170,560	501,744	5.47
1980	13,159,633	716,858	5.45
1990	15,268,549	880,458	5.77
2000	16,181,781	828,015	5.12
2010	18,435,750	1,036,029	5.62

NOTE: Based on Census Metropolitan Area estimates. 1950 data incomplete.

places. Developed within the broader westward expansions and manifest destiny policies in the United States, Out South is constituted by Black enclaves in the West Coast and Northwest (i.e., Anchorage, the Bay Area, Denver, Fargo, Honolulu, Portland, Sacramento, and Seattle).

DEEP SOUTH

Nina Simone's 1964 "Mississippi Goddam" is a sweeping critique of southern segregation and the Black and White political interests that advocated for a "slow" progress and respectability politics in the wake of the murder of Medgar Evers and the violence of Freedom Summer. Her refrain— "Alabama's got me so upset / Tennessee's made me lose my rest / and everybody knows about Mississippi, *goddam!*"—responded to specific instances of racist physical and political violence in those places. In the years since its release, however, the song—especially the rallying cry of "Mississippi, Goddam!," and particularly for people outside of the South— has become shorthand for the unconscionable aspects of the Deep South, from continued racial violence to racist policies that disadvantage com-

Table 5   Deep South Black population: U.S. census, 1900–2010

Year	Total population	Black population	Black population (%)
1900	991,242	410,613	41.42
1910	3,094,993	1,174,523	37.95
1920	3,422,559	1,176,985	34.39
1930	4,038,032	1,233,802	30.55
1940	4,526,456	1,419,449	31.36
1960	6,439,481	1,760,087	27.33
1970	7,168,793	1,823,414	25.44
1980	8,419,919	2,133,095	25.33
1990	8,973,664	2,282,095	25.43
2000	10,197,381	2,679,930	26.28
2010	11,110,870	2,904,008	26.14

NOTE: Based on Census Metropolitan Area estimates. 1950 data incomplete.

munities of color and other marginalized communities, including LGBT groups.

Notions of "Mississippi, Goddamn" reflect ideas about the Deep South as the last bastion of White racism and oppression, highlighting how the region is frequently used—by other southerners and by people outside the South—as an exemplary scapegoat for larger and enduring practices of "separate and unequal." We move within and beyond these discursive constructions to consider the how, why, and where of the Deep South in the twenty-first century. As such, we explore Black areas across the Bible Belt, the East Coast, the South, and the Sunbelt (including Baton Rouge, Birmingham, Chattanooga, the Florida Panhandle, Jackson, Knoxville, Little Rock, Memphis, Mobile, Montgomery, Nashville, New Orleans, and Selma) to map this South that looms largest in the public imagination of the region.

WEST SOUTH

In Gladys Knight's 1973 song "Midnight Train to Georgia," a young man who has moved to Out South to Los Angeles has found that the city has

Table 6   West South Black population: U.S. census, 1900–2010

Year	Total population	Black population	Black population (%)
1900	578,738	66,645	11.52
1910	2,126,565	247,362	11.63
1920	3,030,272	278,532	9.19
1930	5,075,315	388,849	7.66
1940	6,196,392	479,908	7.74
1960	13,331,875	1,236,886	9.28
1970	14,794,087	1,429,585	9.66
1980	20,782,279	2,364,545	11.38
1990	22,521,636	2,187,716	9.71
2000	31,841,644	3,185,449	10.00
2010	37,658,273	3,796,738	10.08

NOTE: Based on Census Metropolitan Area estimates. 1950 data incomplete.

"[proven] too much" for him to handle. Thus, he is "leaving on the midnight train to Georgia" and "going back to find a simpler place and time." This narrative is a common Black migration theme, where one leaves the South and tries to make it in the big city and finds economic marginalization among the "skyscrapers and everything" that make it difficult to survive. However, before the young man took the midnight train to Georgia, in interwar and postwar America, moving Out South was prudent to escape increasing violence Down South and start afresh with new, perhaps less racist, employment opportunities.

We consider West South as composed of the Black communities within the South, the Southwest, and the West Coast (i.e., Albuquerque, Austin, Dallas, Fort Worth, Houston, Las Vegas, Long Beach, Los Angeles, Oklahoma City, Phoenix, San Antonio, and San Diego). Despite a small decline in the interwar period, the West South consistently contains about 10 percent of the nation's Black population. These spaces reflect the promise of the West as a site west of the Mississippi River and beyond the oppression of the Deep South. Still, Black experiences in these places are remarkably similar to those of people in the Deep South, as well as in the Out South, Up South, and Down South.

PART II **The Village**

It takes a village to raise a child.

African proverb

5 The Blacker the Village, the Sweeter the Juice

Where can we be free? Where can we be black?

Solange Knowles, 2015

In the beginning there was the village. Sometimes it was small. Sometimes it was large. It was Black and Brown and in search of freedoms, real and imagined. Black people have been searching for places to be free, safe, and Black since Europe's enslavement and colonization of Africa.

In the nineteenth century, for instance, free Black people inhabited a peculiar and dangerous status in the United States. While legally free, theirs was a freedom contingent on the whims of Whites. We need only look to the life and times of Solomon Northup for an example of the violence and pain visited on free Black Americans by Whites in the context of a fragmented though enduring legalized slavery context.

A free man in New York, Northup was kidnapped in 1841 and taken to the Deep South, where he was enslaved for a period of twelve years. Northup, who was always free up until his capture, was fundamentally changed by the brutality he experienced and witnessed while enslaved. In a twist of luck, he was finally able to muster the gumption and connections needed to be free—again—after twelve years.[1] Passed three years before Northup's rescue, the Fugitive Slave Law of 1850, or what sociologist W. E. B. Du Bois called slavery's "safety valve," heightened the contradiction of being both Black and free in the United States (and in many places abroad).[2]

This contradiction in status as Black but not enslaved compelled many free Black people to move—across the Americas, from Haiti to Nova Scotia and to Sierra Leone and Liberia in Africa in search of a truly free space. Emancipation and its promise of freedom created the legal environment for Black people to finally move within the United States without fear of capture and enslavement. This new freedom spurred them toward the urbanizing American South, to North Buxton, Ontario, Liberia, and to newly created towns in the rural South and the American frontier. "Safety in numbers," which manifested as a racial survival strategy during slavery, persisted in a new and tenuous freedom, influencing patterns of Black urbanization, migration, and immigration forever. The Black Belt began to form across urban America, especially as growing opportunities in manufacturing and other professions combined with the "American Apartheid" of racial residential segregation to constrain Black settlement choices.[3] The modern Black map emerged over the course of the first half of the twentieth century, as across the United States, one by one, Black Belts formed a patchwork of interconnected chocolate cities.

After World War II Black Americans fundamentally transformed the urban core of the Rustbelt, Northeast, and the West Coast, making homes and communities out of ghettoized city space, as municipal and state governments disinvested in Black neighborhoods. This disinvestment in part propelled Black people to return to the rural, urban, and suburban South and reclaim the region as home. Fast-forward: a coalition of activists all across the chocolate map in the Black Lives Matter movement call for an end to police brutality and a reinvestment in Black communities and Black lives. The churning, the movement, and the search continue.

Black Americans have continued to move about the Black diaspora in search of home. Since 1619, then, Black life in the Americas can be defined by this constant movement, migration, resistance, and quest for a place where Black people can be free and Black at the same time. Each generation provided the forward momentum for the next, sprinters in the relay race that is the Black Freedom struggle.

In this historical context, reassessing the wisdom of the African proverb—*it takes a village to raise a child*—is especially fruitful. Often, "the child" of the proverb is imagined as an individual child: it takes all of us to raise Keisha, for instance. But this common use of the proverb obscures its central philosophy. That is, *from many there is one*. Independence and autonomy are born from collective synergy and action. Human collectives—communities, activists, networks, professionals, residents—possess the magic to manifest powerful and often controlling individual creations as leaders, government, places, and geographies.

Conceived in this way, the village is not simply a place whose distinctiveness is based on relative size. Rather, the village is the fundamental unit or nucleus for chocolate cities and Black geographies; it is also a metaphor and evidence for the enduring practice and importance of place making for marginalized and oppressed citizens. In short, it first takes a village to make a chocolate city.

From many villages—small towns, rural communities, small Black sections on the other side of the tracks—chocolate cities were created, surviving and thriving in their respective places on the chocolate map. Even when the northward and westward flows of the Great Migration seemingly reverse, places like Chicago continue to receive a steady stream of residents from their surrounding village cities. Though Black residents began to leave Chicago for the South and West in the early twenty-first century, the village cities in Illinois, Wisconsin, and Indiana continue to feed Chicago more chocolate city citizens every day.

What was this feature, the village, and how did Black residents create and operate within it? How did Black villages evolve into the modern neighborhoods, meccas, South Sides, Black Bottoms, and towns that constitute the chocolate cities? In this chapter, we follow Ida B. Wells's migration from the Black village of Holly Springs, Mississippi, to cities like Memphis, London, and Chicago. Politics, White supremacy, and Black determination of social and physical geographies intersect in Wells's life story, helping us to see the genesis of chocolate cities through the lens of the village intent on raising new generations of chocolate city children.

STRAIGHT OUTTA HOLLY SPRINGS

In 1878 both the White and Black back sides of Mississippi River towns found themselves equally facing a peril that temporarily ruptured the boundaries between these racially separate communities. A yellow fever epidemic had swept through the Mississippi Delta and ravaged communities up and down the river. Cotton's urban distribution capital, Memphis, had ceased to officially exist, save as a taxation district of Shelby County. The disease had caused widespread death and exodus, threatening the distinct but interconnected small towns and rural communities throughout the region.[4]

Just south of Memphis in Marshall County is Holly Springs, Mississippi, the county seat and an active commerce post for area plantations during slavery. After Emancipation many Black Americans, like James Wells, a skilled carpenter, and Elizabeth Warrenton Wells, a sought-after cook, remained in the small but bustling area. Most Black people did not live life in a "pure Negro town" like Zora Neale Hurston's Eatonville. Instead, their village was the "black back-side of the average town." Many lived in places like Farmville, Virginia. Though majority Black and rural, Farmville's geography differed from the racial pureness of Eatonville. "Here in 1890 lived ten thousand Negroes and two thousand whites," Du Bois noted about Farmville. "The country is rich, yet the people are poor. The keynote of the Black Belt is debt; not commercial credit, but debt in the sense of continued inability on the part of the mass of the population to make income cover expense."[5]

In his classic text, *The Souls of Black Folk,* Du Bois further explores Black place making and the emergence of Black geographies of urban America at the dawn of the twentieth century. In a central chapter, "Of the Black Belt," he identifies three different spatial configurations. The first is the half-and-half configuration that arose out of Black laborers settling on the outskirts of a White space: "It is usually possible to draw in nearly every Southern community a physical color-line on the map, on the one side of which Whites dwell and on the other Negroes. The winding and intricacy of the geographical color-lines varies, of course, in different communities. I know some towns where a straight line drawn through the middle of the main street separates nine-tenths of the Whites from nine-tenths of the blacks."[6]

The second consists of the separate rings that came about as Black residents filled in undesirable areas progressively distant from a town center: "In other towns the older settlement of Whites has been encircled by a broad band of blacks." The third reflects the Black sections that emerged in the midst of White spaces: "In still other cases little settlements or nuclei of blacks have sprung up amid surrounding whites." Du Bois further notes the similarities in rural and urban segregation: "Usually in cities each street has its distinctive color, and only now and then do the colors meet in close proximity. Even in the country something of this segregation is manifest in the smaller areas, and of course in the larger phenomena of the Black Belt."[7]

Often wealthy Whites wielded significant control over spatial organization and thus over the physical location of villages. Even still, Black people occupied spaces given to them and those previously off-limits. Whether it was the hills of Pittsburgh, or the plains of Kankakee, Illinois, Black citizens deliberately used their ability to densely occupy space to obscure the White gaze and develop an intricately dynamic lifeworld.

The convergence of rural and urban, pure Negrotown and not, Deep South and Mid South are especially reflected in the life and times for those in places like Alabama, Tennessee, and Mississippi. In the Black village of Holly Springs, the Wells family were members of the village's middle class, politically savvy and committed to Black education, uplift, and self-determination. James and Elizabeth Wells survived enslavement only to succumb to yellow fever while tending to their infant Stanley, who also died in the epidemic. Away at her grandmother's house farther south, a young and focused Ida B. Wells, their eldest daughter, returned to the town despite the ongoing epidemic. She needed to return, she felt, to take responsibility for her younger siblings, striving desperately to keep them together.

To do that, Wells needed a job. Armed with some employment leads from her parents' extensive network in the village, a sixteen-year-old Wells set about securing work to support her family, even posing as older than she was so she could qualify for a teaching position in a rural school on the outskirts of Holly Springs. Her parents were gone, but Wells was determined to continue their example as caring parents and politically sophisticated village citizens endeavoring to create a new life with their new freedom.[8]

Wells's formative years in the largely Black village of Holly Springs shaped her sense of what was possible, as scores of skilled Black folks, like her mother and father, worked toward self-determination after Emancipation. In Holly Springs the realities of race and racism were palpable but still distant from a young Wells living in the relative comfort and privilege provided by her parents' economic self-sufficiency. An avid reader and writer, Wells was sharp and quick-witted, and her smarts propelled her forward on a journey across the chocolate map.

Once financially able, Wells took her sisters and moved to Memphis, where she secured a teaching job and became involved in local salons, conversing, debating, and learning with and from thought leaders from all over the Mid South. From Memphis she launched a career as a journalist and brought international attention to racism and the antilynching cause in late nineteenth- and early twentieth-century America.

It was the experience of Holly Springs that made the 1892 Memphis murder of her friend and goddaughter's father, Thomas Moss, and his friends Calvin McDowell and Will Stewart, so jarring. Wells was not naive about White racism before the lynching at People's Grocery. Her faith in the courts as a place to which Black people could appeal for fairness, for instance, had been shattered by the Tennessee Supreme Court's reversal of the lower court's ruling in her favor in a discrimination suit. But surely Black people were not being brutally executed for simply existing and trying to make a living.[9]

That Whites could murder Black citizens, especially those who were middle class, with impunity was unconscionable to Wells. She questioned and rejected the general popular assumption that Black men were lynched for raping White women. As a result, fighting the injustice of lynching would become her life's work. She would time and again and as much as she could confront head-on what she famously called "that old threadbare lie."[10]

She knew her friend's only crime was Black excellence; he had competed with a White grocer and bested him, and for that—as well as for the audacity to resist assault on his person and property—he and his friends were murdered. Then, as it is now, respectability did not protect Black people from White violence. As this reality became undeniably apparent, Wells knew she needed to investigate and spread the word. In the process, she contributed to the making of social science and the chocolate maps.

Radicalized by the lyceum circuit in Memphis, Wells conducted research on the lived experiences of Black Americans in the post-Reconstruction South, using structural analyses and critical race and gender theories. She investigated the structure and the consequences of lynching as a racialized punishment and policy, illustrating the mutual influence of individual actions and prevailing social attitudes in precipitating such violence. At the outset of *Southern Horrors,* a collection of these research accounts, Wells asserts, "The Afro-American is not a bestial race. If this work can contribute in any way toward proving this, and at the same time arouse the conscience of the American people to a demand for justice to every citizen, and punishment by law for the lawless, I shall feel I have done my race a service."[11]

From 1892 to 1894 Wells collected ethnographic and archival data from across the South, publishing her findings in a pamphlet series titled *Southern Horrors: Lynch Law in All Its Phases.* Detailing more than fifty cases and their murky circumstances, Wells not only offers an accounting of lynching but also explores the rampant and nearly insurmountable hypocrisy that undergirded some of the violence:

> The very week the "leading citizens" of Memphis were making a spectacle of themselves in defense of all White women of every kind, an Afro-American, M. Stricklin, was found in a White woman's room in that city. Although she made no outcry of rape, he was jailed and would have been lynched, but the woman stated she bought curtains of him (he was a furniture dealer) and his business in her room that night was to put them up. A White woman's word was taken as absolutely in this case as when the cry of rape is made, and he was freed.
>
> What is true of Memphis is true of the entire South. The daily papers last year reported a farmer's wife in Alabama had given birth to a Negro child. When the Negro farm hand who was plowing in the field heard it he took the mule from the plow and fled. The dispatches also told of a woman in South Carolina who gave birth to a Negro child and charged three men with being its father, *every one of whom has since disappeared.* In Tuscumbia, Ala., the colored boy who was lynched there last year for assaulting a White girl told her before his accusers that he had met her there in the woods often before.[12]

Wells concluded that this violence, a result of the race and gender codes erected in the postslavery South, could be countered only by Black agency (individual and collective). "Nothing," Wells soberly advised, "is more definitely settled than [the Negro] must act for himself. I have shown how [the Negro] may employ the boycott, emigration and the press, and I feel that by a combination of all these *agencies* can be effectually stamped out lynch law, that last relic of barbarism and slavery."[13] For Wells, boycotting, migration, and the pen are the multiple and effective "agencies" that Black people could and should use to compel equality.

After the lynching of her friend, Wells armed herself, writing in her autobiography: "Although I had been warned repeatedly by my own people that something would happen if I did not cease harping on the lynching of three months before, I had expected the happening to come when I was at home. . . . I had bought a pistol the first thing after Tom Moss was lynched," Wells continues, "because I expected some cowardly retaliation from the lynchers. I felt that one had better die fighting against injustice than to die like a dog or a rat in a trap. I had already determined to sell my life as dearly as possible if attacked. I felt if I could take one lyncher with me, this would even up the score a little bit."[14]

Wells was a tenacious and meticulous investigator. Her "prickliness," as scholar Jacqueline Jones Royster has called it, was distinctive and renowned.[15] She was expelled from Rust College, where her father had been on the board, after a dispute with the institution's president. While being forcibly removed from a White train car on her way to do course work at Fisk University in Nashville, she bit the conductor in resistance and protest.

Then one of the many truth-telling editorials she wrote under the pen name "Iola" got her fired from her teaching post with the Shelby County schools. In these editorials, Wells encouraged Black subscribers of the *Memphis Free Speech*—more than four thousand—to boycott White businesses and streetcars. She implored Black Americans to vote with their feet and cast their lots westward in Oklahoma, since Whites in Memphis had no interest in respecting their humanity.

The first of these editorials drew on her friend's reported dying words— "Tell my people to go west"—and Wells urged Blacks in Memphis who could do so to leave the city. Wells recognized the inherent power of Black people to move, even with constraints, and encouraged them to use this power to shape their futures. After White local papers ran editorials about the pestilence and the violent indigenous people awaiting potential migrants to the West, Wells traveled to Oklahoma and returned to Memphis with a report about her findings that countered those rumors. Ultimately, her emphasis on agency as a counter to racism earned her the ire of powerful southern Whites invested in maintaining the status quo and cost her livelihood and her life in Memphis.

These acts of protest and politics she did at great risk of personal injury. Her life was under constant threat from Whites. Rather than cease her race-conscious writing, Wells resolved to always carry a pistol and "take a lyncher with her" if she were attacked. Wells took on the anti-Black rhetoric of Frances Willard, the Women's Christian Temperance Union leader, calling out her racism in front of an audience halfway across the world in Great Britain. Straight out of Holly Springs, Mississippi, Ida B. Wells's prickliness was a key part of her social science prowess and activism. She was an unparalleled superheroine, working fearlessly on behalf of Black lives.[16]

Serendipitously for the antilynching cause and for the Black Memphians who were ready to defend Wells with their own lives, a vengeful White mob came while she was away in New York City. Working there with T. Thomas Fortune, Wells knew the appropriate White audience was beyond the United States and traveled to Britain to report on her investigations there. Already a frequent target of White media, her international work hardened her infamy among Whites but increased her acclaim among chocolate city masses. Back in the states but unable to return to Memphis, Wells settled several hundred miles up the rail line from Memphis in Chicago's Black Belt, the area sociologists St. Clair Drake and Horace Cayton call the "Black Metropolis."[17] There, in the heart of Chicago's Black Belt, Wells would continue her crusade until her death in March 1931.[18]

UP AND THROUGH (WITH) THE SOUTHS

Wells moved to Memphis, like many other Black folks from Mississippi in the late nineteenth and early twentieth centuries, in search of expanded opportunities in the new urban South. If Holly Springs had been a village with some protections of middle-class naïveté, Memphis laid bare the realities of racism for poor and middle-class Black people alike. There were no tense harmonies to be found in this burgeoning chocolate city. Not twenty years before Wells arrived in Memphis with her sisters, White citizens and police officers rampaged through the city's Black neighborhoods and murdered men, women, and children; raped women; and destroyed homes, schools, churches, and businesses. Wells was only four when this massacre happened, but news of it constantly reverberated across Holly Springs and towns throughout Mississippi, Arkansas, and Tennessee as she came of age.

Among the many things she was, Wells was a chocolate city navigator and challenged fear to move and keep moving about the chocolate map. A pioneer of the public-scholar tradition, she was determined that the power of Black people's agency was rooted in their ability to resist through movement and make places for safety and freedom in the process. She sowed the seeds of truth and justice across the chocolate map, from Holly Springs and Memphis to New York, Chicago, and beyond. Her travels help us understand chocolate maps as a geography of Black people's freedom strivings, illuminating the pathways they took in search of safety and a place to be Black and free. She did the dangerous work she did in the soul city village of Memphis, knowing full well the city's history and reality of unpunished White mob violence and its explicit devaluation of Black lives. She felt she had no choice.

6 The Two Ms. Johnsons

Say her name. #SayHerName

Kimberlé Crenshaw, *African American Policy Forum*, 2014

Explorers and villagers take many forms and have many identities. Although there is a great diversity within the Black American population, often those whose names are lifted up as heroes and sheroes fit within what Evelyn Brooks Higginbotham calls the "politics of respectability"—a version of Black politics and people concerned with aligning freedom goals with being morally unimpeachable.[1] This type of politics has been effective in constructing pathways to civil rights while simultaneously erecting boundaries around Blackness and Black history.

As a result, certain adventurers and villagers and their explorations are obscured. This is especially true when we think about the migrations and lives of Black LGBT Americans. To address this knowledge gap and scientific malpractice and to further expand the various range of viewpoints encompassed in a chocolate cities paradigm, we focus on the life and times of two Black trans women. The two Ms. Johnsons, Marsha P. Johnson and Duanna Johnson, came of age at different times and in different regions of the chocolate map. Both Ms. Johnsons and their journeys, however, exemplify how issues of gender, violence, race, sexuality, and safety motivate the actions and attitudes of Black Americans moving through the multiple Souths that make up the United States.

In this chapter we explore the dynamics of chocolate cities and maps made plain when sexual and gender minorities are centered. As we will find, safety and possibility provide a dynamic call to chocolate cities for Black LGBT villagers. In their quest to survive and thrive, the two Ms. Johnsons (from their respective chocolate cities) engaged in practices of migration and resistance that, at their core, give insights into how Black Americans perceive and move through the United States as a composite of multiple southern regions.

LONG AS I GOT QUEEN JESUS

Whereas antilynching activist Ida B. Wells carried a revolver, Marsha P. Johnson, transgender pioneer of the Stonewall riots, wielded a switchblade. Wells needed to protect herself from lynchers who had put a bounty on her head and sometimes even from Black men uncomfortable with her politics and prickliness who wanted to do her harm. Born at the end of World War II and coming of age during the 1950s in Elizabeth, New Jersey, Johnson needed to protect herself from homophobic violence in and outside of Black communities. Even in the relative safety of the Greenwich Village of 1960s New York, Johnson was constantly aware of the dangers that lurked due to her intersectional status as a genderqueer, Black, gay, drag queen, performance artist, and sex worker.

Even in one of the world's biggest global cities, there was a village. Its function as a space of safety and cultivation for society's marginalized was not unlike that of Wells's Holly Springs. But rather than being an separate segregated space, Greenwich Village, like villages of all kinds Up South and Out South, consisted of a patchwork of safe places, and as Black gay, lesbian, and trans people moved in and out of the Village, they queered the chocolate map, creating places where they could be Black and free in all ways.

For Marsha P. Johnson, those places consisted of streets, rooms, hotels, apartment buildings, and churches of all sorts, from Saint Mary's to the Stonewall Inn. No place lasted, and Johnson's frequent movement throughout New York City and New Jersey was a microcosm for the constant churning of Black people across chocolate maps. Along with other street queens, such as Sylvia Rivera, Marsha P. Johnson "made the road by walking" and is exemplary of how chocolate maps reflect a multifaceted, nuanced set of Black experiences at various identity intersections.[2]

Not everyone's view of the chocolate map is the same. Johnson's vantage point, for example, necessarily included red flags on sites of violence against Black women specifically and Black LGBT people more generally. Johnson's view of the map likely had to anticipate and integrate what Black feminist sociologist Deborah King calls "multiple jeopardy"—how Black women are oppressed by their statuses as Black *and* women *and* also as often economically disadvantaged.[3] Reflecting multiple identities and multiple oppressions, Johnson also embodies what legal scholar Kimberlé Crenshaw called "intersectionality"—the consciousness and experience wherein race, class, gender, sexuality, gender identity, and ability co-occur and create disadvantages or opportunities in status-based societies.[4]

In her 1975 Andy Warhol portrait, an air of coyness almost bordering on timidity belies her "larger than life" status in New York.[5] But only a fool would mistake Marsha P. Johnson's kindness for weakness. Quick-witted and fast with her blade and tongue, she was known for her ability to rise above the foolish, nonbelievers, and dangerous folks who attempted to harm her or those in the communities she held dear.[6]

Up and down the concrete rainbows of Christopher Street in the 1960s, 1970s, and 1980s, Marsha P. Johnson did the work of Jesus. Having gotten "married to Jesus Christ at 16 because he was the only man I could really trust," Johnson walked and talked with Jesus, prayed to Jesus for strength, knew Jesus heard her pleas and prayers, and had the spirit of Jesus on earth. Adorned with masterfully crafted crowns of flowers, she could be found prostrate in churches, worshipping and meditating at the altar.[7]

Out in the streets she spread the gospel of humanity not through a heavy-handed evangelism but through acts of kindness and miracles of survival only queens of color from the Stonewall era know. She greeted folks with that familiar glow and wide smile, gave people her last penny, hustled, and nursed the sick. People called her a saint and knew she was a queen, and they saw her works near the Hudson River like the works of Jesus near Jordan.

Johnson had come across the harbor to New York City at age eighteen to make a freer life for herself. In the volatile Up South village, gay, trans, and genderqueer youth had negotiated tenuous relationships with crime syndicates for protection from police raids and other systematic and ongoing violence that threatened sexual minorities in the 1960s and 1970s. Johnson was frequently persecuted as Black, gay, and a pretty boy in drag.

She, too, had survived the routine hazards of her status as a sex worker: jail, assault, threats with guns, and once a gunshot wound. "Pay it no mind," Johnson would answer when asked what the "P" in her middle name meant. Standing in as a clever philosophy of defiance and survival, the phrase "pay it no mind" helped Marsha forgive those who had harmed her while also keeping her attentions focused on her own struggle and life's work. She adopted this mantra to cope with her precarious life and the things that happened to her because of who she was and what she represented. But it was also a shorthand for her faith, as she strived to live as free as possible of worry and to thank Jesus for her life.[8]

On June 28, 1969, she was at the Stonewall Inn when the police disrupted the fragile safety of the space with one of their usual, but this time unexpected, raids. These raids served as state-sanctioned antigay violence and gender policing, as drag queens and butch lesbians were targeted in particular for rejecting hegemonic gender rules. But on that evening, as police lined people up for gender "checks," arrested some, dragged others out, and beat people, the village had had enough. If Jesus had flipped a table, Marsha P. Johnson is rumored to have thrown a glass and cried out for rights. After that night the riots continued, and Johnson was there organizing, agitating, and resisting. In a 1992 interview with Michael Kasino, she recalled, "In 1969 when the Stonewall riot started is when I started my little rioting."[9]

Johnson's "little rioting" consisted of groundbreaking organizing that created the infrastructure and framework for modern LGBT advocacy. Beyond her everyday activism of feeding, clothing, and giving to those needier than her despite her own palpable need, she cofounded STAR (Street Transvestite Action Revolutionaries) with Rivera. Together they worked to end homelessness among young queens, trans, and gay people, organizing for space, advocacy, and survival. She walked each year in the June pride walk, preferring the labor of walking to riding as a symbol of the labor it took to be alive, to survive, to mourn the dead, and to fight for those coming up. Her "little rioting" was accompanied by an ongoing battle with depression, likely a result of childhood and adult traumas coupled with the stresses of organizing against oppression and losing friends each year. By the 1980s Marsha was a common fixture at vigils, weeping for her friends lost to violence and AIDS.

Though she never had the money to do "serious" drag, she was not preoccupied with being that kind of queen. A queen of and for the people, the People's Queen, Johnson's captivating brand of drag entertainment made her legendary before that quality was available through ball and pageant wins and extravagant gowns. After walking in the June pride march in 1992, Johnson went to her place of comfort, the Hudson River, and it is unclear what happened next. People reported seeing someone harassing her, and it would not have been the first time Johnson met violence at the Hudson. Along with her wig, she had once been thrown in the river, making her way out by some miracle. But this time, she did not. Her body was found floating in the Hudson, and, with little investigation, police ruled her death a suicide.

Like other Up South villages, including Harlem, that nurtured Black gay, lesbian, bisexual, genderqueer, and trans people, the landscape of place and belonging has changed dramatically. Stonewall Inn is now a national landmark in a transformed and trendy Greenwich Village, a sterile preservation imploring us to remember a time when queer and trans people were perpetual targets of violence. In some ways Stonewall's historic preservation mutes the real violence, policing, and surveillance, rendering it politically distant in an era of marriage rights, hate crime legislation, advances in employment law, and increased gay, lesbian, and trans media visibility.[10]

Johnson's movement in and through the chocolate map highlights how the village feature of chocolate cities is used to inform political behavior and Black primary and secondary migration. Johnson was compelled to choose places on the chocolate map that afforded her the most safety. In defense of herself and scores of women, men, and gender-nonconforming people who looked to her as an example and pioneer, Johnson created, took, and took up space.

Made through a lifetime of works, Marsha P. Johnson was a village in and of herself, making a place for herself and others like her on the chocolate maps. Despite advances in LGBT rights and visibility, the intersection of race and sexuality renders that visceral violence that propelled Marsha

P. Johnson to riot ever closer. The queer village Johnson made through a network of sites in Greenwich Village dissolved as New York City "cleaned up," displacing some people and ignoring the epidemic of homelessness and AIDS killing off others. Beyond this spatial violence, a half century after Johnson resisted the police, threw a glass, and insisted on her rights, Black femmes and Black trans women continue to have to defend themselves, by pistol or switchblades or Jesus, as they navigate places that still are not safe for girl children on the chocolate map.

CAUGHT ON CANDID CAMERA

As one Ms. Johnson went up yonder, another had been born. Duanna Johnson had spent her childhood in the 1960s and 1970s between the Down South villages of North Memphis and the Mid South migration destination of Chicago. Twenty years later, like others before her, Johnson moved back to where she started on the chocolate map in the wake of her grandmother's death, starting life again in North Memphis, hoping she could make her old neighborhood and chocolate city into a place where she could be Black, trans, and free.

The North Memphis communities where Johnson spent much of her life began as a separate city of relatively elite Black neighborhoods settled by Black people migrating to the city in the early years after Emancipation. North Memphis persisted as an enclave of Black homeowners and business elites but declined, like many Black neighborhoods, in the wake of postwar highway construction that bifurcated communities and caused neighborhood disinvestment. A small child when Martin Luther King Jr. was assassinated, Johnson came of age as an interstate bypass originally planned through a wealthy White community was blocked by a Supreme Court decision and rerouted through North Memphis.

This racial and political context served as the pushes and pulls toward home and migration over Johnson to leave and come back from places as close as Nashville and as far as Chicago. After some time away, by 2007 the call to home had pulled her back to Memphis. Within a year a violent interaction with Memphis police would put her intersectional disadvantages on full and painful display.

In June 2008 a video from February surfaced and was shown as an exclusive on WMC Action News 5 (Memphis's local NBC affiliate). Unlike today's social media onslaught of videos of violence against Black people on autoplay, beforehand the newscaster warned that what we were about to view "might be considered disturbing." Ready, we were not.[11]

Through the eye of a camera perched in a top corner of an intake room, we survey the action in the entire space. Twenty-eight-year-old Memphis police officer Bridges Sutton McRae repeatedly punches a seated forty-two-year-old Duanna Johnson, pausing to wrap handcuffs around his knuckles to heighten the torture. We then see James Swain, a twenty-five-year-old probationary officer, holding Johnson's shoulders down at one point as McRae continues his assault.

After a severe blow Johnson jumps up and swings back, fearing the next one could end her life. By the video's end Johnson has been hand-cuffed, maced, and critically beaten. Then a nurse enters our view, bypassing a writhing and traumatized Johnson and choosing instead to tend to the officer. Despite the videotaped police assault of Rodney King being etched in our subconsciousness, in 2008 we still were not as practiced at watching and critiquing the spectacle of violence against Black bodies and Black death as we have unfortunately become today.

In a June interview with Donna Davis, the journalist who broke the story and video and who was fired six months later, Johnson recounts how she refused to respond to McRae's homophobic and transphobic epithets as he demanded that she come over to be fingerprinted.[12] Then the attack ensued. As the interview proceeds, Johnson visibly begins reliving the pain of both the attack and the inaction of the multiple witnesses, officers, and the nurse. "I couldn't breathe, and they just made me lay there," a traumatized Johnson says, recalling the ordeal with sobering detail. "And then about 15 other officers came in, and they ran to him to see if he was okay. Nobody checked to see if I was okay. My eyes were burning; my skin was burning. I was scared to death. . . . I didn't feel like I was a human being then. Even the nurse came in and she just ignored me, and I begged her to help me."[13]

McRae and Swain, both White, were fired. McRae's Memphis trial for violating Johnson's civil rights resulted in a hung jury after five days of deliberation, with eleven people for conviction and one holdout. He later pled guilty to federal charges of civil rights violations, receiving only two years in jail.

Johnson had been mounting a case against the city of Memphis and the Memphis Police Department, armed with the powerful visual evidence of abuse and violation, when she was found murdered in November of that same year. Her death reflects the constellation of racism, misogyny, transmisogyny, and police brutality that Black trans women live with every day. Unfortunately, her murder, like the murder of scores of other Black trans women, remains unsolved.[14]

Battling anti-Black transphobia, misogyny, and violence directed specifically at Black trans women because of their intersecting race, gender, and gender identity statuses, Duanna Johnson survived homelessness, constant police harassment, and police brutality and spoke a truth rooted in the neighborhood resistance practices deeply influenced by her life in the villages of North Memphis. Although she was silenced by violence, we still speak Duanna Johnson's name and amplify her important mark on and movement through the chocolate map.

WHERE WE CAN ALL BE FREE

> For those of us who live at the shoreline
> standing upon the constant edges of decision
> crucial and alone . . .
> and when we speak we are afraid
> our words will not be heard
> nor welcomed
> but then we are silent
> we are still afraid
> So it is better to speak
> remembering
> we were not meant to survive.

Audre Lorde, "A Litany for Survival," *Black Unicorn: Poems*, 1978

The early unfolding of the movement that has come to be known popularly as Black Lives Matter or the Movement for Black Lives was criticized for its lack of focus on the experiences of Black people on the margins. These fissures were not new. As political scientist Cathy Cohen has noted, activism against HIV/AIDS in Black communities was impeded by respectability politics and homophobia in Black churches.[15]

Duanna Johnson was brutally beaten by police and murdered under extraordinarily suspicious circumstances. The Black church community was sure to mention its condemnation of Johnson's "lifestyle" while offering tepid outrage at her beating and death. When women are murdered, police narratives abound about their "sassiness" or "violent tendencies," as in the case of Sandra Bland and Korryn Gaines. Women, queer and heterosexual, cis and trans, are often at the front lines of the movement but are frequently obscured in migration narratives and social movement politics and commonly mistreated by their cisgender and heterosexual comrades.

The twenty-first-century Black social movements brought forth a reminder of the still-fraught strategies of collective racial resistance that resonated in Black women's rights and Black lesbian, gay, and trans rights movements in the 1960s and 1970s. Can we organize against police brutality against Black men and also challenge rape in Black communities? Can we recognize how Black women experience police brutality? Can we recognize how being Black and trans and a woman means a particular kind of jeopardy that is especially dangerous for our Black trans women compatriots? In her critique of My Brother's Keeper, former president Barack Obama's initiative aimed at improving the lives of Black boys, Kimberlé Crenshaw simply asks if Black girls are not also disproportionately experiencing racial oppression.[16] Are all the Black people still only men?

Crenshaw has also implored us to "say her name," to lift up the names of Black women murdered by the police, and to also acknowledge the specific ways Black women are in danger in an anti-Black misogynist society.[17] These women, femme, butch, woman-loving, trans, like all Black people, at all of their intersections, are looking for, moving to, creating, and demanding places to be Black and free. The two Ms. Johnsons, Marsha and Duanna, the former from Up South who lived by the Hudson and the latter from the Deep South who lived by the Mississippi, embody this aspiration, motivating a Black geography of the United States. Countering the conventional White landscape forced on Black Americans to develop their horizon of expectation and pathways to and through chocolate cities, both Ms. Johnsons endeavored to make a place in the world where all people could be free.

7 Making Negrotown

> The African past lies camouflaged in the collective
> African American memory, transformed by the middle
> passage, sharecropping, industrialization, [and]
> urbanization.
>
> E. Frances White, "Africa on My Mind," 1990

Despite the relatively short geographic distances between the rural and urban South, internal migration within the South was an equally transformative feat in the making of chocolate maps. Many rural migrants that eventually ended up Out South and Up South were first urbanized Deep South and Down South, where they stopped off to visit, shop, and sometimes stay for a bit, like when the writer Richard Wright went to Memphis from Natchez, Mississippi, before heading to other places on the chocolate map in the United States and beyond.[1] Some people got off the train or the bus where they could or where they had to. Others intended to stay and see family for a bit and then made the urban South their home. Still others who left the Deep South and Mid South returned later from their Up South and Out South lives to tend to the places from whence they came.

As cultural anthropologist Carol Stack reminds us, links between Great Migration destinations and the traditional South endured long after folks left.[2] It was and is common for Black families to send wayward children to the South to get their behavior and minds right or to protect them from dangers, perceived and imminent, in their own communities. Funerals, weddings, and family reunions are the strong cultural incentives pulling

Black people back to the South or across another South. Two popular sources play this social fact out with great flair.

In his award-winning novel, *Long Division,* scholar Kiese Laymon writes of a young Black boy's movement between time, dimension, and place, traveling from the civil rights era to the era of Reaganomics to post-Katrina Mississippi from Chicago, Jackson, and the Mississippi Delta. One protagonist is sent to the Delta from Jackson, Mississippi, because of a viral video of an outburst he made on a televised spelling bee. There, in the Delta, a whipping awaits. But so do profound time-travelling experiences that illustrate where and how his life is connected to those before and after him. These experiences also make plain the importance of place making and time making, as the protagonists live a more beautiful world in a book.[3]

Alongside this novel, we can also look to the popular comedic film *Welcome Home, Roscoe Jenkins* for evidence of recurrent themes of returning home to the South and sometimes making a home there in the context of difficulty or the aftermath of a life-changing event. Though *Long Division* is a speculative novel with time travel as one of its primary devices, *Welcome Home, Roscoe Jenkins* features the kind of comedic fantasy that abounds when a citified Black prodigal son returns to his country family. Starring Black comedian Martin Lawrence as the titular protagonist, the film centers on the less-than-triumphant return of Roscoe Jenkins to rural Georgia for his parents' fiftieth wedding anniversary celebration. Jenkins, a middle-aged single dad and host of a syndicated talk show, quickly finds his Hollywood trappings—a reality TV star girlfriend, a focus on the individual instead of the collective, veganism—in conflict with the simple life of his small-town Georgia kinfolk. He learns, sometimes painfully and hilariously, the kinds of lessons about self, family, and home that are often only possible with a return home.[4]

The story of the Great Migration is often the story of the movement of small-town and farm people from Down South to big cities Up South and Out South, and later reversing course and returning to their Down South origins. We know how they transformed the urban landscape, and we know how they brought Down South customs, mores, and traditions all over the country to make chocolate maps. But what about how they made the places in between? The revival of *The Negro Travelers' Green Book* (see also chapter 12), a crowd-sourced account of safe places to eat, sleep, and picnic during Jim Crow, evidences that we are now learning more about the process and strategy it took to make a life, to make a place to be free, in an anti-Black country. It is this shared cultural knowledge, now hidden in the spatial organization of Black places, that made a Black world in spaces everywhere below Canada.

This chapter explores these connections between the villages wherein Black people find themselves. Through migration, branches of Black family trees grew across the United States but also provided multiple roots for return. Family events, like reunions, weddings, funerals, or an elder's birthday, can draw even the farthest family member back. While differences abound, it is clear that the village is a central feature of the chocolate city, no matter where Black folks are located on chocolate maps. As we will see, Black villages are not simply a hodgepodge arrangement of locales but instead a purposely created set of places, cultures, and resistive practices that help forge bonds that are able to be sustained across space and time.

Using the adventures of Arthur Lee Robinson and chocolate city imaginings of comedy duo Keegan Michael Key and Jordan Peele's "Negrotown" as bookends, this chapter illustrates how migration, culture, and Black density matter. Villages are not simply small southern towns with Black people. Rather, they are a pervasive practice of Black people getting in formation. Simply put, there is an art to making Negrotown.

ARTHUR LEE AND THE TALLAHATCHIE

As he rounded the winding highway in the overfull U-Haul, the lights of the city came into view. His daughter, ahead of him in her equally packed car, called him up, trying to hold in her excitement about the sparkling urban sight. "Daddy!" she said. "Look at them lights! You seen anything like that before?" She was teasing, keeping the city mouse–country mouse joke going, which they had always shared. Recognizing the banter, he replied calmly but with a twinkle of excitement peeping through his voice too, "I know something 'bout that." They said their good-byes and hung up, proceeding all the way up Lake Shore to Sheridan to her new apartment in Chicago.

By all accounts Arthur Lee Robinson was a headstrong child, a dangerous attribute anywhere in 1950s America for a Black child, but especially behind the curtain that socially walled off the Mississippi Delta from the rest of the nation. His mother, Celia Mae Robinson, had been widowed in her youth and was raising her children with assistance from her mother, Rosie Robinson, and community support. Celia Mae did whatever was necessary to provide for Arthur Lee and his siblings, striving to protect them from physical, social, and economic death.

Arthur Lee knew Chicago and all spots in between there and the Mississippi Delta.[5] He had a sister in the south suburbs, cousins in Kankakee, a brother in Saint Louis, siblings in Memphis and Clarksdale, and nieces in Starkville, Mississippi. People on both sides of his family were everywhere east of the Mississippi, including all the way Up South in Albany, New York.

In 2016 he had planned a trip to the semiannual Rose family reunion, being held Memorial Day weekend that year in the Catskills, but he died the week before he was to fly out. He was sixty-four, and it would have been his first time in New York and all the way Up South. But Robinson's life and times up and down Highway 61, known as Blues Highway, teach us a great deal about one of the most common movements across chocolate maps: from the Deep South village to the southern city.

Big Mama, as Rosie Robinson was called, knew Arthur Lee was a different kind of child and got after him with her switch as often as possible, striving to compel conformity. He would curse grown folks when he felt slighted and frequently manipulated the White sharecropper boy on the next farm out of his bike, returning it only when he tired of it. When Arthur Lee heard Rosie Robinson's voice echoing and calling for him from her house to his, he sometimes ignored it, knowing full well what the consequences would be. The adults in the community did not know what else to do with this child.

If Arthur Lee had hell in him, perhaps baptism would cure it. All the children of Persimmon Grove Baptist Church in Glendora, Mississippi, in Tallahatchie County were baptized in the Tallahatchie River, plunged into it to be absolved of their sins and to receive eternal life. Neither Glendora or any of the other towns in the Mississippi Delta were a Black utopic Eatonville. So baptism was an important spiritual protection and rite of passage for when, at ages eight or nine or ten, Black children were inevitably and jarringly stripped of their childhoods. The preacher and the Tallahatchie provided the protection of eternal salvation and the blood of Jesus. But not even the blood of the Savior worked on Arthur Lee, nor could it spare him Big Mama Rosie Robinson's whippings.

The Tallahatchie is a rocky river that is not navigable in places for dozens of miles. During Arthur Lee's childhood, it had flowed south with a grave contradiction: it gave eternal life when the preacher plunged one into it but was a violent resting place, temporary and final, when murderous Whites used it to abet and conceal Black death. Arthur Lee was approaching his fourth birthday when the beaten, shot, and burdened body of fourteen-year-old Emmett Till was plunged into the river in the next county south of Tallahatchie, the county of Leflore, by J. W. Milam and Roy Bryant. The Tallahatchie had refused to harbor Till's body for long, and the murder, trial, and subsequent confession of the murderers rocked and rippled across the chocolate map. One of the murderers, Milam, lived in Glendora.

The specter, threat, and reality of death that surrounded Arthur Lee in Glendora in the 1950s and 1960s had sent many families from Mississippi Up South and Out South but also to the relative safety of the urban places Down South and Mid South. Arthur Lee's grandmother, Rosie Robinson, had come west to Glendora to make a life. And so her daughter Celia Mae stayed in Glendora until her children were mostly raised and then moved to the big county, Coahoma. Celia Mae had made unspeakable and unknowable sacrifices to shield her children from sharecropping, ensure they finished school, and help some of them go to college. They were poor, but, ensconced in the village she and scores of other Black people made, they had a small bit of freedom. For her dedication to them, Celia Mae's children repaid her—to the extent that money can compensate for trauma—by providing for her until her death in 1996.

Rosie Mae Robinson and her daughter Celia Mae Robinson were among the scores of people who stayed in the rural South, making chocolate maps in the village places between the prominent markers on the map. These places are the roots of chocolate maps, places to return and remember and forget, where Black life was lived and forged in the face of palpable and seemingly imminent Black death. Three of Celia Mae's children settled along a familiar route in the middle of the chocolate map: Willie Mae in Chicago, Jesse in Saint Louis, and Arthur Lee in Memphis. Arthur Lee was one of these mapmakers who moved along a path from rural to small town to city in the Deep South.

MR. ROBINSON GOES TO MEMPHIS

Arthur Lee managed to survive Big Mama and White supremacy, finishing West Tallahatchie High School in 1970 and moving to Coahoma County to attend junior college. Clarksdale is one of the Delta's biggest towns and a hub of music, commerce, and culture through which scores of blues musicians traveled on their way to carry the Delta's sound across chocolate maps. They also brought with them what the late geographer Clyde Woods called a "blues epistemology." Woods wrote that the blues emerged

> in a new era of censorship, suppression, and persecution [and] conveyed the sorrow of the individual and collective tragedy that had befallen African Americans. It also operated to instill pride in a people facing daily denigration, as well as channeling folk wisdom, descriptions of life and labor, travelogues, hoodoo, and critiques of individuals and institutions. It is often forgotten that those songs, music, stories, jokes, dances, and other visual and physical practices that raise the spirit of the audience to unimaginable heights also define the blues. The men and women who performed the blues were sociologists, reporters, counselors, advocates, preservers of language and customs, and summoners of life, love, laughter, and much, much more.[6]

It is this epistemology, a blues-informed worldview and interpretative template, that people like Arthur Lee took with them as they moved throughout and beyond the Deep South.

Memphis was not only the nearest big city when Arthur Lee was growing up, but was also where his father, Jack Rose, lived. His brother Jesse had already headed for Saint Louis, where the demand for skilled labor was plentiful. When Arthur Lee finished Coahoma Junior College in 1972 with an engineering degree, he planned to follow Jesse to Saint Louis. There the two children of Celia Mae Robinson and Jack Rose were going to make a life up the Mississippi River. Arthur Lee just wanted to stop in

Memphis for a few days and spend time with his Pops and meet his Memphis siblings before heading on to meet Jesse in Saint Louis.

But Arthur Lee never moved to Saint Louis. When he arrived at his father's house in Memphis, around the corner from Stax Records, he was overwhelmed by the warm reception from his Memphis family, including his father's wife, Lula Mae. The Roses convinced him to stay in the city, where the new turn in the soul sound coming from Stax echoed the kind of defiance that characterized his childhood. After the assassination of King, the music from around the corner on 926 East McLemore Avenue had grown ever more resistant.

Black Memphis was still shaken and in mourning, but its will to defy and resist ossified White power made it a perfect fit for Arthur Lee. He channeled the restlessness that made people think he had hell in him in Glendora into the rumbling labor movement in Memphis, which had won significant victories in the aftermath of the sanitation workers' strike. He joined Local 149 of the Bakery, Confectionery, Tobacco Workers, and Grain Millers International Union and labored and advocated for labor for the rest of his life. The 1970s Memphis milieu Arthur Lee entered into had been in the making since Ida B. Wells was on the city's burgeoning lyceum circuit.

Over the nineteenth and twentieth centuries, Black Memphians had survived two yellow fever epidemics, despite being segregated in the north and south sections of the city without sanitation protections. Afterward, in the 1890s, they built their own neighborhood east of South Memphis, on the site of an old plantation. This new neighborhood was the first to be built by and for Black people and was largely populated initially by people from northern Mississippi.

Yellow fever would not be the only epidemic to strike the growing Memphis village. Not long after the fevers passed, a new unknown illness emerged that contributed to an especially high infant-mortality rate for Black babies in the city. Despite Black citizens' protests that something was wrong, White Memphians assumed this high mortality rate could be attributed to Black people's cleanliness or biological inferiority. Yet Black people's folk knowledge would not be so easily dismissed.

In his work on the city, historian Keith Wailoo shows how even before the disease was named and known, Black people were tracking and documenting it in blues music and culture.[7] Although it had been scientifically discovered in the United States in the early twentieth century, little was known about its epidemiology. It was Black folk knowledge and resistance, rooted in the blues, that brought attention to the disease as Black people advocated for better health care and conditions. By the 1950s the disease that had for so long ravaged Black communities across the chocolate map had gained national attention. Within twenty years cases of sickle cell anemia had dramatically decreased.

The city of Memphis had long been a regional medical leader, and sickle cell solidified Memphis's place as a center of Black medical innovation. It was the village in the predominantly Black city, though, that made the city's status possible. On the one hand, the city built its fortunes on the backs of Black pain and disease. On the other, Black people built their lives by making moral and ethical claims that sprung from a blues resistance that had been forged during their movement from rural communities to small towns to the city.

Black people in Memphis, then, had been demanding justice and a better life for Black people for generations. They had cared for the sick during the epidemics and demanded to be treated as equal citizens when Whites returned to the city when the proverbial coast was clear. The epidemic had brought Ida B. Wells to Memphis, and she had then spearheaded and galvanized a movement against lynching. Meanwhile, Black people gathered and shared folk knowledge about an illness that was taking their children and kept demanding that someone investigate the health of their communities and treat them with dignity.

When they won recognition, attention, and funding for sickle cell anemia treatment, they pointed to the dangerous work conditions of laborers throughout the city, focusing on its sanitation workers in particular. They survived after the massive spiritual and psychological blow that was King's murder and pressed on with work in their communities. It was into this moment in time on the chocolate map, four years after King's assassination, that Arthur Lee came to Memphis.

The woman who would make Arthur Lee into Mr. Robinson had been born in Grand Junction, Tennessee, twenty days before him. Her family moved to Orange Mound, which was still a thriving Black community in the 1950s, though the ominous hum of urban renewal could be heard from surrounding neighborhoods. She was a teenager when the city began to move with "all deliberate speed" to desegregate schools. She was a sixteen-year-old in Orange Mound when King was killed, and the assassination reflected her mother's cautions about activism. If Arthur Lee was a rambunctious handful as a child, Janice was the opposite. She stayed to herself and played by herself, never troubling anyone.

But Orange Mound, like so many other communities, underwent some significant changes in tandem with the growing movement for labor rights and civil rights. Deindustrialization shuttered some nearby factories that were sources of income in the community. People left as neighborhoods east began to desegregate. In the midst of this neighborhood upheaval, Janice began college in 1970 on the edge of Orange Mound at Memphis State University. Orange Mound had nurtured a quiet upheaval within her too. Her childhood introversion and silent rejection of her mother's admonishment against activism had converged to create a grown city sophisticate with modern ideas about race, womanhood, and partnership and sharp critiques of racism and sexism in the South.

Armed with a journalism baccalaureate and an ingrained awareness, Janice opted to escape the confines of racist and sexist work environments to work as a parent community organizer. She used her post as a substitute teacher to observe conditions and practices in a range of Black schools in the city's public school system, demanding resources for students and conjuring resources from her own funds when the system failed, which happened frequently.

Arthur from Glendora, Mississippi, and Janice from Orange Mound in Memphis, Tennessee, met in 1974, married in 1977, and moved to Whitehaven, known widely as Blackhaven by its now predominantly Black residents. Arthur worked for labor, rallying union members for negotiations and critiquing the changing nature of work brought on by fast deindustrialization. Janice worked for parents in communities, curating and collating information and pressuring school officials, board members, and nonprofit organizations to give Black students what they were entitled to as citizens and taxpayers.

In their Whitehaven home Arthur and Janice used their combined village experiences, which were more similar than they liked to admit, to rear two daughters at the beginning of the millennial generation. Together they gave them, these second-generation city daughters, a multidimensional village sensibility born of the place-making practices of Black people. As they moved, they made a world, bringing with them their previous worlds as the rich soil with which to lay the foundation anew.

In Memphis Arthur Lee became Mr. Robinson, but the blues epistemology of Glendora remained. Memphis was where many country boys grew into misters, as they navigated a changing post–civil rights chocolate city that was different but also sometimes glaringly similar to the rural communities and small towns in which they came of age. Black migrants had been flowing into Memphis since before Emancipation, following the Mississippi to what some people called the Delta's capital. The city's character and spatial arrangements had been shaped by these people's experiences, and Mr. Robinson was among the many who made and expanded the Memphis village.

The notion of the village is an inherently nostalgic concept, and not just because the world has changed significantly. "Village" carries with it an idea of naive simplicity, sameness, and ease that is difficult to imagine in a hypermedia world where anti-Blackness is constant. The increasing visibility of Black death has almost erased this notion of village, even as it persists as an intergenerational set of lived experiences and a spatial fact.

In the Obama era Black artists and intellectuals grappled publicly with two competing representations of the village—that it (1) no longer exists at all or that it (2) could exist if Black people only would return to earlier, supposedly simpler eras of community. They were interested in how protracted anti-Blackness in the United States and beyond fostered Black people's longings for a place insulated from White supremacy. These artists imagined a future, like Arthur and Janice had done, that could be made different through resistance. They also used these possible futures to highlight the failings of the present.

EASE ON DOWN TO NEGROTOWN

Where does the village end and the city begin? We see the village in multiple ways. It is at once a precursor to the places on chocolate maps; a description of existing places, small towns, neighborhoods in big cities, and

Black back sides of places on the chocolate maps; and a disposition toward community life that reflects Black people's collective practices of resistance in and through place. Mr. Robinson may have left the village of Glendora and gone to college in the village of Clarksdale, but he brought those villages with him, like so many others did, when he settled in Memphis.

Comedians Keegan Michael Key and Jordan Peele reflect on this movement of Black people, this quest to make place and futures, in the fifth and final season of their acclaimed Comedy Central sketch comedy show, *Key and Peele*.[8] Between sketches Key and Peele are on a long journey through a barren territory. They are headed somewhere on the discursive Black map they have traveled throughout the show's tenure, deftly exploring a multidimensional Black experience in an unequal America. Previous seasons had featured the duo on stage in front of a live audience between sketches; in the final season the men are together in an old beater, driving through the desert headed somewhere for some reason the audience does not know. In the finale we learn their journey throughout the season is a metaphor for the unending search for where Black people can be free.

The sketch begins with an uncomfortable but all-too-familiar scenario. One protagonist, played by Key, is walking alone at night and accosted by a police officer who asks for his identification, pulls a gun on him, handcuffs him, and not-so-accidentally bangs his head on the top of the police car as he is forcing him into the vehicle. Wally, an unhoused man played by Peele who has previously asked Key's character for change, steps in to take over for the officer, who inexplicably removes the handcuffs. Together the two travel through a wardrobe-like portal into a Black Narnia: Negrotown.

Negrotown is sunny and bright and colorful, "a place to be if your skin is brown," one even more magical than Atlanta. It is an actual "utopia for Black people." Wally, now donning a pink three-piece suit, begins what turns out to be a spectacular musical dance number in several ways. An array of Negrotown constituents, clad psychedelically in garb of the past and present, help Wally introduce Key's character to Negrotown. In Negrotown loan applications are always approved, Black people can walk the streets without police harassment; cabs always stop; there is no shortage of Black men for Black women; no cultural appropriation, no racial health disparities, no "trigger-happy cops or scared cashiers" exist; no one is followed while shopping; and no is murdered for wearing a hoodie. The choreographed number ends with smiles and all fists raised in a Black power salute.

The sketch's perhaps expected ending is that Negrotown is a delusion. There is no village where one can be safe from these everyday experiences of racism in the world. Key's character awakens from a period of unconsciousness caused by the officer's brutality, exclaiming in a state of frightened confusion, "I thought I was going to Negrotown!" The police office responds flippantly, "Oh, you are," as he puts him into the car and drives away. It is a heartbreaking but anticipated ending that answers Solange Knowles's questions with devastating brevity. "Where can we be Black and free?" Key and Peele answer: only in our imaginations.

"Negrotown" reflects a fantastical longing for a place where Black people can be Black and free, gesturing toward what a twenty-first-century Eatonville, a "pure Negro town," might be like.[9] Searching for greener pastures, Black people have always envisioned, and when possible attempted to create, a less complicated freedom, whether in an imagined and generic African past, a Jim Crow southern past in separate cities and on Black back sides, or in the New South Black mecca of Atlanta.

From Emancipation and Reconstruction, to the unrest of the civil rights movement, to the ramifications of the declining urban core, Black people in the United States have moved, shifted, responded, resisted, and created town and neighborhood spaces where they could be both Black and free. As the daily assaults on Black lives continue to play on loop in traditional and social media, Black people's desire for a place to be has become increasingly evident in the ways they imagine alternative Black villages in science fiction, satire, and music. This is not, as political scientist Adolph Reed Jr. has called it, "romancing Jim Crow," or wallowing in nostalgia for a mythical and segregated all-Black past.[10] This is a political imagining and reimagining of the village as a site of past, present, and future resistance. Strong villages became the bricks for chocolate cities, expanding chocolate maps and cementing together the fortunes of Black places with a new kind of blues epistemology: *soul power.*

PART III   The Soul

I'm a rebel, soul rebel
I'm a capturer, soul adventurer.

Bob Marley and the Wailers, "Soul Rebel," 1970

8 When and Where the Spirit Moves You

I believe in living. . . .
And I believe that seeds grow into sprouts.
And sprouts grow into trees.
I believe in the magic of the hands.
And in the wisdom of the eyes.
I believe in rain and tears.
And in the blood of infinity.

Assata Shakur, "I Believe in Living," 1987

The house at 406 Lucy Avenue in South Memphis was on the docket for demolition again. Surrounded by other boarded-up properties, the small shotgun house was in violation of county environmental codes and had been deemed a hazard since 2012. In the four years following the initial citation, things had only gotten worse. Part of the roof had collapsed, the home had caught fire, and the building had fallen further into general disrepair. Historic preservationists pleaded again with donors and community stakeholders to rally to save the landmark. Taking the lead, LeMoyne-Owen Community Development Corporation, a neighborhood entity, hoped to move the house to a location nearby if it could not be preserved in place. Once again the home was saved from immediate destruction, and advocates bought a little more time to figure out a permanent solution.

The property at 406 Lucy Avenue was not just some abandoned hazard, people had contended. There, during World War II, a soul prodigy had been born in its front room. The place had taken on a near-biblical significance, alternately cast as anointed manger of the savior as well as a body in need of resurrection. It was the birthplace of Aretha Franklin,

Queen of Soul.[1] To preserve the place where she came into the world was to mark and maintain the spirit that changed American sound at the height of American social upheaval in the 1960s.

For two years Aretha lived on Lucy Avenue, one of many stops for the Franklins as they moved throughout the Mississippi Delta, then all the way to Buffalo, then New York, before finally settling in Detroit, Michigan.[2] She traveled the gospel Chitlin' Circuit with her father, preacher C. L. Franklin, but her travels across the chocolate map as a musician in her own right reflect how Black people fundamentally transformed urban America between World War II and the civil rights era. Aretha crafted and carried the soul sound that served as the sonic harbinger of this urban transformation. This chapter explores her indelible mark on the chocolate map by tracing her sound and spirit from Mississippi to Los Angeles, from blues to soul, and from civil rights to Black Power.

SPIRIT OF A QUEEN

> I am a black woman
> The music of my song
> Some sweet arpeggio of tears
> Is written in a minor key
> and I
> can be heard humming in the night

> Mari Evans, "I Am a Black Woman," 1970

There had been spirit all around Clarence LaVaughn Franklin in interwar Mississippi: a fervent religious spirit nurtured by his father's preaching; a sound spirit embedded in the intermingled sounds of gospel and blues; and a spirit of striving for freedom in the Mississippi Delta. Though Franklin's family lived in several Delta towns, he was born in Sunflower County, home to Parchman Farm state penitentiary. The prison was a hulking, sprawling manifestation of the state's systems of exploitation and oppression, from enslavement to sharecropping, and foreshadowed its later exploitative structures of mass incarceration and the prison industrial complex. It was a warning and inevitable in a region and nation committed to containing and punishing Black people.

Songs from Parchman, which were later recorded by folklorist Alan Lomax, surrounded C. L. and moved in and out of the prison, as people from all over the state were held there. Life outside of Parchman for Black people was a kind of prison of its own, but music was an ephemeral but palpable freedom on both sides of the gates. Franklin knew well the sacred and secular parts of the musical coin, singing both blues and gospel and always managing to infuse the latter with the former.

C. L. looked to the road, to the Blues Highway, watching the train that traveled through the Delta to New Orleans, determined to escape this inevitability. Still, even as far north as Benton Harbor, Michigan, where he had done migrant farm labor with his family in a post-Depression summer, he would experience the threat and reality of White violence and oppression. Franklin quickly discovered, like so many other Black people traveling across the country from the Deep South, that there was no place where Black people could be free.

C. L. would start out a traveling preacher like his father, beginning on the Delta Baptist circuit as an adolescent in the 1920s. He longed for a permanent and prominent position and nurtured his call to preach by receiving some education at Greenville Industrial Institute and practicing in various congregations. By 1939, married for the second time and father of one, a twenty-four-year-old C. L. got his first permanent post. His guest preaching had netted him an invitation from New Salem Baptist Church in Memphis. The Franklins settled in South Memphis near the church, as C. L.'s wife, Barbara, came to Memphis with their daughter, Erma, and her son, Vaughn; Aretha was born three years later. It was in Memphis that C. L. honed an artful blend of the sacred and profane, the spirit of the holy word with the lived experience of Blackness in Memphis.

Franklin's sermons did not exist only in the ecstatic moments of town revivals and in the pulpit at New Salem. His "million dollar voice" boomed around the country, with sermons archived on records alongside gospel songs and broadcasted on the radio.[3] From his seat at the head of New Bethel Baptist Church in Detroit, which he held from 1946 to 1979, his voice, words, and sermons went viral across chocolate maps.

Aretha certainly inherited her parents' musical gifts. Her mother, Barbara Franklin, was a gifted singer and pianist, and she nurtured these talents in her children. Aretha quickly caught on to melody, harmony, and rhythm conventions in gospel and blues, both of which were intertwined staples in the Franklin home, and could replicate and experiment with them with ease.

She had also inherited their blues worldview. Like many Black people, they had a moving spirit, one compelled into existence by racial violence and inequities and also driven by the search for a better kind of freedom. From her father in particular Aretha learned about organizing and activism, as he became not only a prominent preacher but also an influential political figure for Detroit labor. C. L.'s dual status as music celebrity and community figure attracted a range of politically active artists who frequented their Detroit home, modeling for Aretha how the spirit of a people and the spirit of a sound could intersect.

From the time she sang her first solo in church at age ten, it was clear that Aretha was unique. The social environment provided by C. L.'s position, her inheritance of Barbara's and C. L.'s blues epistemology and musical gifts, and an urban situation on the verge of cracking under the weight of racial oppression made Aretha and the sound she made distinct. She dutifully worked in the gospel genre, as it was her genealogy and social life, pushing it to its limits with her voice's simultaneous soaring and deep qualities. At age eighteen, though, she told C. L. that she wanted to pursue a pop career and sing secular music and headed off to New York to sign with Columbia Records.[4]

MAKING PLACE, MAKING SOUND

The sum total of who Aretha was—her inherited spirit, the specificities of her dual gospel and blues aptitude, and her experience of coming of age in postwar Detroit—was beyond the comprehension of Columbia Records' executives and producers in New York City. The cosmopolitan character of New York City, composed of Black populations who had made their way Up South from the eastern seaboard, was different than that of the manufacturing hub of Detroit, with its large share of folks from the Mississippi Delta and the urban Mid South. Aretha's voice could certainly be stuffed into this or that popular trend, whether it was big-band jazz standards or swing, but this practice ignored the chocolate map and the place Aretha had already made on it before she was an adult. After a successful but creatively and politically frustrating six years in New York with Columbia, Aretha would have to return to the Deep South, to Muscle Shoals, Alabama, to get back to the sound that reared her and to remix that sound into soul.

Aretha was made as much by Detroit and its milieu as she was by her parents' influence. Like other Up South destinations, Detroit had not been ready for steady and cyclical influxes of Black migrants from the Deep South, even as Henry Ford was among the earliest of major factory operations to recruit and employ Black people. Racialized labor tensions and White racial violence meant Detroit was always on the verge of eruption, with at least one riot during the civil war and two riots during World War II. The more infamous 1967 riot had thus been long in the making, as had Aretha's four albums released that year: *Take It Like You Give It, Take a Look,* the gold *I Never Loved a Man the Way I Loved You,* and the aptly titled *Aretha Arrives.*[5]

When the Franklins arrived in Detroit after the war, the city was still teeming from the 1943 riots. Wartime labor needs had been significant, and people from all over the Black map, and especially from the Deep South, had come to Detroit in search of new work opportunities. This had created a host of new tensions, between Black people who had been in the city for generations and newcomers and between still-segregated union outfits and Black workers who were used to challenging them. Detroit's riots exposed extreme racial inequality in housing and employment in the city, along with the unpleasant fact that the city's prosperity had indeed been made in no small part through the exploitation of Black labor.

C. L. stepped into this era of labor and civil rights organizing in Detroit, still young but with a reputation for preaching and singing that preceded him. In the Motor City he developed a reputation for activism and used New Bethel both for uplifting assaulted spirits and for supporting a labor-based Black resistance that challenged the older generation's ideas about how civil rights activism should be undertaken. Aretha thus came of age integrating a spirit of working-class resistance into her musical expression, despite her relative economic privilege. Going back and forth between Detroit and her mother's home in Buffalo, cared for at times by a range of talented Black women musicians, including Mahalia Jackson, Aretha crafted sound with the precision the factory folks used to produce cars. When the Detroit uprisings broke out in 1967, Aretha was breaking the conventional sonic mold from Alabama to New York City.

In the postwar era the blues and gospel spirit shifted. The conventions that had constituted a significant portion of the soundtrack of Black life and place making since enslavement shifted too. Though traces of chocolate maps are evident in grapevine accounts as early as the United States began to enslave people, the remaking of sound conventions in the 1960s and 1970s reflected Black people's increasing awareness of chocolate maps and of the power they exerted in making and transforming space wherever they went. These sound innovations were concerted attempts to unify voices and sounds across place, both in response to pressures from a changing and racialized music industry and in response to the imperatives of Black resistance across chocolate maps in the civil rights era.

Record executives' naming of this new sound reflected their lack of understanding of the chocolate map and the relationship between place and sound. It was blues, they thought, with rhythm. This simplistic conceptualization of the sound missed its import as a marker of a significant shift.

To be sure, soul was a new instantiation of the familiar language of the blues. Black people had certainly brought the village epistemology and its discursive and aesthetic practices with them as they made chocolate maps. But the new rhythms of urban life and creation shifted the cadence of Blackness, as soul came to occupy the place in the spirit that had once been held by blues and gospel.

Soul was a new articulation of that moving spirit and spoke directly and unapologetically about the conditions of Black life, striving for freedom in this life, and not the afterlife, and a determination for rights and respect. It embodied the pleasures of Black love and life, explicitly muddying the line between spiritual and fleshly ecstasy. It presented the pain of Black life, pointed out systemic and individual perpetrators, and made explicit moral, ethical, and social political claims on the state. Through soul music, the sacred and profane in Black life and resistance were forever intertwined.[6]

FAITH, PLEASURE, PROTEST

C. L. believed in the integration of the sacred and profane as a theological and social practice. To reach the people, he had to meet the people where they were all days of the week, and not just Sunday. Moreover, movement activists hailed from all walks of life, and his Detroit home served as a meeting and collaboration space. But Aretha elevated this practice, simultaneously expanding soul to its ecstatic and transformative limits.

While the spirituals and gospel were in and of themselves a protest, even if they were a protest to God about the earthly conditions of Black people caused by White supremacy, Aretha used her voice and altered arrangements of traditional songs toward new ends. Her work made visible Black people's faith but also highlighted the works—organizing, resistance, protest, and pleasure—that they were engaged in to give life to that faith.

Columbia Records admittedly did not understand the significance of Aretha's gospel roots to her artistry, but she still managed to include songs that signified the spiritual protest that was soul music in her early work there. At age twenty she recorded Billie Holiday's "God Bless the Child," underlining the racial disparity in "those that got shall get" and "them that's not shall lose." Beyond the overt references to money, there is also a nod toward Black pride inherent in the child who can "stand up anywhere and say he's got his own." Accompanied by strings, piano, and muted horns, Aretha put gospel crescendos over a jazz rhythm to advocate for the disadvantaged, "the child," who needs to make a way to survive. Ten years later a gospel organ and blues piano have an instrumental discussion of the sacred and profane in "Bridge over Troubled Waters." The organ and piano conversation prefaces Aretha's offering of her body, labor, and voice up to the movement. "Yes it do," she sings quickly and affirmatively after her background singers declare "still water runs deep."[7]

Aretha lingers after and runs ahead of the beat sometimes, letting the marching bass and drums and singers keep the rhythm as she complements, reflects, and sings alongside the movement. Within the context of Black Power, the Simon and Garfunkel tune takes on an insistent quality, increasing in tempo and fervor toward its close.

Over a couple of days in Los Angeles in January 1972, Aretha recorded *Amazing Grace,* a soul album that drew directly on her gospel roots and status as a preacher's daughter and soul leader.[8] *Amazing Grace* opens with "Mary, Don't You Weep," the biblical story of the death of Lazarus and his resurrection by Jesus. It is at once a funeral dirge and a march onward, the Southern California Community Choir chanting, "Oh, oh, Mary," for a full eight measures before they give her the titular directive: "Oh, Mary, don't you weep; tell Martha not to moan." When Aretha sings, she almost whispers, "Mary, Mary, listen Mary, tell your sister to don't moan." Beginning with a definitive miracle of God as evidence of why she should not weep, Aretha notes the fate of Pharaoh's army in the Red Sea and shouts go up from the live audience and choir.[9]

"We gon' review the story of two sisters," Aretha preach-sings in the next verse, focusing on the women's pain at Lazarus's death. She approximates Mary's wails to Jesus, "my sweet Lord," about how his presence might have prevented Lazarus's death. Mary's wails, as reenacted by Aretha, also function to approximate Black women's wails about the deaths of Black men more broadly, including Martin Luther King Jr. Above the steady march of the blues bass on the first and fourth beats of the six-beat measure, fervent eighth-note claps come on the second, third, fifth, and sixth beats from the choir and the audience. When Aretha calls Lazarus forth for the third time, stretching the first syllable of his name across an entire measure, she temporarily resurrects everyone lost to racial injustice. She reminds women in particular that with faith and works, a miracle relief is on the horizon.[10]

Los Angeles was a prime Out South destination in the postwar era, and its Black population increased tenfold between the war and 1970, creating several chocolate city communities in South Central that had been in the works since the early twentieth century. By the 1970s the city had elected its first Black mayor, Thomas Bradley, and had become a destination for Black artists and entertainers that offered a change of pace from New York City. Like other chocolate cities, though, it had erupted in violence the decade previous, the frustrations of hyperpolicing and police brutality, as well as rising unemployment and entrenched segregation, had erupted in the Watts Riots.

New Temple Missionary Baptist Church was similar to the church in Detroit in which Aretha had come of age singing. The reverend Dr. James Cleveland was a gospel star like C. L. and had been born and raised in Chicago before moving Out South. The choir and congregation, composed of people from all over the chocolate map, melded the distinctiveness of their place-based experiences into a sound that resonated across places and in turn increased awareness of shared cultural roots. At the soloist's helm like she had been in her father's church, Aretha recorded her best-selling album of all time.

The church and religious experience offered up a cultural link and implored Black people to continue working and believing until the kind of miracle relief Mary and Martha received from Jesus, or that the Jews had received from God from Pharaoh's army, came forth. Aretha, though, had also offered up some suggestions for earthly relief. In her corpus women's pleasure, as a form of protest against racism and sexism, was both a right and a salve in a painful world. The protagonist in "Dr. Feelgood" eases her pain in one visit in ways that no medical doctor "filling her up with pills" could. Even when the person providing the pleasure is not the best part-ner, the pleasure of loving that is "just too strong" endures as a temporary reprieve from pain.[11]

Not all relief comes without anguish, and certainly Aretha's corpus rumi-nates on hurt. Respect is perhaps the most capacious soul concept Aretha forwards, and so "Respect" remains popular with a wide range of audiences who can situate themselves as the aggrieved. Aretha asks repeatedly to be given her propers, doing so in a way that does not come off as too demand-ing—"just a little bit," her background singers say—but that also is simulta-neously explicitly demanding: "sock it to me." Although "Respect" is osten-sibly about a lover or partner, Aretha, like other Black women performers, invites us to read "Respect" as also being about demanding respect from White people who are "runnin' outta foolin'" and might walk in and find Black people have left. The theme of respect within the context of romantic relationships between men and women forms the basis of the kind of pro-tests in and out of the home in which Black women have to engage for freedom.[12]

Aretha's work sowed the seeds of faith, pleasure, and protest that made up the soul sound all over the chocolate map. Up South, Out South, Down South, and Deep South, Aretha's voice connects and introduces chocolate cities to one another. While Black people had long been aware of chocolate maps, soul had given it a new visibility that highlights their power as place makers.

CHOCOLATE CITY, SOUL POWER

Aretha Franklin's chocolate city roots are located in the Mississippi Delta, a space and place dominating our public imagination about the origins of the Great Migration. Although she never lived in Sunflower County, Mississippi, her father's experiences there shaped her early life, situating her in a gospel-inspired activist practice that complemented her musical prodigiousness. But it was in postwar Detroit, squarely between two riots, in the midst of a network of artists and activists, that Aretha went further than what is even now imaginable.

With Mississippi roots, Detroit sensibilities, and a spiritual drive toward freedom, Aretha's migrations are key to her career and music. In her quest for a sound, Aretha provided new ways to navigate chocolate maps that supplanted easy North-South arguments about differences in Black experiences. She had made plain and expanded the parameters of a new language of soul, a blended language of gospel and blues that made chocolate maps sonically visible. This language was power, a broad soul power that developed alongside the civil rights, Black arts, and Black Power movements. All over the chocolate map, Black people had—through faith, pleasure, and protest—survived, thrived, and came to local, municipal, and state political power.

From Detroit to New York, Muscle Shoals to Los Angeles, and back to Detroit, Aretha's diverse chocolate city experiences reinforced the overwhelmingly unifying similarities of rural communities, small towns, Black neighborhoods, Black back sides, and majority Black cities. Other soul artists followed Aretha's lead around the chocolate map and went beyond, with Stax artists traveling to Watts, Los Angeles, and artists from all over the Americas traveling to Kinshasa, Zaire, in 1974. They mapped new soul routes and new avenues to soul power. Aretha's music was then, and continues to be, a soul anthem for places across chocolate maps.

For all the ecstasy and promise of soul, by the late 1970s the sound, the culture it represented, and its call to power were being rapidly fractured by the dogged persistence of racial inequality in chocolate cities. Deindustrialization and increasing unemployment, a shrinking welfare state, assassinations, state surveillance, drug epidemics, hyperpolicing, and the beginnings of mass incarceration assailed an increasingly weary

Black populace. The soul power that had ushered in Black mayors and other municipal elected officials, in some places for the first time since Reconstruction, was under threat, and a post-soul sound emerged to capture and assess these changing structural realities.

Music scholar Mark Anthony Neal has called the generation who came of age shouldering the ramifications of these changes "soul babies."[13] One of these soul babies was conceived while Aretha was finishing up recording *Young, Gifted, and Black* in New York City. His mother-to-be, a young movement participant, was being held in New York City on charges that she was a part of a Black Panther terrorist bombing conspiracy. Precisely the kind of person Aretha was singing to and about on the album, the woman spent most of her second and third trimester defending herself in court, prevailing just weeks before the soul baby was born. The North Carolina–born woman continued her activist work, moved down south to Baltimore to give her son more opportunities but was swept up by addiction, and settled Out South in the Bay Area to try to start anew, to rediscover the spark of soul power that had driven her toward an impassioned and brilliant defense of herself not twenty years earlier.

She had named herself Afeni Shakur. She named her son Tupac.

9 How Brenda's Baby Got California Love

There's a rose in black at Spanish Harlem
A rose in black at Spanish Harlem
It is a special one
It never sees the sun. . . .
It's growing in the street
Right up through the concrete

Aretha Franklin, "Spanish Harlem," 1971

On August 3, 1995, Black music, especially rap, was forever changed.[1] As the sun set on legendary Black music houses—Detroit's Motown, Memphis's Stax, and Philly's Philadelphia International—a new era had begun for a new generation of sound and artists. These artists had gathered together for the *Source Awards*, an annual recognition of the accomplishments of hip-hop artists hosted by the magazine that had become the central hip-hop authority.[2]

Having started as a small publication, *Source* magazine had grown since the early 1990s into the major publication for journalism, reviews, and interviews with and about hip-hop and hip-hop artists. Seeking to counter the mainstream move of the Grammy Awards' inclusion of a Best Rap category in 1988, the magazine focused on the hip-hop voices and talents that had not nor would likely ever reach White audiences. Former co-owner of the magazine Dave Mays recalled the broad criticism of the Grammy move, saying, "that set a tone of mainstream awards shows snubbing real hip-hop, [and] not televising awards, and the process of nominations was very suspect."[3]

By 1994 the *Source* had garnered enough clout and readership to produce an awards show specifically for acts in hip-hop and R&B. While the
inaugural show wasn't televised, interest and popularity led to the ability
to nationally televise the awards program from New York City. The hip-
hop industry was heavily involved and invested, with the awards based on
a ballot system. "DJs, some of them at radio and others who were just
influential," were among those who cast ballots, as well as small "mom-
and-pop" retailers, whose influence on music was key "because they were
in the trenches in the community." The votes were in by late July 1995, and
the production staff moved to get the awards and performers ready for the
August show.[4]

Though awards shows tend to err on the side of pure celebration of its
celebrities and their commercial success, the 1995 show proved to be an
intense battleground over Black music. Held at Madison Square Garden's
Paramount Theater, the 1995 *Source Awards* brought out hip-hop's bright-
est and newest stars to bring to life the hits that had given the mid-1990s
their sonic fire. All the big names, including Snoop, Puffy, Biggie Smalls,
Outkast, Flavor Flav, Q-Tip, Dr. Dre, and many more, were in the building.
Missing, however, was Tupac Shakur, who after having been near-fatally
shot, was serving time in jail on a sexual-abuse conviction. His absence and
the emerging animus between East and West Coast hip-hop became a
springboard for a whirlwind of drama and music that would end only with
Shakur's and Christopher "Biggie Smalls" Wallace's still-unsolved murders.

Sauntering triumphantly to the microphone to accept the award for
Best Motion Picture Soundtrack for the gritty basketball film *Above the
Rim*, Death Row Records CEO Suge Knight eased onstage with an ominous smile. "Regulator," the winning surprise hit and anthem by Warren G
and Nate Dogg, boomed overhead. Its samples of Michael McDonald's
"I Keep Forgettin'" and Dr. Dre's Parliament-inspired "Let Me Ride," which
had sampled the 1976 song "Mother Starship Connection (Starchild)"
reflected hip-hop's conversation with place through soul and funk.

In a blatant shout out to Shakur and diss of Bad Boy records founder
Sean "Puffy" Combs, Knight raised his award high and looked straight into
the camera. "First of all, I'd like to thank God. Second of all, I'd like to
thank my whole entire Death Row family, on both sides. Like to tell Tupac

keep his guard up. We ridin' wit 'em." And venturing even further off-script with what has now become an innocuous and funny meme but was a grave read at the time, Knight declared, "Any artist out there that want to be an artist and wanna stay a star and don't wanna have to worry about the executive producer tryna be all up in the videos dancing and on the records, come to Death Row."[5] The real-time diss, aimed specifically at Puffy and Biggie but also at the East Coast more generally, quickly shifted the awards show into a coastal beef, with artists and audience alike choosing sides.

Who owned Black music and, in this case, hip-hop? What places and people were the spokesmen and spokeswomen on this new expression of the souls of Black folk? Reagan- and Bush-era conservatism had given way to Clinton's centrism, leaving Black communities all over the country ravaged by the war on drugs and the prison boom. As demonstrated by scholars Imani Perry, Tricia Rose, and H. Samy Alim the emerging hip-hop genre became a new and dominant musical expression of the souls of Black folk.[6] Police brutality, consumerism, poverty, partying, and dancing melded with the new genre, influencing a rising tension and competition within and across chocolate maps.

The role of "coasts" particularly took on added significance. Serving as a musical signifier for Black cultural expression, especially in hip-hop, the coasts, East and West, became dominant and divisive cultural tools and regional markers. The headquarters of Black popular culture is a moving target. From the Harlem Renaissance, to Bronzeville, to Clarksdale-inspired Blues to Atlanta trap to the police brutality of Compton and Oakland, many chocolate cities have served as the source of images, sounds, and explorations of Blackness. In the era scholar Nelson George dubs "Post-Soul," hip-hop rose as a master template for the expression of Black culture and consciousness.[7]

To understand how hip-hop music, culture, soul, and Black geography overlap, this chapter revisits the life of Tupac Shakur, whose life was ended in the heat of an intense debate about Black regional difference that reflected the fracturing of Black communities in the postindustrial, neoliberal era. Having moved across the map, from New York to Maryland to the Bay Area and then Los Angeles, Shakur and his music offer great insight into the role of chocolate cities in Black cultural production in the postsoul era. A rapper-actor, Shakur had a critical political and racial consciousness yielded when Black Panther–styled Black nationalism collided with the drug epidemic and the movement of soul through the medium of hip-hop.

THE ADVENTURES OF TUPAC

Born in North Carolina in 1947, Afeni Shakur (born Alice Faye Williams) moved with her older sister Gloria Williams to New York when she was in middle school. By the mid-1960s Shakur had become politically engaged. In an effort to keep Black schools open in New York under the threat of a massive teachers' strike, Shakur joined the Black Panther Party in 1968.

Within a year Shakur quickly rose in the organization's ranks and was soon embroiled in a legal case that became better known as the "New York Panther 21."[8] Charged with conspiracy against the U.S. government and conspiracy to commit and organize a domestic terror attack, Shakur and her twenty codefendants and comrades spent eleven months in jail. Though she would later post $100,000 bail ($610,000 in 2017 dollars), when her bail was revoked months later, she returned to prison five months pregnant.

Deciding to serve as her own legal counsel, Shakur successfully achieved acquittal, listening to the sound of "not guilty, not guilty repeated more than 100 times for the number of offenses against her and other members of the Black Panther Party."[9] Thirty-six days later in East Harlem on June 16, 1971, she gave birth to a baby boy, Lesane Parish Crooks. By 1972 Shakur had renamed her son, drawing inspiration from the Peruvian revolutionary who challenged the colonial Spanish Armada, Tupac Amaru II. Added to the African origin of her chosen last name, Lesane Parish Crooks was officially redubbed Tupac Amaru Shakur.

Deeply embedded in the networks and figures of the Black Panther Party and Black liberation, Tupac Shakur was raised with an acute sensitivity to the oppressive government forces in Black American lives, witnessing the surveillance of and violence sown against Black freedom fighters. For example, his stepfather, Mutulu, and aunt-in-law, Assata, were on the run, seeking refuge from FBI forces and charges. Nearly born in prison, he had creatively channeled his racial consciousness from an early age.

Spending his formative schooling years in a variety of creative and performing-arts productions and programs in Harlem, Tupac's star shown brightly, even as his mother found it increasingly difficult to make ends meet working as a community and tenant's rights activist. By his fifteenth birthday, the family moved to Baltimore, Maryland. There, just below the Mason-Dixon Line, Tupac honed his talents at the Baltimore School for the Arts, where he began a lifetime friendship with fellow classmate Jada Pinkett-Smith. Combatting drug addiction and waning opportunities, in the late spring of 1988 Afeni Shakur moved the family to Marin City, just a few miles north of San Francisco.[10]

"Come to Marin City, and there's even more poverty," Tupac remembers about arriving in June 1988. "I was finally starting to see it. The one thing we do have in common as Black people," Shakur intimates, "is that we share that poverty." Having traveled through the multiple Souths, Tupac found he had a critical racial consciousness with geographic implications: "I made it to where I had knowledge that it wasn't just me; it was a bigger picture. It was my people that was getting dogged out. It wasn't just my family; it was all of US."[11] A linked fate–minded chocolate citizen was formed.

After completing school, a teenage Tupac sought to make the most of the creative talents he had cultivated from Harlem to Baltimore to the Bay Area. The first few years proved relatively uneventful. After a chance 1990 meeting with a record executive who had attended a poetry event in which he performed, Shakur was signed to be a dancer and roadie for the emergent West Coast group, the Digital Underground.

"All around the world, the same song," the hook went as Tupac entered the booth. The hook, containing the track's title "Same Song," was an upbeat, up-tempo party song with the laid-back flair that had come to be a hallmark of West Coast party anthems. With his New York–influenced flow, Shakur didn't waste anytime adding his verse in memorable fashion, ending in his characteristic unapologetic charisma: "I remain, still the same (Why Tu?) 'cause it's the same song."[12] His migrations had brought many things, and an attention to the consistencies across Black space was one of them. No matter where he was on the chocolate map, it was the same, for a Black geography influenced by Harlem, West Baltimore, and the Bay Area was embedded in Shakur's own migration story.

In the years that followed, the pushes and pulls of the East and West Coasts played a key role in the evolution and struggles of Shakur, now branded 2pac, as a rapper. By 1994 he had been the breakout star of *Juice*, the coming-of-age drama about wayward teenage Black boys in Harlem; played "Lucky," Janet Jackson's love interest in *Poetic Justice;* and released a series of well-received hip-hop songs, including the classic "Brenda's Got a Baby"—telling the story of teenage pregnancy from the perspective of a young Black woman in New York. Shakur had revealed his music and acting dexterity to much acclaim. Unlike many others, he had managed to create a bicoastal life of success, with Hollywood and New York City providing fertile ground for sharing and disseminating his creative gifts.[13]

Those years were not without their difficulties. Having had "no [police] record all [his] life until he made a record," Tupac became well acquainted with the criminal justice system during the early to mid-1990s. Like his mother, Afeni, before him, Tupac found himself both the target and accused culprit. After being brutally assaulted by police in 1991, Shakur filed a civil suit against the Oakland Police Department (OPD) for $10 million dollars ($17.4 million in 2017 dollars). "As my video was debuting on MTV, I was beaten behind bars by the police department," Tupac remembered, recalling personal photos taken by family and friends of his bloodied face and swollen eyes after his release.[14]

Flanked by his lawyers and the Digital Underground, Shakur held a press conference, where he shared the photos and told the media of his ordeal. Because it occurred just seven months after Rodney King's vicious and recorded assault at the hands of the Los Angeles Police Department, the mainstream media was primed for Tupac's retelling of the events leading to the attack. In a red hoodie with a matching ball cap and black denim jacket, Shakur looked into the cameras and broke his silence:

> Basically I walked 'cross the street between Seventeenth and Broadway [in Oakland]. The police officer stopped me on the sidewalk and asked to see my ID. They sweated me about my name. The officers said, "You have to learn your place." They were charging me with jaywalking. So I was riffing and arguing about why would they try to charge me with such a petty crime. So I kept yelling, asking them to give me my citation and let me go about my business. Next thing I know, my face was being buried into the concrete, and I was laying face down in the gutter. Waking up from being unconscious in

cuffs with blood on my face. And I am going to jail for "resisting arrest." That's harassment to me. That I have to be stopped in the middle of the street and be checked like we are in South Africa and asked for my ID.[15]

His face had been repeatedly banged against the floor and multiple officers took part in or watched the assault. After several months of ongoing litigation, Tupac would eventually settle with the Oakland Police Department for $42,000 ($73,100 in 2017 dollars). After the settlement he would often show the lasting damage of the police beating. "All that Hollywood stuff ain't mean nothing; to OPD I was just a nigger," he said, referring to the lasting marks across his face as the "learn-to-be-a-nigger scars."[16]

An altercation with off-duty police in 1993 in Atlanta and a fifteen-day sentence for beating codirector of *Menace II Society* Allen Hughes solidified Shakur's reputation as troubled. These experiences with the criminal justice system influenced his emphasis on "Thug Life." "I diagnosed thug life," a sociologically minded Shakur remarked, adding that for him "thug" meant something very different: "Thug is not a criminal, not someone to beat you over the head; I mean the underdog," and especially Black people.[17]

By the time the 1995 *Source Awards* aired, Shakur had released one of the year's most successful albums, *Me against the World,* an homage to his hometown of New York City. Tupac watched his album explode on the Billboard charts from the New York State's Clinton Correctional Facility, where he had been incarcerated since a first-degree sexual abuse conviction the previous December for an assault on a nineteen-year-old Brooklyn woman in November 1993. Shakur proclaimed his innocence at the sentencing, apologizing to the victim but declaring that he had not committed a crime. Assumed guilty before the verdict, the case added to Tupac's designation as both troubled and a troublemaker.

It was common knowledge that Tupac's appeal and the $1.4 million bail ($2.18 million in 2017 dollars) prevented him from being able to leave New York. Seizing the opportunity, Knight posted Shakur's bail a few months after the awards show and signed him to Death Row Records. Though an album about his hometown had taken over the airwaves and music charts, Tupac felt that New York City and the East Coast had not cared for East Harlem's Black concrete rose and had conspired in his demise.[18]

This feeling of anger, loss, and musical revenge would motivate the sound of his next album, *All Eyez on Me*. A decided shift away from his New York City roots, his Death Row album threw fuel on the flames of the West Coast–East Coast rivalry with new passion. The fire raged, and soon videos by Death Row and Bad Boy artists featured reenactments, bizarre and caricatured imitations of the other, and sometimes outright violent threats. The Zapp Band–influenced auto-tune opening of the Dr. Dre–produced anthem "California Love" sealed the deal for many fans that Shakur had cast his lot with the West Coast, never to return home again.

Once with Death Row he also developed his own group, called the Outlawz. Composed of his kinfolk, his new group wasn't merely a rap group but instead a Black nationalistic formation of resistive hip-hop. "Now I got a military," Tupac announced, explaining his new group. "Not mob like mob Italians. Mob like we've been mob orientated all our lives. . . . Because, everybody saying we choose to organize now because we emulating Italians, and we shouldn't emulate them because they don't like us. Muthafuckas got it twisted. We got organization because we peeped game. And it's not the mob really that we seeing, it's really the government—they the biggest mob. That's who we studyin', governments."[19]

Unfortunately, within a year he would find himself in an altercation in Las Vegas. Alongside Knight, Shakur had been involved in a violent episode with a group of men, many of whom remain unidentified by authorities. On September 13, 1996, just after attending a boxing match at the MGM Grand, Bruce Sheldon versus Mike Tyson, Shakur would die from gunshot wounds he suffered in a drive-by shooting while his car was at a red light. His former friend–turned–East Coast rival, Christopher Wallace, would be murdered months later in a drive-by shooting in Los Angeles on March 9, 1997.

CHOCOLATE CITIES GOT SOMETHING TO SAY

> I see no changes, wake up in the morning and I ask myself
> Is life worth living, should I blast myself?
> I'm tired of bein' poor and even worse I'm Black
> My stomach hurts, so I'm lookin' for a purse to snatch

Cops give a damn about a negro
Pull the trigger, kill a nigga, he's a hero. . . .
I see no changes, all I see is racist faces
Misplaced hate makes disgrace to races
We under, I wonder what it takes to make this

2Pac, "Changes," 1992

Tupac's untimely death sent shock waves through the industry. Still, even today, contemporary artists look to his racial geographic sensibility. For example, on his critically acclaimed album *To Pimp a Butterfly*, Compton-based artist Kendrick Lamar concludes the album with the song "Mortal Man." The song, a meditation on fame, wealth, race, and masculinity, ends with Lamar asking a boisterous Shakur about "the ground" often mentioned in his music. "The ground is gonna open up and swallow the evil . . . I see and the ground is the symbol for the poor people. The poor people is gonna open up this whole world and swallow up the rich people. 'Cause the rich people gonna be so fat, they gonna be so appetizing, you know what I'm saying, wealthy, appetizing. The poor gonna be so poor and hungry, you know what I'm saying, it's gonna be like . . . there might be some cannibalism out this mutha; they might eat the rich."[20] The linkages Tupac's migration demonstrated between Black poverty across the map in each chocolate city he knew eerily resonates from the grave, as Lamar's contemporary and imagined interview fades to black: "Pac, Pac, Pac . . . "

As Tupac Shakur likely watched the *Source Awards* from prison, he saw not just a tense battle over music territory. The child of a North Carolina migrant–turned Black Panther–turned Bay Area activist, Tupac would have also been taken with witnessing the pushback from the traditional South later that evening. Upon receiving the award for Best New Artist, the Atlanta-based duo Outkast approached the stage. Where East Coast and West Coast artists had been received with a mixture of claps and boos, Andre 2000 (now Andre 3000) and Big Boi were booed like they had written and signed the Clinton welfare reform policy.

Knowing that the air was thick with tension, Andre cut it straight down the middle like a hot knife through butter. Making plain a point that had been lost in the 2Pac versus Biggie–motivated tension, Andre unapologetically exclaimed, "The South got sumthin' to say." Like an exclamation point he held the award high and embraced his rap partner. They looked at each other and smiled.[21]

Outkast knew that Los Angeles and New York would soon be looking to Atlanta, North Carolina, Florida, Tennessee, and Texas for hip-hop inspiration. While coasts won the night, Outkast's South won the future. Indeed, we need only look to the current intersection of soul and chocolate cities, as the next chapter does, to find the traditional South at the vanguard of Black cultural production. Though absent that night in August 1995, given his travels in and through the multiple Souths that make up chocolate maps, Shakur probably appreciated Andre 3000's reminder. After all, Tupac's geographic sensibility was key to his musical awareness of the connections between Brenda and her Baby, his "Dear Mama" Afeni Shakur, and Rodney King's body covered in "learn-to-be-a-nigger scars."

10 Bounce to the Chocolate City Future

> The future is filled with vast and marvelous possibilities.
> This is a great time to be alive. Let us not despair. Let us
> realize that as we struggle for justice and freedom we have
> cosmic companionship.
>
> Martin Luther King Jr., "A Look to the Future," 1957

In 2013 bounce star Big Freedia and her dancers took over Canal Street, a main artery in downtown New Orleans, near the French Quarter. The women stopped traffic temporarily with their twerking in the street and on top of cars, asses in the air in defiance of and resistance to established norms, disrupting the humdrum of the every day. Big Freedia's temporary disruption of public space designed for the wealthy, the White, and tourist visitors prefigured the national Black call to "shut it down" that would come the next year as the Black Lives Matter movement rose to prominence in the wake of the murder of Mike Brown in Ferguson. From bridges to politicians' offices to police headquarters, Black people used their bodies to occupy symbolic and physical space and draw attention to the vast inequities and state violence that characterize their lives.[1]

Just like that of Black Lives Matter movement participants, Freedia's disruption of Canal Street calls up a long tradition of Black people asserting, taking up, and appropriating spaces and places to which they have been denied access by racism and other forms of structural inequality. Freedia's method, a Black queer disruption with the body, allows us to explore how chocolate maps often speak from the margins of Blackness to center the lives of the most vulnerable.

When Black people have been constrained in their ability to move from place to place, they have insisted on moving their bodies in protest. In the process they mapped new geographies of Blackness onto bodies, providing a corporeal complement to the chocolate map's sonic attributes. How bodies move in place says a great deal about how they make and lay claim to places. In New Orleans, which had outlawed dancing of enslaved people in its Congo Square several years before the Civil War, a confluence of African ethnic groups left a legacy of motion that persists today. To gather and to dance, even in the face of repression, is a place-making practice of chocolate maps.

AZZ EVERYWHERE

In 2014 viral videos of Black women twerking in public places—at checkout registers, in the aisles of Walmart, at gas stations, on top of cars in the street—drew ire from the usual respectability corners. Still bodies, these critics contend, are proper, respectable, and safe bodies.[2] However, as Black people continue to be murdered by police for all manner of innocuous movements, sitting, standing, and walking being among them, Black people on the margins have increasingly put their Black backsides in the face of violent establishment politics.

In early twentieth-century New Orleans, Congo Square's dance competitions and celebrations had evolved into another kind of subversive set of dance practices. In her eloquent analysis of the Baby Doll tradition in New Orleans Mardi Gras culture, gender scholar Kim Marie Vaz gives the history of Black Storyville, a Back o' Town neighborhood off the French Quarter that housed a range of working-class Black people and institutions as well as artists and entertainers, including Louis Armstrong.

The neighborhood was a designated vice district, a Black corollary to White Storyville. Working women in the community created a carnival club that evolved into a staple Mardi Gras organization. These women masked themselves in short, silky skirts and elaborately adorned or elegantly constructed baby bonnets and also sometimes dressed in men's clothing, "playing with conventional, paradoxical notions of gender."[3] The earliest Baby Doll organization, the Million Dollar Baby Dolls, emerged from the Storyville neighborhood, with other organizations springing up in other predominantly Black quarters. Culture workers, sex workers, and entrepreneurs, these women created place through their industriousness and determination to be free, at least in their own bodies.

Masking offered Black people, and Black women in particular, an opportunity to subvert the intersecting expectations of race and gender. Bodily autonomy was essential to this subversion, and the Baby Dolls moved in ways that expressed this freedom and pushed against hetero, male-centered, and capitalist norms. Masking allowed Black women to speculate about their place in society and invite new possibilities for resistance.

As Vaz notes, bounce culture is in the Baby Dolls' lineage. Bounce, New Orleans' distinctive chocolate city hip-hop, is as much sonic as it is corporeal. Bounce draws heavily on the production of "Drag Rap," also known as "Triggerman," a song by the duo The Showboys, from Queens, New York. "Drag Rap" samples the police siren from the popular television series "Dragnet." In bounce, with synth sounds on the off-beat, the siren becomes the rhythm that punctuates and compels the fast-paced rotation of bottoms that is twerking. Electronic sounds, whistles, and break beats round out the sound, as voices chant directions and descriptions. "Azz everywhere!" declares Big Freedia on a song of the same title, commanding us to dance. Darting from sample to sample, "Azz Everywhere" approximates the frenetic pace and fracturing of postsoul life.

Black women have been long reduced to their backsides, from Saartje Bartmann to Michelle Obama. Yet, just as Black people have had to make a life on the Black back side of towns, Black women have used their rear ends to protest their exploitation. Black women, cis and trans, and queer Black men in bounce turned an offensive gesture—turning around, bending over, and showing off one's butt as a sign of disrespect—into a liberatory resistance practice. Although her performance name is inspired by her given name, it is no accident that Freedia chose a name that broadcasts her status as liberated. Suggested by a friend, the name "Freedia" is a full acknowledgement of her status as gay and genderqueer.

Translated on to a mainstream stage, twerk's embodied liberation was obscured by subjective understandings of booty and hypersexuality. Many folks across the chocolate map, especially those in the Deep South, understood the broader contexts of twerking as a space of celebration, pleasure, and taking up space, a set of practices that politicized partying. Yet that message often never reached the national stage.

The 1999 video for Juvenile's "Back that Azz Up," still one of the most popular mainstream bounce songs outside of New Orleans, sought to visually replicate the feeling of the club. With a bounce beat produced by local deejay Mannie Fresh, the video begins with two men, one in a wheelchair, one playing the violin, preparing participants for the dance. When the beat drops, the once-still bodies the camera lens scans are now in unstoppable motion. Like Master P's No Limit Records had done, the Cash Money Records single put New Orleans on the rap map. "Back That Azz Up" was a reflection of a local sound, the people's sound, as well an archive of the way people had moved, and it resonated across the chocolate map.

While a bounce-inspired New Orleans rap was going mainstream in the early 2000s, Big Freedia was becoming a big name on the local scene. Freedia was famous but also a local, which made her vulnerable to violence. Her sometimes-volatile crew at times also put her at risk, though she writes of the pain and joy of surviving the intersections of race, gender, and sexuality in a poor chocolate city. While the threat of violence was always present, especially as competition between bounce artists increased, that threat was made real when a boy from the Ninth Ward shot her, sending her into a deep depression that she eventually struggled her way out of. Back to music in 2005, Freedia seemed to be finally on her way to a big break.

The levees broke before that break came, pushing Freedia out into other places on chocolate maps. The aftermath of Katrina had stalled and complicated her hustle, but it ultimately changed Freedia's trajectory from that of local phenom to international superstar. Freedia learned quickly how to use chocolate maps outside of New Orleans to her advantage to survive, promote bounce, and find and re-create home.

A HOME WITHOUT HOUSES

> After 'trina hit I had to transfer campus[es]
> Your apartment out in Houston's where I waited
> Staying with you when I didn't have an address
> F—king on you when I didn't own a mattress

Working on a way to make it out of Texas
Every night.

Frank Ocean, "Nights," 2016

Seven years before the levees broke, Katey Red had transformed bounce, declaring that she was a "punk under pressure," commanding "when you finish put my money on the dresser." Her first moment on the microphone in Melpomene made Black gay desire visible in a place that had been accustomed to sexual explicitness, but typically only of the hetero variety, since its inception. Indeed, "put my money on the dresser" calls up some of the sex workers who were also Baby Dolls. Their unapologetic and entrepreneurial transgression of gender norms on and off the stage, masked and unmasked, set the stage for Katey Red, who in turn set the stage for Freedia. Bounce's predominantly woman and Black gay audience bound the Arethas to the Kateys and Freedias as they collectively shook, moved, and protested their marginalization in a hetero male-dominated society.[4]

Like Aretha in Detroit, Freedia had gotten her start singing in church at age ten, invited by a friend to Uptown Third Ward's Pressing Onward Baptist Church. And just as Aretha had been dubbed the Queen of Soul during her ascendancy, Freedia would become the Queen Diva. Navigating an antigay environment where Black gay men and Black lesbians were maligned, attacked, and killed, Freedia writes of balancing her early knowledge of her sexuality with an almost relentlessly homophobic home and neighborhood environment.

Her mother, Vera, had been a host of contradictions but later accepted and supported Freedia wholeheartedly, while her stepfather had been verbally abusive and homophobic. Her experiences were compounded by the fact that she was both fat and feminine and thus endured homophobic fat and femme shaming. Still, like for many Black gay and nonbinary boys and men in the South, the church was a refuge, as was the hair salon, a gay uncle who designed costumes for Mardi Gras drag queens, and a community of older Black gay men and lesbians who housed and cared for younger Black gay and lesbian people whose parents had kicked them out after they came out. At home in her body but under constant threat because she was sometimes compelled to deny it until she found safe spaces to be herself, Freedia dealt with displacement as a familiar but nonetheless disorienting feeling.

Hurricane Katrina rocked chocolate maps, piling physical displacement on top of cognitive and social displacement. New Orleans and other chocolate cities on the Mississippi Gulf Coast were disproportionately affected by the damage, a product of strategic failure to protect Black communities and Black back sides of town. Sickened; subject to state violence, including police corruption and murder; and dislocated, Black New Orleanians were further disenfranchised by policies that overhauled their public school system for private profit. Entities, largely White, from nonprofit organizations to contracting firms to realtors benefited from the structural and spatial arrangements that disadvantaged Black people, poor people, and most especially poor and working-class Black people. The city's Black population declined, as people who could do so moved to other places on chocolate maps, from Atlanta to Chattanooga to Birmingham, to Baton Rouge and Houston, to Memphis and Nashville.

Houston in particular, a five-hour drive straight west from New Orleans, became a patchwork of temporary homes and addresses when houses and homes in New Orleans had been destroyed. There had long been a movement of culture and people between Houston and New Orleans, so the exodus across the state line to Texas after Katrina continued a twentieth-century pattern that had been shaped by war booms and economic change. As in New Orleans and other places across chocolate maps, Black people in Houston had made places and shaped the landscape of the city as they came west after Emancipation, and then during the interwar and postwar periods, and then again in the 1970s. Building a strong working-class culture, Houston gave birth to both the screw sound and the Geto Boys and Destiny's Child and Beyoncé. It was to Louisiana, the birthplace of her mother and grandmother, that Beyoncé turned in 2016 to rally Black women across the chocolate map to "get in-formation" for the movement for Black lives.[5]

Despite its familiarities and shared cultures, though, Houston was not home and screw was no sonic salve. In *God Save the Queen Diva*, her 2015 memoir, Big Freedia recalls the longing for the taste, sound, and feel of home that swept New Orleans and the New Orleans community in Houston after the storm. Part of the city's sonic landscape since the early 1990s, bounce—which after its distinctive rise in the late 1990s and early

2000s was nearly silenced after the storm—was made to do the work of nostalgia, resistance, anger, protest, and mourning. The fracturing that had come to be characteristic of life all over chocolate maps in the post-soul era was made physically manifest by the devastation.

Other places people went on the chocolate map after Katrina were not home. Nevertheless, chocolate maps enabled people to see where they could go—a cousin's home in Oakland, a friend's home in the south suburbs of Chicago, a distant aunt in Birmingham, a sister in Decatur—through their existing extended networks of real and fictive kin. Thus, in response to the neglect that rendered the effects of Katrina especially devastating for poor Black people, Black New Orleanians who could move influenced chocolate maps as they made homes out of pain and promise. We can see their mark all over chocolate maps, especially in the Deep and Out Souths.

Some say that when they returned to New Orleans after the storm it was not home either, not anymore. Talk of revitalization crowded out talks of restitution. Calls for artists, culture producers, and characters to return and give the city its charm again never came in full earnest. The myth that artists could play and sing and dance in and through anything floated above the reality of people trying to piece together their lives with little or no insurance or social assistance.

The word had been that this particular arrangement of events, the mass displacement of poor people and Black people, was just the kind of opportunity wealthy White investors had been waiting for. Others knew that, whether or not they had been anticipating it, they would rapidly capitalize on it. Housing projects were torn down. New mixed-income communities went up. Public school teachers were fired. Charter organizations moved in. Poor Black people were crowded into fewer areas. Prices went up and so did incarceration. The chocolate city had changed. There was still bounce, but the people were different. Familiar places and spaces for block parties were gone. It was home, but there was no shelter.

QUEEN BOUNCED

Eleven years after the storm sent an oak tree crashing into the living room of her new place and pushed her out on to the chocolate map, Big Freedia was in court being sentenced to three years' probation for theft of government resources. The courts charged that she had unfairly benefited from approximately $35,000 of Section 8 Housing voucher assistance between 2010 and 2014, a time when she was out on the chocolate map, bringing attention to New Orleans and bringing the bounce of NOLA to homesick New Orleanians across the country. She had a highly rated reality show on Fuse TV that documented this rise as well as her still-precarious economic circumstances. The vouchers provided a payment toward housing for qualified low-income residents. Freedia contended that she had made a mistake by not reporting the changes in her income caused by her meteoric rise.[6]

Freedia's circumstances had changed but did not provide stability in the way a steady and predictable income at a traditional job would have. As a culture worker and entrepreneur, it cost Freedia to do business, and in the aftermath of Katrina with an increasingly ill mother, Freedia opted to stay put to make the most of her resources. Besides, while her new economic realities were dramatically different from her previous circumstances, the cost of housing had changed even more dramatically, pricing her out of markets increased by wealthier young White people moving to New Orleans from New York and Los Angeles. In short, Freedia had too much money for Section 8 housing, not enough money to live in the gentrifying neighborhoods across the city that were outside of her social network, and there was not enough stock of the kind of housing that she could have simultaneously afforded and been in a Black community.

The judge in the case had been determined to make an example out of Freedia, especially after she had violated the terms of her bail by testing positive for marijuana. Chiding her for attempting to use her celebrity to be above the law, the judge had reminded Freedia of her economic reality, but perhaps not in the way intended. To be sure, Freedia had taken one spot for which thousands of people were waiting—a place on the Section 8 voucher roll. But even if there were funding for those thousands of people, there would not be enough housing stock for them. New Orleans had run out of shelter for poor Black people, even as poor Black people did the culture work that kept people flocking to the city.

Like housing, the body is a form of shelter, a chocolate city, an embodied place for resisting oppression and articulating freedom. After Katrina, bodies had in some ways become the most predictable shelter, and they were increasingly unreliable because of the lingering health effects of the storm, post-traumatic stress disorder, loss, and haunting anxiety. Bodies needed to move, and they did so all over chocolate maps. Black people had reshaped the nation's landscape with their movement. If they could not move from place to place, perhaps they could reshape their lives by moving their bodies.

Black people have used the resources at their disposal to change their circumstances and change the places in which they find themselves to make them a bit more amenable for survival, even in places where they are not meant to survive or thrive. They have sometimes used their culture work and sometimes their physical labor and bodies to transform the world around them. And where physical, intellectual, and culture work converge in chocolate cities, power is born. The next section is about how Black people accrued and used power, despite the racist structures of American society, to make a place where they could be free.

PART IV   The Power

Fight the Power!
Fight the Powers that be.

Public Enemy, "Fight the Power," 1990

11 The House That Jane Built

Well, I wish I could be like a bird in the sky
How sweet it would be
If I found I could fly
I'd soar to the sun
And look down at the sea
And I'd sing 'cause I know
How it feels to be free

Nina Simone, "I Wish I Knew How It Would Feel to Be Free,"
Silk and Soul, 1967

A melodic steel drum echoes. Black women chant down Babylon. The funk is infected with the skank of Lee Scratch Perry. "If you are a big, big tree," Bob Marley announces in rhythm, "then we are a small axe." In a four-part harmonious refrain, Marley coos "Ready to cut you down, to cut you down." In a modest studio under a Jamaican sun, "Small Axe," recorded in 1973, would appear that same year on Marley's album *Burnin'.*

The song, performed in the key of Black power, gives musical trappings to an important truth. Marginalized and oppressed peoples wield small axes to chop down systems and establish new vantage points that allow them the power to clear and see through the wilderness. This wilderness is geographic and legal, historical and contemporary, changing yet persistent. Black power is the small axe.

Black power. Soul Power. Power to the people. There are many ways that power can take shape. In the lives of oppressed and marginalized people, this power can look as large as the Haitian Revolution led by Toussaint-Louverture, the Arab Spring of 2008–10, or the rise of the Bolsheviks in Russia. These larger acts of power like revolution and resistance often begin from everyday small acts, small axes, and small places: small groups of unhoused Black people squatting in an old tenement; Black students marching across the city to protest the exclusion of Black history in American educational curricula; a Black journalist or activist sitting at a computer, creating pamphlets, leaflets, newsletters, and newspapers to circulate the goings-on and freedom struggles for Black people near and far; a Black scholar fighting for peace and freedom of movement.

Part 4 explores chocolate cities as intersections of power and place. Borrowing from political theorist Steven Lukes, we look for the multiple, sometimes "indirect and hidden," ways that power operates. Lukes contends that "human powers are abilities activated by agents choosing to do so (though the choice may be highly constrained and alternative paths unlikely to be taken) and also passive powers which the agents may possess irrespective of their wills."[1]

Power, then, especially as expressed by Black people, can and is often obscured by the common focus on the dominant elite. It is common in scholarship for Black power to take a backseat in favor of an emphasis on its White dominant counterpart. This tendency has led to a limited focus on the impact and dynamics of Black power, as scholars seek to uncover how the dominant elite works "to maintain and extend its material and symbolic reach." Counteracting this tendency, political scientist James Scott reminds us that those who are marginalized and oppressed actively devise "strategies to thwart and reverse that appropriation and take symbolic liberties as well."[2]

Chocolate cities have served as the "weapons of the weak," sites on which strategies of resistance and Black power have taken shape and taken hold.[3] Majority-Black projects, blocks, schools, encampments, plantation fields, farms, churches, neighborhoods, and homes have been key to forming and sharpening the small axe that is Black power. Many of these sites that serve as the built environment of chocolate cities have an important role in the Black Freedom struggle. As time passes, though, due to the dispossession and displacement of Black residents by forces of suburbanization and gentrification post–World War II, these sites have literally and figuratively disappeared. The home of a former resident of Washington, DC's U-Street Corridor animates this point.

There is a brick house squeezed in a row of homes on W Street in the historical yet rapidly gentrifying Black U-Street Corridor/Shaw neighborhood of northwest Washington, DC.[4] About a mile away sits the historically Black college Howard University. Less colorful on the outside than the red and silvery houses to its left and right, a small garden and patterned sidewalk of gray concrete lead to 1421 W Street's wooden door. For more than a century students and residents alike have passed by 1421 each day, the house's plain facade belying its status as one of the unlikely headquarters of the Black Freedom struggle. Only a historical marker outside of 1421 notes the building's distinctiveness, detailing the life of its first and most extraordinary owner: Mary Ann Shadd Cary.[5] Spending the last three years of her life at the residence, Shadd Cary was a pioneer and mastermind of the iconic chocolate city's Black resistance movement.

At age twenty-seven, in the wake of the passage of the Fugitive Slave Act of 1850, she promptly immigrated to Windsor, Ontario, in Canada. Once she arrived, she ran the abolitionist newspaper the *Provincial Freeman*, becoming the first Black woman to run a newspaper in North America. Shadd Cary would ultimately migrate back to the United States, becoming a longtime resident of the U-Street Corridor.[6] Shadd Cary's long migration toward freedom across Up South and Canada is pregnant with insight, especially as it relates to issues of power and place.

Shadd Cary was a sophisticated political actor whose life choices reflect that of a broader Black public and politics. Her formative years were a collision of escaped slaves, legally free Black people, slave owners, and poor Whites looking for work. This was the context that would propel Shadd Cary into action and history making.

This chapter explores the conditions under which chocolate cities serve explicitly as sites of Black power and agency. Shadd Cary's long migration, across multiple sites on the chocolate maps and her last stop in the Black mecca of Washington, DC, serves as a guide and compass. By highlighting the key stops, debates, and policy shifts along Cary's journey, this chapter reveals how place and power collide in chocolate cities. Indeed, 1421 came to function as a key node in U-Street Corridor chocolate cities network. In the intertwined history of 1421, Mary Ann Shadd Cary, and America's beloved chocolate city, Washington, DC, we are able to locate the importance of place and power in the formation, progress, and contraction of chocolate cities.

ON THE RUN, PART ONE

Washington, DC, was not Mary Ann Shadd's hometown. She had, like many Black Americans, filtered into the city after a long migration. She and many Black migrants throughout the Souths were the added cocoa that made Washington, DC's U-Street Corridor's one of America's first Black meccas.

In 1823 Shadd was born free in a relatively well-off family in Delaware, a slave state. Raised in Wilmington by Black professional and abolitionist parents, Shadd had been actively engaged in antislavery efforts since childhood. Tenacious and assertive, Shadd inherited her social consciousness from her parents, cultivating them among Pennsylvania Quakers at her boarding school in West Chester.

Throughout Shadd's adolescence, Delaware abolitionists had been engaged in a long and relatively unsuccessful campaign to convince leaders to shift in favor of freeing all slaves. Having to be doubly conscious of her Blackness and her freedom, Shadd didn't take her distance from enslavement lightly. Time and again reports and rumors about the loss of friends and family to bandits who sold free Black folks illegally in the Deep South put her and other legally free Black Americans on edge. Shadd was especially sensitive to the fact that capture and enslavement also meant sexual violence for Black women. Gang rape, involuntary pregnancy, and other horrors were common violations endured by Black women at the hands of White slave owners and bounty hunters. Although Shadd was just above the Mason-Dixon Line, she knew she was in the South.[7]

Shadd's fears were not mere paranoia. Even as a legally free Black person, at any moment she could be kidnapped by bounty hunters seeking the cash incentives within fugitive slave laws. With minimal legal checks on the practice of snatching those legally free and placing them in bondage for pay, escape from slavery in the United States was not assured in the states above the Mason-Dixon Line.

Sessions and resolutions from the 1849–50 Virginia State legislature illustrate that Shadd's intuition was entirely founded. "In the language of an acute and enlightened foreigner," the legislature resolved, "slavery at the North was a question of commerce and manufactures—in the South it was a question of life and death."[8] As a forceful leader and proponent of slavery, Virginia's politics forecasted what would ultimately happen in nation's capital on the issue of slavery. And in the mind's of Virginia's leaders a smart observer would easily notice that slavery was everywhere in the United States. Black freedom held no guarantee even for those legally free.

By 1850 a more aggressive fugitive slave policy was headed for President Zachary Taylor's desk. As the leader of the short-lived Whig Party, Taylor's political loyalties cut across the divides of the two major political factions divided on the issue of slavery—the Free Soilers and the abolitionists. The Free Soilers, largely White, poor, and working class, was a prolabor party with a relatively soft stance on slavery, as freedom would allow Black workers to charge for their work and thus upend the pecking order among laborers.

Though the Fugitive Slave Act of 1793 had been in place for more than fifty years, charges of unfairness by slaveholders mounted, with claims that "fugitive slaves were harbored and protected." Slave owners and southern legislatures alike also protested that "suits and prosecutions were instituted against the owner," usually ending in short imprisonment for "irresponsible mobs, composed of fanatics, ruffians and fugitive slaves, who had already found asylum abroad."[9] Slave owner after slave owner complained and filed suits against other localities and state governments for harboring escaped slaves. Local, state, and federal courts were inundated with lawsuits involving slave owners who charged that the enforcement measures of the 1793 law were laissez-faire. This, alongside the strength of the proslavery coalition, signaled to Shadd that a change, for the worse, was on the horizon.

With a quick stroke of his pen, the president authorized the Fugitive Slave Act of 1850. Whereas the 1793 law placed the responsibility of fugitive laws and authority on federal agents, the Fugitive Slave Act of 1850 was a significant policy shift, wherein local, municipal, and even individual slave owners would be the enforcers of America's fugitive laws.[10] By the time the news of the law's enactment broke, Shadd was already passing through Michigan on her way to Windsor, the Canadian city just opposite of Detroit.

Once she arrived, Shadd took up work as a teacher and aided free and enslaved Black Americans in seeking asylum in Canada. Though the fear and reality of slavery pervaded the United States. Shadd found many Black Americans, free and enslaved, reluctant to leave the country, especially for Canada, which was a relatively unknown mythological place for some Black Americans. For others it was the United States' stepcousin, whose wintry tundra and long cold seasons were of little appeal, despite the promise of freedom.

In response, Shadd embarked on a geographic survey of Canada, intimating that "the absence of condensed information accessible to all, is my excuse for offering this tract to the notice of the public . . . [so they can] become thoroughly informed respecting the Canadas, and particularly that part of the province called Canada West." She was determined to offer a sincere and rigorous assessment of Canada for Black people. Spending two years analyzing Canada's landscape, seasons, work opportunities, rural and urban environments, and racial attitudes, Shadd developed a historical antislavery pro-Black geographic manifesto. Black "people are in a strait,—on the one hand, a proslavery administration with its entire controllable force, is bearing upon them with fatal effect: on the other, the Colonization Society . . . is seconding the efforts of the first named power, by bringing into the list a vast social and immoral influence."[11]

The "passage of the odious Fugitive Slave Law has made residence in the United States to many [Black Americans] dangerous in the extreme," Shadd writes at the outset of the study. "Again, many look with dreadful forebodings" she continues, "to the probability of worse than inquisitorial inhumanity in the Southern States, from the operation of the Fugitive Law. Certain that neither a home in Africa, nor in the Southern States, is desirable under present circumstances, inquiry is made respecting Canada."[12]

Titled *A Plea for Emigration; or, Notes of Canada West, in Its Moral, Social, and Political Aspect: With Suggestions respecting Mexico, W. Indies and Vancouver's Island, for the Information of Colored Emigrants,* the study was published and disseminated in pamphlet form in 1852 by Shadd and her associates. As a literal plea to implore Canadian immigration as a Black divestment strategy, the geographic survey did not seek to ignore key differences in weather and opportunity. Appealing to Black Americans in rural and urban areas, the plea suggested that in addition to guaranteed freedom a financial comeuppance can also be easily achieved in Canada: "Those whose capital invested in it is their own, are sure to increase their means and wealth." Further, Shadd identifies critical juridical differences between Canada and the United States after an inventory of policies and laws in the province: "There is no legal discrimination what[so]ever [a] ffecting colored emigrants in Canada, nor from any cause whatever are their privileges sought to be abridged."[13]

As the *Plea for Emigration* made its way throughout chocolate maps, Shadd gained tremendous respect and support for her antislavery efforts from a network of activists and Black people in the United States and Canada. Following the completion of the geographic survey, Shadd was convinced that a weekly paper that reported on the crisis of the Fugitive Slave Law, Black life across the African diaspora, and general information on local and global affairs was the next necessary step in her Black liberation campaign. She channeled her support into the monies needed to finance her takeover of the *Provincial Freeman*, a weekly Black newspaper headquartered in Windsor. Founded in 1853, the *Provincial Freeman*, with Shadd serving as editor in chief, reported on crimes against Black people in United States and abroad and published letters from fugitive slaves who had successfully immigrated to Canada.

The first Black woman to run a newspaper in North America, Shadd used each issue to reiterate her belief in the importance of Black people's agency. "Self reliance is the fine road to Independence," Shadd proudly and defiantly wrote in an early issue of the newspaper. Upon heading up the *Provincial Freeman*, Shadd placed it into wide circulation: "A number of persons as yet, probably, unacquainted with the intention to publish this paper, will receive a copy of this issue, by which it is hoped they may be induced to subscribe; numbers who have pledged themselves to aid in its support will, in like manner, be reminded of their promises."[14]

Under Shadd's leadership, a major goal of the newspaper was also to develop an intergenerational network of subscribers and supporters of Black liberation and emigration:

We do hope that young people and old will help to forward a good work. Canadians are not too well supplied with papers advocating the measures herein set forth, so we are not prepared for the cry in this quarter of "papers enough!" The matter is settled for another paper here. Persons abroad want reliable information of Canada, *from* Canada; that they shall have, if they will speak and act encouragingly. The advocates of emigration will have an opportunity to compare the facilities of this country, with others on which their attention is now fixed. The lovers of the ridiculous will also be highly entertained, no doubt, when they hear, as they will if they *take the paper*, of the somersets, manoeuvres and antics now in full tide of operation, especially at the "west end." We have now, awaiting forthcoming issues, resolutions and counter-resolutions, accounts of meetings held and the resolves passed thereat, and of resolutions published, but *not* passed at any meeting, for begging and against it, for the Provincial Council and against it, for the United States National Council and against it, and for exclusive institutions and against them, all showing that some among colored Canadians, as among all other people, intend to kill, while others try to cure. Canadians, East and West, see and speak freely of the importance of the enterprise, and from them we hopefully look for patronage.[15]

The *Provincial Freeman* was indeed a paper of ambition, seeking to manifest an internal Black political dialogue centered on questions and possibilities of freedom.

Shadd also meant for the paper to reach Black youth near and far. "We hope they will not be slow to assume their proper duties, to relieve the old men of a portion of the labor, never failing, meanwhile, to profit by their counsel," Shadd wrote, seeking to charge Black youth with taking over the movement as elders pass on. Her paper would be one truly meant for the Black masses, explicitly and implicitly.

As common sensical as Shadd's propositions of self-reliance and movement away from slavery may seem, it was a serious source of discord among abolitionists. Her call for emigration as a strategy of freedom and resistance put her at odds with Frederick Douglass, who was for the duration of his life a major figure and spokesperson against slavery. For Douglass, however, emigration was the opposite of the approach he believed should be promoted.

In 1855, a year after taking the reins of the *Provincial Freeman*, Shadd's and Douglass's differences of opinion collided in Philadelphia. In a rare return to the United States, Shadd arrived in Philadelphia to participate in the Colored Convention, a gathering of the major figures in the antislavery movement, including Douglass. Shadd's presence riled up the convention, leading to a standoff about whether or not she could be admitted as a delegate. For some antislavery proponents like Douglass, staying put in the United States was fundamental to Black freedom and ending slavery. By emigrating to Canada and also advocating such, Shadd was a lightning rod in the antislavery movement. Despite Douglass's dissension, Shadd was later admitted, though by the slimmest odds of any delegate, a margin of fifteen votes.[16]

Although her visit to United States had been uneasy, Shadd returned to Windsor motivated by the synergy of the convention. Seeing the growth and vibrancy of the antislavery movement, Shadd continued churning issues of the *Provincial Freeman,* attempting to increase circulation. Shortly after her return from Philadelphia, Shadd's romance with Thomas F. Cary, Black barber and Torontonian, deepened.

The couple wed in Windsor in 1856. Following the wedding, they moved from Windsor to the emergent chocolate city of Chatham, Ontario. Over the previous thirty years, Chatham had grown into a dense Black village. A favorite final destination for Black Americans crossing the border at the end of Underground Railroad, Chatham teemed with Black diversity and dialects; former slaves and free Blacks from across the Souths built a high-functioning chocolate city in a matter of decades. Though the *Provincial Freeman* was in wide circulation in both the United States and Canada, the production costs mounted, and Shadd Cary began to have a difficult time keeping the paper's finances out of the red.

The move to Chatham, then, seemed economically wise at the time. A larger local Black population might sustain the paper enough to cover the continued cost of dissemination beyond the Canadian border. Further, because of its proximity and relationship with the Underground Railroad, Chatham contained a critical mass of Black activists and antislavery proponents who could serve as interlocutors for newly married Shadd Cary. Upon her arrival, she and Martin Delany, for example, had become fast friends, providing mutual support to each other. Delany, a Black antislavery activist and journalist, also arrived in Chatham in 1856. Having been one of the first three Black Americans admitted to Harvard University's Medical School, Delany believed that collaboration and emigration were a necessary part of the antislavery activist arsenal against the status quo in the United States.[17]

Born free in Charles Town, West Virginia, Delany had lived and worked throughout the Souths, especially the Mid South chocolate city of Pittsburgh (where he met and married his wife, Catherine Richards, in 1843). Although Delany arrived in Canada after Shadd Cary, he had done so for similar reasons. Delany had been an ally to Shadd Cary as a proponent of emigration as a strategy of Black resistance and freedom.

Shadd Cary's and Delany's mutual support of each other and of emigration as a worthy antislavery strategy, along with the critical mass of socially conscious Black Chathamites, gave the *Provincial Freeman* a renewed opportunity. Shadd Cary used the transition to further amplify the works and words of Black feminists and abolitionists, such as Lucretia Mott and Lucy Stone Blackwell. In one of the first issues from its new Chatham headquarters, the *Provincial Freeman* featured reporting on a fiery and moving speech by Blackwell who had "been at the stations of the U.G.R.R. [Underground Railroad], up and down the river, and had heard of parties—one, two, five, ten, and even twenty in a party—moving northward." Blackwell "held in her hand a paper where pots and kettles, and traces and carts, and oxen and horses, men and women, all mingled in one advertisement, were announced to be sold on New Year's; and one of these chattels, a girl of 14, brought $1,245 [$35,900 in 2017 dollars]!" The South was all one den of infamy. No woman was safe there, if her skin were dark, from the brutal violence of any libertine."[18]

With her new husband and newspaper headquartered in Chatham, Shadd Cary soon gave birth to two children, Sarah and Linton Cary. While the move to Chatham proved successful initially, expenses mounted and Shadd Cary was forced to suspend publication of the *Provincial Freeman* on August 22, 1857. The shuttering of the paper was coupled with the sudden death of her husband just three years later in 1860.

ON THE RUN, PART TWO

Despite losing her husband and her paper and becoming a single mother, Shadd Cary forged ahead. Though 1860 proved to be a difficult personal and professional year, a new development compelled Shadd Cary to return to the United States for good: the Civil War. Her friend and Chatham neighbor, Martin Delany, had joined the Union Army and was appointed by Abraham Lincoln to develop a recruitment apparatus for Black soldiers.[19]

Both Delany and Shadd Cary had been inspired and encouraged by the White abolitionist John Brown and his 1859 raid on Harpers Ferry, Virginia, a central ammunition site for the Confederate coalition. From October 16 to 18, Brown and a motley crew of Black and White comrades had taken hold of the fort at Harpers Ferry without shooting one bullet. Though Confederate general Robert E. Lee and his troops would suppress their efforts, the raid at Harpers Ferry sent shock waves through the nation, illustrating that the proslavery contingent across the Souths were more vulnerable to planned attack than was previously believed.[20]

For her part, Shadd Cary moved her family to Indiana. Once there, she worked as one of the few women recruiting Black men into service for the Union Army in the Civil War. That she would do for the next three years, until Lincoln's issuing of the Emancipation Proclamation, in 1863. In this presidential executive order Lincoln proclaimed, "on the first day of January, in the year of our Lord one thousand eight hundred and sixty-three, all persons held as slaves within any State or designated part of a State, the people whereof shall then be in rebellion against the United States, shall be then, thenceforward, and forever free; and the Executive Government of the United States, including the military and naval authority thereof, will recognize and maintain the freedom of such persons, and will do no act or acts to repress such persons, or any of them, in any efforts they may make for their actual freedom."[21]

The Emancipation Proclamation did not apply to all States, however; it focused particularly on Confederate states as a means of further crippling the southern economy, creating a legal incentive for enslaved Black Americans to emigrate from the rural plantations to which they had been bound for generations.[22] Limitations notwithstanding, Lincoln's proclamation had been the first major and legally enforceable antislavery government effort in Shadd Cary's lifetime. It was music to her ears, after a long journey prompted by the Fugitive Slave Act of 1850.

Although the Emancipation Proclamation was not a full guarantee of Black freedom and the complete end of slavery, it was just the right legal salve to heal Shadd Cary's earlier scars from the fears of enslavement and sexual violence in the wake of the 1850 fortification of the fugitive slave laws. Two years later, at the Civil War's conclusion, Shadd Cary brought her children to her birthplace of Wilmington, Delaware. It was her first time home, and south of Philadelphia, since she had left fifteen years earlier.

Upon her return to her hometown, Shadd Cary did as she had always done, taught and raised social consciousness. She worked at local Black schools and continued her activism, this time focused on generating a lasting legal checks-and-balance system that would help ensure that the Reconstruction's constitutional amendments (thirteenth, fourteenth, and fifteenth) were implemented and enacted properly. This interest began to attract Shadd Cary to Washington, DC's Black U-Street Corridor. Once in the nation's capital, Shadd Cary believed she would gain the proximity and skills needed to work on the frontlines of ensuring that the legal protections of the newly amended Constitution would cover Black Americans.[23]

And, just like that, the family left Wilmington and was off to Washington, DC, where Shadd Cary could be closer to and involved in the post–Civil War racial realignment process. Soon after arriving to the U-Street Corridor, Shadd Cary was promoted to the rank of principal, spending her seventeen-year tenure at the helm of three different schools in Washington, DC. At the same time, her legal studies were underway at the nearby Howard University School of Law.

Having spent her entire life teaching, her movement in and through law school presented many of the same difficulties she endured over her life. Always an outspoken and assertive Black woman, Shadd Cary had become accustomed to fighting men who dominated leadership and authority positions. Because she was a woman, professors and lawyers were dubious and often thwarted her attempts to move forward, notably blocking her attempt to join the Bar Association.

In the face of these odds, Shadd Cary earned her law degree from Howard in 1884, becoming the second Black women to accomplish this feat. Thereafter she resigned from the school district. Following her resignation, she worked alongside Susan B. Anthony on women's suffrage and developed her own legal practice.

While the success of her legal practice was modest, it generated broad respect for her across the Washington, DC, metro area and provided her the money to purchase the house at 1421 W Street. She moved in shortly after its completion in 1890. For the next three years she continued her tireless advocacy and legal work. In the late spring of 1893, Shadd Cary succumbed to pancreatic cancer and was mourned on both sides of the U.S.-Canadian border for her courage and accomplishments.[24]

MAPPING FREEDOM

Shadd Cary's story has many lessons. Her life and times demonstrate the fluidity of the South as a legal and political apparatus. Its omnipresence compelled her journey of emigration, protest, and activism that placed her at odds even with other Black Americans for whom Canada was a bridge too far.

She developed a Black mapping of Canada to incentivize Black Americans, Caribbeans, and Africans to divest from the world dominated by White supremacy. Looking to jurisprudence, Shadd Cary was acutely aware of how slavery and enslavement worked as legal powers. Seeking to use the press and her feet as expressions and platforms for Black discontent, Shadd Cary represents how fears and realities of racial and sexual violence pervade every place on the U.S. map. No place was safe for a Black person, free or otherwise, in a post–Fugitive Slave Act of 1850 world.

Shadd Cary's life makes plain the freedom geography Malcolm X uncovered in situating everywhere below Canada as the South. Though seeking freedom and safety, Shadd Cary was also especially American, never letting go of her attachment to and investment in the American project. Drawing on her networks and training as a lawyer at Howard University, Cary's adventures and activism make legible the contours of the South that extend well beyond traditional borders. Finding refuge and a critical mass of Black people in the province of Ontario, Canada, Shadd Cary sought to remind all that life for Black people across the United States occurred legally, socially, politically, and culturally above and below the Mason-Dixon Line; only hers truly lay north of Michigan.

12 Mary, Dionne, and Alma

> Undoubtedly black women are cultivating new attitudes,
> most of which will have political repercussions in the
> future. They are attempting to change their conditions. . . .
> From their experiences they learned that the real sources
> of power lay at the root of the political system.
>
> Shirley Chisholm, "The Black Woman in Contemporary
> America," 1974

On a warm evening in 2015, a dusty box in a South Philadelphia basement sat just along the beige walls, among a bunch of nondescript boxes. Cobwebs strung across the wall and attached to the intertwined four flaps, connecting its lid to those in the stack beside it. Outside the noises of urban living and change were in the air.[1]

The set of nondescript boxes, which had been on quite a journey, contained items saved in a fire that consumed the family's home. Only blocks from the South Street of the old Black Seventh Ward studied by W. E. B. Du Bois in 1896, the smoke and fury blazed on for hours in the late summer of 2007. Otherwise empty, the house at 1237 Christian Street began to melt under the pressure of the combined humidity and heat of the flames.

Though the family lost nearly everything, a few items managed to escape the fiery episode. After collecting them in a swift and unmemorable fashion, the survivors packed them in bunches, relieved that all had not been lost. For the next eight years the items made their way around the city in a set of boxes that traveled across the villages of South Philadelphia.

From one basement to the next, the boxes and their contents began to fade as the house fire and the forced migration it set in motion brought new events, people, and locations into the family's orbit. By 2015 a few of those boxes made it to a two-story row house within the racially and ethnically eclectic Bella Vista neighborhood. Near the Delaware River, this South Philadelphia neighborhood contains a bright and sometimes clashing mix of Puerto Rican, Black American, Black African, Italian American, Irish American, and Southeast Asian residents.

A long uneventful day after years of eventfulness provided an opportunity to explore. Long forgotten, the contents of the boxes in the basement now seemed like a curious collection of possible treasures or long-kept family secrets. The spiders seemed to think so too, covering them in a noticeably thick layer of webbing.

Flipping open the boxes at random led to the discovery of an item steeped in mystery, history, and migration. At the bottom of the box, wrapped ever so tightly in an old edition of the *Philadelphia Inquirer,* was an orangey-brown soft fox stole. "Mary Sanders," was engraved in the silk lining in meticulously stitched and bonded cursive. Her daughter, Shelley, who had not seen this item since her mother's untimely death in 1970, took a deep sniff and rubbed the stole against her face, feeling as it did like warm sunshine in the dead of winter. The stole's long migration had finally ended, discovered in Sanders's birthplace of Philadelphia.

Mary Sanders (née Mary Syneatha Hill) was born in between the two world wars on September 11, 1934, just a few miles north of her daughter's current South Philadelphia home. Though given the last name "Hill," after her mother's husband, Timothy Hill, Sanders was the product of a romance outside of their wedlock. Her mother, Mozelle Morrison, lived the life of a hustler, cobbling together money to support her family through a well-known speakeasy in the heart of North Philadelphia. And so when Shelly Scott, a local Black laborer, came around, Morrison's fast life led to a fast romance, and soon enough Mary Syneatha was born. Mozelle's husband, Timothy, after a reconciliation, lent his last name and fatherly oversight to the bouncing brown baby girl.

By 1947 Mozelle's lifestyle had been the subject of great scrutiny, leading her eldest sister, Sheraldina Randolph, to take a young Mary further Up South to the emerging chocolate city of Newark, New Jersey, known as "Brick City" to Black residents. A profoundly religious woman, Randolph felt the Holy Ghost had guided her to swoop into the North Philly den of hustle to save her niece and teach her the right ways of the world. Over the next two decades, Mary would meet, marry, and divorce George Sanders, father of her four children, George Jr., Denise, Bruce, and Shelley, whom she named after her biological father.

At the same time, Sanders had become a staple of Newark's Black political elite. Actively involved in local politics, by 1964 she was director of the Area 4 of Newark's United Community Corporation, assisting "low-income, disadvantaged and at-risk individuals and families to become self-supporting, while enhancing their quality of life and standard of living . . . to ameliorate the impact of poverty in Newark."[2] A former resident of Newark's Bruce Street's housing projects, Mary was well aware of the difficulties for Black residents to achieve and sustain mobility and opportunity.

Activist-minded and organized, Sanders worked and advocated for aspiring local Black leaders such as Donald Paine, future and longtime congressman in the U.S. House of Representatives; and Earl Harris, city council president from 1974 to 1982. Known around town as one of the "Gibson Girls," Sanders also spent much of her time alongside Black women across Newark in support of local politician Kenneth A. Gibson's ambitions. Gibson, active in Newark's civil rights movement, aimed his political aspirations at the mayor's office.

Though Sanders was part of an arsenal of Black residents dedicated to liberating Black Newark from the ills of poverty, redlining, and police brutality, things came to a head in the hot summer of July 1967. When Black residents of the Hayes projects witnessed two White police officers dragging and beating an unarmed taxi driver, John Weerd Smith, word and protests quickly spread. Within hours the incident had reverberated throughout Black Newark, and soon Sanders's neighbors at the Bruce Street projects had joined their fellow protesters. For five days national cameras recorded as tanks, police, Molotov cocktails, busted storefronts, and heavily beaten Black residents painted the streets of Newark. From July 12 to 17, the sights and sounds of Newark looked much like its 1965 predecessor Out South in Watts, Los Angeles. Less than a week later, the Twelfth Street rebellion would bring similar attention, protest, and devastation to Detroit.

The rebellion caused many Newark residents, Black and White, to migrate to neighboring suburbs of East Orange, Montclair, and South

Orange. Many others stayed, impassioned to shift the geography of opportunity in favor of Black Newark. Among them was Sanders, who began a tireless campaign to get Gibson elected as the city's first Black mayor. By 1968 change was afoot, and Newark was at the vanguard, both locally and nationally.

Just as the smoke was clearing in the city, a local singer turned pop star, Dionne Warwick, had taken over the music charts and seemed a shoo-in to win the Grammy Award for Best Pop Vocal Performance for the up-tempo Burt Bacharach and Hal David tune "Do You Know the Way to San Jose." A sonic postcard and roadmap to California's South Bay, the song was a breezy unapologetic take on the distinctive differences between Northern and Southern California. Where Los Angeles offered freeways and fame, San Jose provided clean air and space. Brown-skinned and slender, adorned in a gown shimmering like a clear evening sky, Warwick would take home the 1969 Grammy Award, a historic feat for a Black singer.

As Sanders and the rest of the Gibson Girls campaigned, the record and celebration of Warwick's achievement filled the streets and reflected the power of Black women in Newark to change and make history locally and nationally. Sanders could often be found dancing and singing the song as she campaigned. Adorned in her fox stole, Sanders spent 1969 and 1970 attending galas, fund-raising events, and cabarets, taking to the floor in her dashing heels whenever the Warwick tune made its way into the hall.

Her work soon paid off. By January 1970 Gibson's campaign was on the upswing and the Gibson Girls continued their quest. A year later, in January 1971, Gibson was sworn in as the mayor of Newark, becoming the first Black person to be mayor Up South. Though the out-migration meant that many middle-class Black residents had left for the suburbs, the Gibson victory brought everyone home, even Warwick, if only for an evening of exuberant celebration and song.

Sanders, however, would never cast her ballot for Gibson. An Independence Day headache had turned her vision blurry, and she had gone to the bathroom at a friend's house in search of relief, likely hoping that a quick splash of water and a few deep breaths would be just the remedy she needed to return to the festivities. But after a few minutes Sanders collapsed there on the floor, lying unconscious until her friends, noticing her absence, rushed to the bathroom and got her to the local hospital.

Succumbing to an unknown brain aneurysm, Sanders was pronounced dead on July 5, 1970, at thirty-six years old. Her youngest daughter, Shelley, then age nine, would inherit her mother's Warwick-infused dreams of California. Wiping tears from her eyes as she placed the stole over her shoulder in a South Philly basement in 2015, Shelley took stock of how her mother had changed urban America before age forty.

This chapter explores the power of chocolate cities through the explicit lens of Black women connected by the everyday inequalities Black residents face across the chocolate maps. Linked by the sonic call to migration and opportunity offered in Dionne Warwick's Grammy-winning song, this chapter travels from Up South to West South to Out South, where we learn about life for Black people in San Jose today.

Located on opposite coasts, Newark and San Jose, as we will see, share more than a song. While Newark has gone on to become a majority-Black city with high rates of poverty and a poor educational infrastructure, San Jose—like the rest of Out South and West South—has witnessed a declining Black population. Disenchanted with the hopes of prosperity and unable to keep pace with the cost of living, many Black residents have left since Warwick brought San Jose into the popular imagination. Left behind, a village of highly educated, middle-class, and wealthy Black residents have found themselves plagued by glass ceilings and health, financial, professional, and familial outcomes on par with their poorer, less educated counterparts in places across the Souths, like Newark.

"DO YOU KNOW THE WAY TO SAN JOSE?"

Boom. Boom. Boom. Boom. The light bass prefaces the signature harmonic woh, woh, woh-woh, woh, woh, who-who-woh, woh. The bass guitar melds with the harmonies of the Sweet Inspirations, the legendary background trio of Black women. With effortless timing Dionne Warwick's voice breezes into the musical introduction, floating over the melody with elegant whimsy with a seemingly simple query: "Do you know the way to San Jose?"

Singing from the perspective of "being born and raised in San Jose," Warwick sings about searching for an easier life back at home. The song centers on a call to home and a longing for a place that is not Los Angeles.

Cautious to take any old road back to San Jose, Warwick melodically confesses, "I've been away so long. I may go wrong and lose my way."[3]

As the song notes, then, as now, it was and is quite important for a Black traveler to have racially sensitive pathways to whatever the destination in the United States may be. Established much later than its East Coast counterparts, the frontier state of California existed largely as a majority-White space of two million people in the early 1900s. It would grow rapidly over the first half of the twentieth century, particularly during World War II, with its population swelling to five times its turn-of-the-century size by midcentury. "Black 49ers," Black migrants chasing and searching gold in the frontier, along with the Great Migration, helped generate a significant Black population in the West South, and in California especially.[4] Added to this mix was a combination of immigrant populations from across Asia, Mexico, and Latin America. The result: "California's population nearly tripled in the last half of the 20th century, and its growth rate remained much higher than that of the rest of the United States."[5]

Despite the state's rapid growth, at its peak the Black population only constituted roughly 10 percent, a majority of whom called Los Angeles and the Bay Area home. Thus, as Warwick's song suggests, it would be quite easy and dangerous for a Black migrant to make a wrong turn or take the wrong road while moving through California. Not unlike Pennsylvania or Kansas or Wisconsin, the roads of California required a racial sensibility to navigate its terrains safely. Here, we can imagine that on the way back to San Jose from Los Angeles, the song's Black protagonist would have made use of the directions from other Black friends and a broader Black network of travel information, like that provided in *The Negro-Motorist Green Book*.

Victor H. Green, a Black activist and postal worker in Harlem, published the book, known simply as the *Green Book*, from 1936 to 1964. He had developed the *Green Book* "to save the travelers of his race as many difficulties and embarrassments as possible," after he and "several friends and acquaintances complained of difficulties encountered . . . [and] painful embarrassments suffered which ruined a vacation or business trip." Though Green was hopeful that one day Black Americans would "enjoy the rights and privileges guaranteed" by the Constitution, he knew that such freedoms were "withheld in certain areas of these United States." A traveler's guide based on the geography of Black freedom, safety, and interests, the *Green Book* provides lists "of hotels, boarding houses, restaurants, beauty shops, barber shops and various other services [that] can most only help solve your travel problems."[6]

"Carry the *Green Book* with you," the 1949 edition cover warns. "You may need it."[7] For nearly three decades the *Green Book* served as a popular Black travel resource guide, selling out of each of its fifteen thousand copies of every edition. Though California is a large state, the *Green Book* illustrated the limited options and racial contours there for Black people. Indeed, Los Angeles and the San Francisco Bay Area are the two major destinations for Black travelers in California in the *Green Book*. Whether headed toward Watts, Baldwin Hills, the Fillmore District, Hunter's Point, Oakland, or San Jose, Black travelers needed to be prepared to travel long distances to go from West South (Southern California) to Out South (Northern California). And as filmmaker Byron Hurt notes about the sociopolitical context of the *Green Book* in *Soul Food Junkies,* Black travelers commonly packed boxed lunches and dinners and drank little water to anticipate and avoid being turned away or denied services by White proprietors.[8]

So Warwick's worries of getting lost, though breezily sung alongside a full Bacharach-directed orchestra, reflected the real fears and dangers of moving across and within the Souths of the West Coast. Desperate to escape West South, the singer continues, "LA is a great big freeway. Put a hundred down and buy a car. In a week, maybe two, they'll make you a star," Warwick sings with lightness highlighting the pull of stardom for migrants to Los Angeles. Alas, all cannot be successful as "all the stars that never were are parking cars and pumping gas. . . . [Their] dreams turn into dust and blow away. And there you are without a friend. You pack your car and ride away." Disenchanted with the magnetism of fame and fortune, Warwick's soprano modulates to alto declaring, "I'm going back to find some peace of mind in San Jose."[9]

The web of post–World War II freeways and racial discrimination made Los Angeles difficult to navigate physically, socially, politically, and economically for Black residents. As their numbers increased during the postwar period, so too had police supervision and brutality in California's Black communities. The frustrations, along with limited success and hyperpolicing, led to the Watts Riots of 1965 and fomented the seeds of the early Black Panther Party in the Bay Area. Peace of mind was a commodity, and Warwick tells us that the chocolate city in San Jose is a refuge, a place where Black neighborhoods are clean and relatively safe. Indeed, data as shown in table 7 affirms that Black residents in San Jose (Santa Clara County) agree with Warwick's sentiment.

"Do You Know the Way to San Jose" depicts somewhat accurate distinctions in life and possibility between Northern and Southern California. Where Black communities in Southern California and most of the Bay Area had mixed fortunes, over the twentieth century San Jose had become an exceptional, if isolated, place of Black success. The lion share of Santa Clara County, San Jose, like the majority-Black Maryland suburb Prince George's County, has become an unlikely site of Black upward mobility.

Situated within a network of small cities, now known as the Silicon Valley, at its peak San Jose was 8 percent Black. Today it has seen its Black population on a steady decline, falling to approximately 2.5 percent as of 2015. San Jose, however, is unlike traditional stories of Black out-migration, where middle-class and wealthy Black residents leave for greener pastures, leaving behind their vulnerable, poorer, and less educated Black counterparts.

Rather, San Jose is a place where those who have stayed (or have been left behind, depending on the vantage point) are more solidly middle class. Most Black residents hold a college degree and make a median household income of $65,347 (see tables 9–10) compared to the $35,481 for Black households nationally. Black poverty in San Jose is 10 percent, while the national average is 27 percent (see tables 12–13).

These demographic facts perhaps constitute the peace of mind Warwick seeks in the song. Such facts, however, belie others that underscore consistencies between Black San Jose and Black people everywhere else. That is, while Black residents in San Jose rank higher on key indicators of mobility such as education and household income, others, like health and infant mortality, tell a different story. With respect to health, as table 18 demonstrates, despite their small numbers, Black folk in San Jose are disproportionately suspended and expelled from school, affected by cancer, have lower life expectancy, and are inordinately unemployed and hospitalized.

Table 7 Adults with clean neighborhoods by race and ethnicity,
Santa Clara County, 2009

Race and ethnicity	Neighborhood cleanliness, excellent or good (%)
African American	92
Asian/Pacific Islander	91
Latino/Latina	91
Non-Hispanic White	94
Santa Clara County	92

SOURCE: Santa Clara County Public Health Department, *Behavioral Risk Factor Survey* (San Jose, CA: Santa Clara County Public Health Department, 2009).

Table 8 Household income by race and ethnicity, Santa Clara County, 2012 (%)

	$0–$24,999	$25,000–$49,999	$50,000–$74,999	$75,000+	Median household income
African American	19	19	21	41	$65,347
Asian/Pacific Islander	13	10	11	66	$105,088
Latino/Latina	20	26	16	37	$55,220
Non-Hispanic White	12	14	13	62	$100,480
Santa Clara County	14	15	13	58	$91,425

SOURCE: U.S. Census Bureau, *American Community Survey: 1-Year Estimates* (Washington, DC: U.S. Government Printing Office, 2012).

NOTE: Some percentages may not equal 100 percent due to rounding.

Table 9 Household income, California and the United States, 2012 (%)

Income	California		United States	
	African American	Overall	African American	Overall
$0–$24,999	34	22	39	24
$25,000–$49,999	23	22	26	24
$50,000–$74,999	17	17	15	18
$75,000+	26	40	19	34
Median household income	$41,275	$58,328	$33,764	$51,371

SOURCE: U.S. Census Bureau, *American Community Survey: 1-Year Estimates* (Washington, DC: U.S. Government Printing Office, 2012).

NOTE: "African American" includes both Hispanic and non-Hispanic Black Americans.

Table 10 Educational attainment by race and ethnicity, Santa Clara County, 2012 (%)

Race and ethnicity	Less than high school	High school graduate	Some college or associate's degree	Bachelor's degree or higher
African American	8	14	43	35
Asian	12	10	17	61
Latino/Latina	36	24	27	14
Non-Hispanic White	4	13	28	55
Santa Clara County	14	15	24	47

SOURCE: U.S. Census Bureau, *American Community Survey: 1-Year Estimates* (Washington, DC: U.S. Government Printing Office, 2012).

NOTE: Some percentages may not equal 100 percent due to rounding. Educational attainment is reported for adults twenty-five and older.

Table 11 Marital status by race and ethnicity, Santa Clara County, 2012 (%)

Race and ethnicity	Married	Divorced or separated	Widowed	Never married
African American	37	15	4	44
Asian/Pacific Islander	62	5	4	28
Latino/Latina	44	10	3	43
Non-Hispanic White	53	13	6	29
Santa Clara County	53	9	5	33

SOURCE: U.S. Census Bureau, *American Community Survey: 1-Year Estimates* (Washington, DC: U.S. Government Printing Office, 2012).

NOTE: Some percentages may not equal 100 percent due to rounding. Marital status is reported for residents ages fifteen and older.

Table 12 Individuals living in poverty by race and ethnicity, Santa Clara County, 2000–2012 (%)

Race and ethnicity	2000	2010	2012
African American	10	14	10
Asian/Pacific Islander	7	7	9
Latino/Latina	13	16	19
Non-Hispanic White	4	6	6
Santa Clara County	8	9	11

SOURCE: U.S. Census Bureau, *American Community Survey: 1-Year Estimates* (Washington, DC: U.S. Government Printing Office, 2012).

NOTE: Poverty is defined as living at or below 100 percent of the Federal Poverty Level.

Table 13   Individuals living in poverty in California and
the United States, 2012 (%)

	California	United States
African American	26	27
Overall	17	16

SOURCE: U.S. Census Bureau, *American Community Survey: 1-Year Estimates* (Washington, DC: U.S. Government Printing Office, 2012).

NOTE: Poverty is defined as living at or below 100 percent of the Federal Poverty Level. "African American" includes both Hispanic and non-Hispanic Black Americans.

Table 14   Unemployed residents by race and ethnicity, Santa Clara County, 2000–2012 (%)

Race and ethnicity	2000	2005	2006	2007	2008	2009	2010	2011	2012
African American	6	—	9	10	10	14	16	15	18
Asian/Pacific Islander	3	7	5	5	5	9	10	8	8
Latino/Latina	6	9	8	6	6	12	15	13	12
Non-Hispanic White	3	6	5	5	6	10	9	9	7
Santa Clara County	4	7	6	5	6	10	11	10	9

SOURCE: Santa Clara County Public Health Department, *2008–12 Death Database*, accessed August 11, 2013, https://chhs.data.ca.gov/; State of California Department of Finance, *State and County Population Projection, 2010–60* (Sacramento, CA: State of California Department of Finance, 2013).

Table 15   Felony arrests for violent offenses among adults ages eighteen
and older by race and ethnicity, Santa Clara County, 2012

Race and ethnicity	Number	Rate per 100,000
African American	411	1,099
Latino/Latina	1,563	454
Non-Hispanic White	842	162
Santa Clara County	3,246	233

SOURCE: State of California Department of Justice, *Crime Statistics and Demographics* (Sacramento, CA: Criminal Justice Statistics Center, 2012).

NOTE: Data not available for Asian/Pacific Islander.

Table 16 Felony arrests for violent offenses among juveniles ages
zero to seventeen, by race and ethnicity, Santa Clara
County, 2012

Race and ethnicity	Number	Rate per 100,000
African American	21	225
Latino/Latina	138	86
Non-Hispanic White	41	40
Santa Clara County	213	49

SOURCE: State of California Department of Justice, *Crime Statistics and Demographics* (Sacramento, CA: Criminal Justice Statistics Center, 2012).

NOTE: Data not available for Asian/Pacific Islander.

Table 17 School suspensions and expulsions by race, Santa Clara County, 2012–2013

Race and ethnicity	Total suspensions	Violence and drug-related suspensions (%)	Total expulsions	Violence and drug-related expulsions (%)
African American	1,066	62	14	100
Asian	1,318	70	17	88
Latino/Latina	9,587	60	180	92
Non-Hispanic White	2,057	66	15	87
Santa Clara County	14,589	62	231	92

SOURCE: California Department of Education, "Demographics and Statistics: Education in the State of California," *DataQuest, 2012–2013,* accessed June 12, 2017, http://data1.cde.ca.gov/dataquest/.

Table 18   Cancer deaths, Santa Clara County, 2012

	African American	Asian/Pacific Islander	Latino/ Latina	Non-Hispanic White	Santa Clara County
All sites					
Men	272	169	200	243	216
Women	236	120	133	193	163
Total	248	141	161	213	185
Breast					
Women	35	15	18	32	25
Colon and rectal					
Men	36	17	20	19	19
Women	31	11	13	17	15
Total	32	14	16	18	17
Lung					
Men	52	42	33	54	47
Women	58	22	13	43	33
Total	56	31	21	48	39
Prostate					
Men	47	11	17	27	22

SOURCE: Santa Clara County Public Health Department, *2008–12 Death Database*, accessed August 11, 2013, https://chhs.data.ca.gov/; State of California Department of Finance, *State and County Population Projection, 2010–60* (Sacramento, CA: State of California Department of Finance, 2013).

Table 19   Adults reported experiencing racism and discrimination, Santa Clara County, 2013 (%)

Race and ethnicity	Think about their race at least once a month	Emotional symptoms in the past thirty days*	Physical symptoms in the past thirty days**
African American	59	13	7
Asian/Pacific Islander	53	6	3
Latino/Latina	65	10	7
Non-Hispanic White	34	5	3
Santa Clara County	48	7	4

SOURCE: Santa Clara County Public Health Department, *Behavioral Risk Factor Survey* (San Jose, CA: Santa Clara County Public Health Department, 2013).

* Indicator is defined as adults who felt emotionally upset, for instance, angry, sad or frustrated, as a result of how they were treated based on their race or ethnicity.

** Indicator is defined as adults who experienced any physical symptoms, for instance, a headache, an upset stomach, a pounding heart, or tensing of their muscles as a result of how they were treated based on their race or ethnicity.

Since the postwar and civil rights eras, higher education and gainful employment have been put forth as poverty panaceas, ensuring the livelihood and well-being that upward mobility affords. San Jose, as the tables demonstrate, offers a more complicated story. Here, in the South Bay, aka Silicon Valley, resides an exceptionally upwardly mobile Black population whose outcomes mirror their poor and undereducated Black counterparts across the United States. Money and education can do many things. Protecting and insulating Black people from the harms and injuries of racism and glass ceilings is not one of them (see table 19).

To delve into these dynamics further, we turn our attention to the 2013 civil lawsuit *Alma Burrell v. County of Santa Clara*. The case centered on three Black woman employees of Santa Clara County's Health Department, who claimed that they had been purposefully locked out of key promotions while also being given more responsibilities at stagnant wages. As we will see, Black people's dreams have turned into dust not only in the freeways of Los Angeles of the West South but also in the Out South of Silicon Valley, the global technology capital.

INTERSECTIONALITY ON TRIAL

As Mary Sanders was being laid to rest on one coast, a young Alma Burrell was coming of age on the other. A child of the Out South, Burrell had been raised under the sun and palm trees of the South Bay. Burrell spent her teenage years excelling at Sequoia High School in Redwood City. After graduating in 1976, she went on to earn a bachelor's degree of science in health and a master's in public health from San José State University.[10]

Through her formative education, she developed a keen interest in health, especially for Black populations. While completing her master's thesis, she "worked for a nonprofit, the American Lung Association, for about a year." Burrell then left and "went to work for Santa Clara County Public Health Department (PHD) in 1998," where she had been "hired as a health education specialist . . . working in the tobacco control program." A standout at work, she was quickly "recruited to work in the Black Infant Health Program." Though a lateral transfer, Burrell was excited to coordinate the "state-sponsored program that works with African-American women" who are "pregnant or parenting small children." The program was a response to the alarming "high infant mortality rate among African-Americans" in California.[11]

Her expertise and work were soon again noticed and rewarded. A year later Burrell was promoted from coordinator to manager of the Black Infant Health Program. This she would do with great effectiveness for all of 2001. Soon after she was promoted again. This promotion, to "Program Manager II," came with "additional duties to manage the Maternal Child and Adolescent Health Program, along with the Black Infant Health Program."[12] Burrell and her team of sixteen worked with obstetricians, gynecologists, and other doctors to get women in the county linked to care and, when possible, matched to a primary-care physician.

Despite her record of achievement and her acceleration through the ranks of the PHD, by 2004 things came to a sudden and screeching halt. Without notice or conversation, Burrell was demoted. On August 16, 2004, she received an unceremonious notice that as of September 12, 2004, she had two options: "1. Take a voluntary demotion to the new class, without loss of current salary; or, 2. Be laid off in accordance with the appropriate layoff provisions." Committed to her work on behalf of Black women and children, Burrell settled for the first option, a voluntary demotion. Though the letter noted her salary of approximately $93,000 ($112,000 in 2017 dollars) would not change, after accepting the demotion she found there was indeed an impact on her wages. Unlike her colleagues, Burrell in her demotion was not "able to experience the cost of living adjustments" others across the department received.[13]

After expressing her disappointment and confusion to her manager, Dolores Alvarado, a middle-aged Latina, Burrell was assured time and again that her work was top-notch and that budget cuts were to blame. She was told that there would be more opportunities for promotion on the horizon and that she should keep upcoming job announcements on her radar. Alvarado also mentioned that those being placed in senior positions in the health programs were responsible for larger staffs and navigating positions with more complexity and a "larger span of control." "Not true," Burrell rebuffed Alvarado. Burrell went on to note that there were senior individuals who did not meet this criteria, and yet despite this fact, "people [she] was comparable with had been promoted to the senior health care program manager position."[14] Where most were managing a staff of five or six, Burrell, even with a demotion, still oversaw and managed a staff of sixteen, more than double the average.

For the next six years Burrell worked up the chain of command and responsibility to seek the appropriate readjustments. While her title, income, and status were reduced, her duties only increased over those years. She even, at times, served in senior positions, covering the responsibilities and tasks of colleagues on leave or vacation. Openings for senior positions had either flown under the radar, such as announcements missing from Burrell's inbox, or required her to leave the work with and for Black women and children that had been a central focus of her education and career.

After witnessing the rise of many of her peers, even those junior to her, to the senior ranks of the department and exhausting all available options through Human Resources, Burrell decided enough was enough, and in 2011 filed a civil suit against Santa Clara County. Facing mounting health issues, going on a missionary pilgrimage to Nigeria, and seeing two Black women colleagues—Vickye Hayter and Margaret Headd—experience the same glass ceiling compelled Burrell to take her claims to federal court. Each woman, Burrell, Hayter, and Headd, had previously filed claims with the Equal Employment Opportunity Commission, the federal entity responsible for adjudicating workplace discrimination claims. Joined by her Black women colleagues, a mix of courage, anxiety, and sadness filled Burrell as she instructed her lawyers to file the claim.

Filed September 13, 2011, the lawsuit contended "that Defendant County Of Santa Clara through Santa Clara County Public Health Department and managing agents of Defendants retaliated against them for engaging in protected activity and speech, and treated them differently based on their gender, female, race, African American, medical disability for Ms. Headd, and pregnancy for Ms. Hayter." The plaintiffs also charged that they had "suffered and continue to suffer substantial losses in earnings, significant loss of reputation and professional injury, loss of promotional opportunities and other employment benefits, lost wages, attorney's fees, medical expenses, loss of future earnings and benefits, cost of suit, embarrassment and anguish, all to their damage in an amount according to proof." Indeed, they charged, Santa Clara County had failed "to take reasonable action to prevent discrimination and retaliation which was a substantial factor in causing plaintiff's harm."[15]

In a nutshell Burrell and her co-claimants charged the county with racial, gender, and ability-based hiring bias, naming these factors as the mechanisms through which Black women had been systematically shut out of the senior positions across county offices like the PHD. Though the county had many highly educated and qualified county employees, across San Jose and other cities, relatively few, if any, were Black Americans. "Filing a lawsuit was my last option," Burrell shared. "I never thought I would end up here. It hasn't mattered how hard I've worked; I still keep hitting the glass ceiling. It makes me so sad that my managers go to these lengths to prevent me from promoting. Since starting my job, I have worked hard and with passion, always been professional in my demeanor. . . . I have never done anything to deserve this type of treatment."[16]

The case, then, reflects not just a claim about discrimination. Rather, it is also a window into the insight of Burrell and others that racial segregation and discrimination, like that associated with the traditional South, were active features of their professional life elsewhere on the chocolate maps. The intersection of race and gender created a separate Black professional and personal world within the county writ large.

There would be nearly two years of depositions and a jury selection before the case was finally heard. That time would not be easy for any of the plaintiffs, especially Burrell. Usually an upbeat and warm person, she had grown tired and was often on edge. Usually able to mask her anguish, as she had for the past decade on the job, in the interim between the filing and the hearing, Burrell lost her grandchild and her ability to rest her mind and body. By the time spring 2013 had approached, Burrell had been working through a variety of prescriptions for depression, insomnia, and acid reflux, among other ailments.

In the first week of May 2013, Burrell would finally get her day in court. During the days of testimony, the plaintiffs each laid out their case. Hayter, a registered nurse and former staff member of the PHD under Burrell's supervision, told of an experience with emotional and professional trauma. During her tenure Hayter had "been denied promotion more than five times, while others with less education and experience ha[d] been promoted." One denial involved a stipulation that she needed to have been in a previous position for at least three years, even though "there ha[d] been non–African American public health nurses who ha[d] been promoted" into the senior nursing ranks before they had worked for three years. Adding insult to injury, Hayter's denial letter also warned that further pursuit of a reallocation of rank could bring termination: "If you pursue this realloca-tion request and your position is successfully reallocated . . . you shall be laid off in accordance with Merit System Rule A25–103(f), which states, 'Should a permanent incumbent of a position that has been reallocated upward not qualify for that new class, the employee shall be laid off.'"[17]

Despite the denial, time and again Hayter found herself completing tasks and responsibilities of the senior nurse class into which she had been consistently denied promotion. Over the next three years she would again apply for reclassification and would again be denied. By 2008 it had become a customary practice and procedure that nurses working in the Black Infant Health Program were excluded from applying to senior posi-tions in the Regional Nursing Services, on the notion that the program was a stand-alone effort requiring differing and less applicable sets of skills than those required in the regional network.

On April 29, 2010, Hayter had a meeting with leading administrators, officials from the Service Employees International Union, and a Labor Relations representative. The meeting proved to be a disheartening fiasco for Hayter. A PHD senior official "stated in that meeting that the African American population in Santa Clara County was so small, only about 2.9%, and could not really be considered a community, especially since Hayter was only serving a percentage of them." With a raised voice, the same PHD offi-cial "degraded Hayter's work level to that of clerical," denying her aptitude and training as a registered nurse altogether. Following the meeting Burrell, Hayter's direct supervisor, was told by the same official that denying her was a favor, especially as she was allowed to keep her current job. Pitching Hayter to Burrell as ungrateful, the supervisor, a middle-aged White woman, intimated to Burrell, "You see what these people do to you."[18]

As the union contract-enforcement specialist pursued the case, an eventual offer of $5,000 ($5,270 in 2017 dollars) compensation for Hayter's work above scale was offered. While mulling over the offer, Hayter was also informed that she was lucky she hadn't been promoted, as "she would have been the first to be laid off during budget cuts because she would have had the least amount of seniority." Pregnant at the time, the compounding denials and the miniscule and dismissive settlement weighed heavily on Hayter. She would soon find herself in preterm labor, forced to delivery her baby months premature.

Where Hayter's pregnancy proved a substantial risk and obstacle to her professional livelihood, Margaret Headd, the other Black PHD employee, found her medical leave had put her at an irreparable professional disadvantage. Employed at the county since January 2003, Headd had enjoyed working in Santa Clara's Valley Health Medical Hospital "for many years." Beginning in 2008, however, "the hostile and adverse treatment she ha[d] experienced ha[d] mounted to an escalating and intolerable level."[19]

After going on approved medical leave for cancer, in December 2008 Headd "received a lay-off notice, by phone, from her manager," which was "followed by a letter from the Santa Clara Human Resource Department." After inquiring with the appropriate parties, Headd found out she had been placed in a lower-ranked and lower-paid position. While in between cancer treatments, Headd waited, as her calls remained unreturned, only later to discover that she had lost her original position and been shuffled into a "county rehire list" and "laid off from her full-time professional position" as a health educator. Upon return from medical leave, Headd was then laid off from the lesser position and made to look through the county's database of job vacancies, hoping to solidify gainful employment to help curb her mounting health bills. Despite her best efforts and some successful interviewing savvy, Headd was passed over for a younger non-Black competitor.[20]

In response, Headd sought to transfer into an area more aligned with her seniority and skill but was halted by a sudden "transfer ban" policy ban at the PHD. From 2008 to 2011 Headd pursued all of the appropriate listings and openings, often making it through several rounds of interviews. Each time, however, she would be passed on. In a final blow Headd had enthusiastically pursued a position as a senior analyst at PHD in the health-care program. Shortly after being notified that her name had been submitted for the position, Headd received a call that the "job was deleted." Her dreams of upward mobility and maintaining were dashed.[21]

Burrell, who had overlapped with Hayter and Headd directly and indirectly, had watched the trials of her Black women colleagues with much anguish. She too had been denied time and again. Often Burrell's attempts at reclassification and promotion were followed by e-mails mentioning, "that now was not a good time to promote her because of budget short-falls."[22] After a series of administrative changes, Burrell had taken her concerns to the top of the ladder. The new director assured her that she was due a promotion and of course deserved it. During what Burrell felt had been a productive meeting, she offered ideas about ways of meeting patient and county demands in more cost-effective ways. Her work, always rated outstanding, seemed to be of great promise to the new director.

At the same time, Hayter's claim was moving forward, and Burrell's supervisor warned that if those claims moved forward, "she would place the blame on Burrell."[23] Refusing to shrink under the threat, Burrell stuck to her guns, only later to find that many of key duties were consequently removed, thus destroying any real chance of promotion for Burrell while also diminishing her stature at the PHD. The toll this had taken proved tremendous and, between a surgery for severe acid reflux and a religious mission to Nigeria, Burrell returned to a hostile and dismissive work environment.

Testimonies from economists and mental health professionals revealed that Burrell was losing anywhere between $6,000 to $10,000 ($8,100 to $12,500 in 2017 dollars) in annual salary relative to her counterparts and had developed a mixture of anxiety and mood disorder, depression, and overall fatigue. Though the higher-ups had "essentially implemented a significant portion of her proposal with no compensation to her," Burrell continued in her diminished job throughout and after the trial.[24]

In the end, though, smaller sums were considered appropriate. As the jury was unable to reach unanimity on the ultimate claims of racial dis-crimination and gender bias, the broader case was limited in success. During a late summer conversation over food from San Jose's West Indian cuisine mainstay Backa Yard, Burrell confessed, "I just had to push it as far as I could. And many of the jurors believed us." Her two-strand twists caught a subtle breeze as she looked up, staring straight ahead as if she could see the past and future at once: "The issue was the jury wanted and needed something that was explicitly racist. Like e-mails or messages or conversations where derogatory and explicit racial language like 'nigger' were used. Because this is the Bay Area, they just couldn't see that this was like the South too. Another South. No Confederate flags but some sinister racism bubbling just beneath the surface. I lived it. We, Black people in San Jose, live it everyday."[25]

THE SOUTH COAST TO COAST

Coasts are not merely a matter of oceans. They are also about experience. As this chapter demonstrates, there is a connection across the multiple Souths of the chocolate maps. Illuminated by the vocal genius of Dionne Warwick, the tenacity of Mary Sanders, and the courage of Alma Burrell, across the United States Black women have stood in the face of White supremacy, health issues, and political lines to forge a more free society for themselves and their communities.

The connections are not always explicit. They can be found in the liberation work and struggles over professional mobility and against police brutality. Black people everywhere at different times, and sometimes at the same time, using their power to gather, to move, to protest, to sing, to party, to campaign, and to file lawsuits make the chocolate map and its understanding of the multiplicity of the South visible.

Though the protagonists centered were often outnumbered and women and experienced a variety of health concerns, each realized the potential of chocolate city citizenship by pushing the envelope. They each sought to provide equal footing between Black and White Americans in the social, economic, and political lives of the places they called home. Health, wealth, education, politics, and courage are key ingredients of the brand of interactive power and agency emanating from chocolate cities across the map.

13 Leaving on a Jet Plane

I bathed in the Euphrates when dawns were young.
I built my hut near the Congo and it lulled me to sleep.
I looked upon the Nile and raised the pyramids above it.
I heard the singing of the Mississippi when Abe Lincoln
went down to New Orleans, and I've seen its muddy
bosom turn all golden in the sunset.
I've known rivers. . . . My soul has grown deep like the rivers.

Langston Hughes, "The Negro Speaks of Rivers"
(for W. E. B. Du Bois), 1920

Kids. Check. Wife. Check. Bags. Check. Passport. Check. He and his family arrived at the Cape Town International Airport in South Africa in enough time to make the flight to Ethiopia. In twelve hours or so, he expected he would be before an audience hungry to see his talents on full display. Standing before customs agents, he supplied his documents.

Despite meticulous preparation, he and his family never made it to Ethiopia that day. Carrying a World Passport, issued by the World Service Authority in Washington, DC, Dante Terrell Smith, aka hip-hop artist Mos Def, aka Yasiin Bey, and his family were denied the ability to leave South Africa. "My country is called Earth," he declared, refusing to furnish and use his U.S. passport.[1]

At odds with U.S. policies and practices, such as police brutality and force-feeding prisoners on hunger strike at the Guantanamo Bay prison, a month earlier Bey sought travel documents that aligned with his opposition to his birthplace, the United States, and to his self-identity as a world citizen. To obtain such documents Bey looked to the World Government, a nonprofit organization founded by Garry Davis, a White American, in 1951.

Davis, who proclaimed to be the first world citizen, founded the organization guided by a philosophy that all people were entitled to the protections of the Universal Declaration of Human Rights adopted by the United Nations in 1948. No matter the national boundaries or country of citizenship, the World Government wanted to ensure that those seeking shelter, food, safety, and asylum had the documents needed to travel across nation-state borders. To this end, Davis developed the World Passport to assist in guaranteeing one of those essential human rights, the right to move freely.[2]

Currently held by millions of people and recognized by more than 120 countries, Bey's World Passport arrived just in time for his January 2016 trip to Ethiopia for a long-awaited performance of his music, most notably from his critically acclaimed 1999 album, *Black on Both Sides.* Not only did the South African authorities refuse Bey's right to fly that day, but they also charged him and his family with illegally staying beyond the time allotted on their initial visas, threatening immediate deportation of his wife and children.

On his album *Yasiin Gaye: The Departure,* deejay and critical mashup artist Amerigo Gazaway, foreshadowing Bey's travel troubles, puts Marvin Gaye in conversation with his postsoul counterpart to contextualize Black people's travel from inner cities around the world and back. Gazaway uses Bey's verses, interview snippets from Marvin Gaye where he discusses his lifelong desire to be an aviator, and the music from Gaye's "Inner City Blues" to weave together a haunting story of leaving, movement, loss, and return. Chronicling his travels as an artist and those of Black people more generally, Bey roll calls a range of chocolate city spaces—"Cali and the Cackalacks [Carolinas]," New York City, Virginia, "the Cadillacs" (southern cities), Chicago, Jamaica, "foreign lands and Japan"—annotating chocolate maps of the United States and beyond. Bey and Gaye are placed in a call-and-response: "I'm leaving," says Bey, and Gaye's voice responds from a sample from *Here My Dear*—"You can leave, but it's going to cost you." What has it cost Black people to leave, for love or freedom or truth, from one place to another on the chocolate maps?

Bey's choice to forgo using his U.S. passport and travel and work as a "world citizen" has certainly cost him. It has led to an ongoing legal battle that jeopardizes his, and his family's, freedom, all of whom remain in South Africa under a fragile arrangement with the government. Unable to leave South Africa, Bey went on to cancel tour date after tour date, losing a significant source of income. Subsequently, Bey announced his retirement from music altogether.

Expatriation and global citizenship are not new among Black Americans—nor is the legal and political trauma that emerges as a consequence. Bey's immigration and migration in search of freedom and peace are a reflection of a broader history and future wherein Black people's quest for power and home space endures. It also highlights how the law has been used against Black Americans who attempt to use the power of their U.S. citizenship to awaken a broader global consciousness on matters of peace and freedom.

We need only look to the life of scholar-activist W. E. B. Du Bois for telling lessons on how the global South, peace, and geopolitics collide. In 1951, just as Davis's World Government was opening its doors and disseminating World Passports, Du Bois and his organization, the Peace Information Center (PIC), were also in Washington, DC. Du Bois and the PIC were, however, facing an indictment in a federal courthouse.

An accomplished and world-renowned professor, at age eighty-three Du Bois would watch his reputation and livelihood be severely damaged by the U.S. government. His crime: having been a proponent of a global peace initiative during the Cold War. By Du Bois's eighty-seventh birthday, he was a permanent resident of Ghana, for even Canada was not free enough to escape the prosecution and persecution he faced.

This chapter tells the story of Du Bois's indictment, illustrating the persistence of the South within and beyond conventional borders. The South is everywhere Black people find themselves. We turn to the circumstances surrounding Du Bois's indictment to tell the intertwined story of Black people and the many Souths they find themselves in on both sides of the Atlantic in the twentieth and twenty-first centuries.

THE UNITED STATES OF AMERICA V. WILLIAM EDWARD BURGHARDT DU BOIS

A child of Up South, Du Bois "was born by a golden river and in the shadow of two great hills, five years after the Emancipation Proclamation, which began the freeing of American Negro slaves." On February 23, 1868, a little brown baby boy took his first breath in his hometown of Great Barrington, "which lay between these mountains in Berkshire County, Western Massachusetts, [and] had a broad Main Street, lined with maples and elms, with white picket fences before the homes."[3]

A gifted student and skilled researcher, Du Bois would go on to become the first Black person to receive a PhD from Harvard University. Over his seventy-plus-year career Du Bois passed through many campuses across the United States, including appointments at Wilberforce University, the University of Pennsylvania, Fisk University, and (Clark) Atlanta University. The author of more than thirty books of fiction and nonfiction, he was a poet at heart.

His exceptional wordsmithing abilities and leadership carried him beyond the ivory tower. As one of the founders of the National Association for the Advancement of Colored People (NAACP), Du Bois was the founding editor of its monthly magazine, which he dubbed *The Crisis*, from 1910 to 1934. Over the next four decades he also built a significant international reputation, traveling across Europe, Asia, and Africa, speaking and teaching on issues of race, labor, class, and politics. As time progressed, he came to be supportive of socialist principles to combat the savage poverty and racism due to American capitalism and its devastating effects abroad.

As his socialist leanings became more pronounced, Du Bois's mission and that of the NAACP were increasingly out of synch. While Du Bois wanted to focus internationally and on the dark side of capitalism, the organization was more invested in domestic racial matters. The aggressive World War II–era suspicion and fear of socialism and communism, especially as embodied by the Soviet Union, intensified these differences. Eventually dismissed from his post as director of Special Research at the NAACP, Du Bois was offered and accepted a nominal, unpaid position, vice chair of the Council on African Affairs, which afforded him work space and secretarial services, but little else. Undeterred, he continued with his pursuit of international issues, turning toward Africa "by sort of a logical deduction," and began to focus exclusively on the continent (343).

Du Bois's mission now was to uncover and solidify Black knowledge and legacies over time and across space and place. He had grown "tired of finding in newspapers, textbooks and history, fulsome lauding of white folk, and either no mention of dark peoples, or mention in disparaging and apologetic phrase." To help find himself and help his people and the world, he made up his mind "that it must be true that Africa had a history and destiny, and that one of [his] jobs was to disinter this unknown past, and help make certain a splendid future." After more than fifty years of focus on race in the United States, Du Bois's shift to the homeland manifested into *The World and Africa* in 1947.

The book, an assessment of the histories and contribution of the continent, illustrated that Black people's fates everywhere were deeply influenced and linked with that of Africa. The Holocaust, the global costs of defeating Hitler's Germany, and the pillaging of Africa loomed large in Du Bois's consciousness as interconnected reasons for a broad push toward peace everywhere. As the world began to heal and the tenuous Cold War peace of bomb shelters and nuclear drills took hold, Du Bois joined the peace effort in earnest.

As a social scientist, skilled internationalist, and researcher, Du Bois's expertise and potential to contribute meaningfully to the cause of peace were initially in high demand. In February 1949 he was personally invited to a Cultural and Scientific Conference for World Peace focused on American-Soviet relations by former U.S. assistant attorney general O. John Rogge. "We are eager to make this Conference a real contribution to the solution of the problems that now block the way to peace," Rogge had written. The conference of more than five hundred American and Soviet "leaders of modern culture and thought" convened the next month at the Waldorf Astoria Hotel in New York City. These kinds of efforts to use intellectual and cultural diplomacy to calm the escalating and feverish pitch of the Cold War were thwarted by a "concerted and directed movement against peace and in favor of war against the Soviet Union" operating to quash peace discourse. So strong was the pushback that "distinguished cultural figures such as Picasso were refused visas to attend" in an attempt to compromise and dampen the conference proceedings (349).

After the conference government war forces made death threats against those who continued to support the peace mission. Despite mounting aggression, Du Bois forged ahead, joining with peace activists such as John Clark, Uta Hagen, Linus Pauling, and Rogge in calling for an

"American Continental Congress for World Peace" (351). In August 1949 Du Bois was the only American to accept the invitation to the all-Soviet peace conference in Moscow, courageously telling the thousand people in attendance: "I represent millions of citizens of the United States who are just as opposed to war as you are. . . . There are millions of other Americans who agree with these leaders of the peace movement. I bring you their greetings" (355). Peace conferences in Mexico, Cuba, and Australia had also proven successful, though underreported in mainstream American press. From these meetings emerged the Stockholm Peace Appeal—a broad resolution advocating global peace and diplomacy in the face of war and an active plan of international nuclear disarmament.

Though the peace mission had been a complicated success, 1950 was also a time of personal loss. In February his "wife of 53 years," Nina, was "buried in the New England hills beside her first-born boy." In April 1950, with upcoming peace conferences scheduled in Paris and Prague and international momentum for peace growing, Du Bois and peace activists began to circulate the Stockholm Peace Appeal widely, disseminating "peacegrams" from the newly formed Peace Information Center in New York City across the globe. Soon after its founding, however, the U.S. government attacked the PIC. In the July 13, 1950, issue of the *New York Times*, Secretary of State Dean Acheson charged, "I am sure that the American people will not be fooled by the so-called 'world peace appeal' or 'Stockholm resolution' now being circulated in this country for signatures. It should be recognized for what it is—a propaganda trick in the spurious 'peace offensive' of the Soviet Union" (358).[4]

Du Bois's response questioned the accusations and reminded the public of broad American sentiment in favor of peace, especially in a time where the anxiety of nuclear war loomed large. "We have got to live in the world with Russia and China," Du Bois reminded them. He asked, "If we worked together with the Soviet Union against the menace of Hitler, can we not work with them again at a time when only faith can save us from utter atomic disaster?" "Today," Du Bois continued, "in this country it is become standard reaction to call anything 'communist' and therefore subversive and unpatriotic. . . . We feel strongly that this tactic has already gone too far. . . . We are a group of Americans, who upon reading this Peace Appeal, regard it as [a] true, fair statement of what we ourselves and many countless other American[s] believed. . . . We [are] united in this organization for the one and only purpose of informing the American people on the issues of peace" (358–59). The U.S. government took Du Bois's emphatic response as palpably defiant, and so began the roots of the legal drama and trauma that came thereafter.

After traveling through Europe on his peace mission, Du Bois headed back to the United States, receiving two bits of news over the wire as he started home that August. The first was from John Abt of the American Labor Party, inquiring if he would run on the party's ticket for U.S. senator from New York in the November election. After some deliberation, Du Bois wired back: "Accept." The other piece of news was more distressing. The PIC's executive secretary Abbott Simon had wired to let Du Bois know of an urgent and hostile Department of Justice inquiry: the DOJ had "demanded our registration as 'agents of a foreign principal'" (356). Du Bois resolved to fight the charges of being a foreign agent upon his return home.

The fall of 1950 found Du Bois was running a twin campaign, then: one for political office, the other to prove his innocence against the DOJ. The Senate campaign was doomed from the outset, as once the charges against Du Bois were publicized by local and national media outlets, lines of social, economic, and political support dried up. Many Black and White elites, schools, institutions, and communities questioned Du Bois's integrity and believed that since the charges were coming from the DOJ, they must have veracity and seriousness.

To win over skeptics, Du Bois traveled through New York, making the case that he was being smeared by erroneous charges but nonetheless beginning the yearlong task of closing the PIC. "Wake up, America. Your liberties are being stolen before your very eyes," a disgruntled Du Bois professed defiantly in September 1950 at a meeting held at Town Hall in New York City in support of his candidacy (375). The meeting was an opportunity to demonstrate his innocence against the implied charges of espionage and terrorism in the DOJ's characterization of him "as a foreign agent." In the end, Du Bois delivered "ten speeches and made seven broadcasts," and though he lost the election, 205,729 "men and women of courage" cast votes in favor of his candidacy (362). With more than five million votes cast in the election, the vote for Du Bois was largely a symbolic and political gesture of bravery and support for which "[Du Bois] was happy" (363).

In January 1951, when the charges hadn't materialized into anything more than warning letters, Du Bois was encouraged to celebrate his eighty-third birthday in a big way. So when the birthday milestone was on the horizon, Du Bois's friends and associates convinced him that February 23, 1951, would be a wonderful time to celebrate his life and feel the love of friends and family. Upon the announcement, preparations for a "birthday dinner at the Essex House, New York City, were being made . . . and the list of sponsors was imposing and growing daily. . . . About 300 people had made reservations and paid over $2,000" [$18,200 in 2017 dollars]" (367).

And then in the first week of February 1951, Du Bois's plans were shattered. He wrote, "on February 8 I was indicted for an alleged crime; on February 14, I was married secretly to Shirley, lest if I were found guilty she might have no right to visit me in jail; February 16 I was arraigned in Washington and on February 19, four days before the dinner, the hotel at which the dinner was planned canceled our contract by telegram."

The indictment, received on February 8, 1951, stated in part:

> Continuously during the period from April 3, 1950 to and including the date of the return of this indictment, Peace Information Center has been an agent of foreign principal, because within the United States . . . at the request of its said foreign principal, [PIC] published and disseminated in the United States the "Stockholm Peace Appeal" and related information pertaining primarily to prohibition of the use of atomic weapons as instruments of war. . . . The defendants deny that peace is a foreign idea; but they gladly admit that they gathered and publicized ideas and news of action for peace from everywhere they could obtain them. They assert that any attempt to curtail such free interchange of thought, opinion, and knowledge of fact the world over is clearly an interference with the constitutional rights of American citizens. (365)

Just weeks before his birthday, he was notified that pressure from the DOJ on vendors had caused him to lose his birthday venue. In fact, almost all New York City establishments declined to host the birthday bash. Despite his reputation of having high integrity and moral character, Du Bois was "indicted as a criminal by a grand jury in Washington, on February 9, 1951, for not registering as an agent of a foreign power in the peace movement" (347). "I can stand a good deal," a weary Du Bois shared, "and [had] done so during my life; but this experience was rather more than I felt like bearing, especially as the blows continued to fall. I had meantime been finger-printed, handcuffed, bailed and remanded for trial" (368).

On a shoestring budget and limited timetable, a group of his closest friends and admirers were able to host the birthday bash in Harlem at Small's Paradise. E. Franklin Frazier, sociologist and past president of the American Sociological Association, served as the party's MC; "Paul Robeson spoke courageously and feelingly"; and Belford Lawson, "head of the Alpha Phi Alpha fraternity, volunteered and made a fighting speech" (368). Du Bois was grateful but deeply wounded.

The indictment and accompanying media onslaught were devastating. It seemed each day a newspaper, Black or White, was adding more fuel to fire the flames. On February 11, 1951, New York's *Herald Tribune* published an editorial excoriating Du Bois and the PIC: "The Du Bois outfit was set up to promote a tricky appeal of Soviet origin, poisonous in its surface innocence, which made it appear that a signature against the use of atomic weapons would forthwith insure peace." Just shy of accusing treason, the article suggested the PIC was "in short, an attempt to disarm America and yet ignore every form of Communist aggression" (369).

Despite support from some Black press and journalists, notably Percival Prattis of the *Pittsburgh Courier* and Carl Murphy of Baltimore's *Afro-American*, others lambasted Du Bois. The legendary Black newspaper, the *Chicago Defender*, for example, characterized Du Bois as an embarrassment, hammering a nail into the coffin of his public life and reputation. In an editorial, the paper corroborated the charges: "Dr. Du Bois has earned many honors and it is a supreme tragedy that he should have been exposed as subversive in the twilight of his years" (370).

Members of the Black intelligentsia believed Du Bois was guilty and spread that position through the Black grapevine, claiming insider knowledge of the evidence and proof against Du Bois held by the DOJ. They often affirmed that the case against him was open-and-shut, and soon even some of Du Bois's most ardent past supporters either stayed silent or provided tepid endorsement. For example, "without passing on the merits of the recent indictment of Dr. Du Bois," wrote and resolved the NAACP on March 12, 1951, "the board of directors of the NAACP expresses the opinion that this action against one of the great champions of civil rights lends color to the charge that efforts are being made to silence spokesmen for full equality of Negroes." Despite his twenty-eight years of distinguished service to the NAACP, the board did not provide the full-throated endorsement of innocence expected or needed, instead couching its defense in the context of other, qualitatively different kinds of silencing efforts against Black activists (372).

Nevertheless, Du Bois's new wife, Shirley Graham, committed her days to tirelessly advocating and seeking support on his behalf, especially from the international community. Though support domestically for Du Bois was middling, messages of support poured in from the West Indies, South America, Africa, Asia, Australia, and more than twenty European nations. Du Bois's global support eventually led to the formation of the International Committee in Defense of Dr. W. E. B. Du Bois and his Colleagues. Unlike the American mainstream press, international news media, like Shanghai's *China News* and Scotland's *Edinburgh Review,* covered the story in earnest, and Du Bois's plight was made known worldwide in multiple languages. The Caribbean was also especially supportive to Du Bois's cause. He received letters "from the professors of the University of Havana and outstanding Cubans like Dr. Fernando Ortiz, Latin America's most famous sociologist; Dr. Domingo Villamil, eminent Catholic jurist; and Juan Marinello, senator and poet" (373).

Du Bois was convinced that his indictment was a dangerous omen for democracy. "This case is a blow at civilization," Du Bois's defiant letter to the DOJ began. Highlighting two injuries to democratic society reflected in the case, Du Bois observed that the DOJ was attempting to thwart free speech "by thought control [and] by seeking to shut off the free flow of culture around the world and reducing all American culture to the level of Mississippi and Nevada" (374). As Du Bois's experience had shown, for Black people, American culture writ large was indistinguishable from places where it was thought to be under the most threat, like behind the door of the closed society of Mississippi. The indictment remained; court was scheduled for November 8, 1951.

"This brought forward the whole question of costs," a reflective Du Bois shared. "It had not occurred to us how costly justice in the United States is. It is not enough to be innocent in order to escape punishment. You must have money and a lot of it" (375). If the case were to make it to the Supreme Court, it could cost as much as $100,000 [$912,000 in 2017 dollars] to defend. "Personally," Du Bois humbly notes, "I had no funds for such a case. I was retired from work, with a pension too small for normal expenses of living. My wife's work and income were seriously curtailed by her complete immersion in the case. We had no rich friends. None of the defendants were able personally to finance the case" (378). Further, no money could be used from international bodies or individuals. But through an appeal to a diverse group of poor and middle-class Black and White Americans and trade unions and community organizations, Du Bois raised nearly $50,000 [$456,000 in 2017 dollars]. He would need and use all this money to the last penny in the lead-up to his November trial.

Du Bois arrived on time to surrender to authorities for the trial. He was again handcuffed and placed in a jail cell. Thick-skinned, Du Bois had during his life faced "many unpleasant experiences; the growl of a mob; the personal threat of murder; the scowling distaste of an audience." Nothing, not even the fiasco around his eighty-third birthday, had traumatized him as had "that day, November 8, 1951, when [he] took his seat in a Washington courtroom as an indicted criminal . . . accused of a felony and liable to be sentenced before leaving this court to five years of imprisonment, a fine of $10,000 [$91,200 in 2017 dollars] and loss of my civil and political rights as a citizen, representing five generations of Americans" (379).

The toll the ordeal had taken was apparent. Du Bois, known for his jovial nature and dapperness, now carried a deep sadness that had begun to etch lines into his usually smooth smiling brown face. His once-regal posture was broken, a sign of Du Bois's pessimism in the case's outcome despite his innocence. By the time he was brought in the courtroom, he looked tired, old, and worn.

Judge Matthew F. McGuire entered the federal courtroom as the audience and Du Bois and his codefendants rose. Assistant Attorney General Maddrix wasted little time addressing the judge and calling his first witness, O. John Rogge. Maddrix added that the "chief dependence of the prosecution was on O. John Rogge." This was a shock and immediately revealed to Du Bois that the claims were always false and fabricated, as Rogge was not only a friend and former U.S. assistant attorney general, but also the person who initiated Du Bois's involvement and organized the first peace congress in New York City just two years earlier. A shadow of his former self, where there was once a passionate peace crusader stood "a worn man, whose clothes hung loosely on him, and who in a courtroom where he had conducted many cases, had difficulty locating [Du Bois] in the defendant's chair" (381).

In his testimony Rogge admitted that he was a member of the PIC and attended the World Peace Congress and declared "its actual objective was not peace, but that it was an agency for the foreign policy of the Soviet Union" (381). This was hearsay at the least, and heresy at best. Du Bois began to sense the situation might shift in his favor for the first time.

Judge McGuire was not so pleased by this display by the prosecution: "Do you expect to show that the World Council for Peace was in fact an agent of another principal, namely the Soviet Union?" To which Maddrix responded, "We do not intend to show the Committee of the Congress of the World Defenders of Peace was an agent of the Soviet Union" (381). After being asked by the judge again about this Soviet connection and evidence thereof, Maddrix repeated that there would be no presentation of any evidence to support that claim by Rogge.

The trial went on for another five days, though the exchange between the judge and prosecutor following Rogge's testimony sealed the deal. Maddrix hoped that a long trial and its lead-up would allow him to draw on the court of public opinion to, if not legally convict Du Bois, publicly do so. Keen on the prosecution's political charade, Judge McGuire abruptly stopped Maddrix on day five and called an end to the proceedings. "The judge's function is exhausted," McGuire declared, meeting the eyes of those in the courtroom, "when he determines that the evidence does or does not permit the conclusion of guilt beyond a reasonable doubt within a fair operation of a reasonable mind. So, therefore, if the case should go to the jury, I would be permitting the jury to conjecture in a field of con-jecture. . . . So the case goes off, in my view, on a conception of law. . . . I think that the position of the defense is maintained and supported by the opinion mentioned, and that opinion is conclusive in my mind; and that is my ruling" (386).

The jury was then brought in and dismissed. Judge McGuire admon-ished Assistant Attorney General Maddrix and his office. Du Bois smiled for what felt like the first time in years. After hugging his friends and legal counsel, he and his wife departed Washington posthaste.

BACK TO AFRICA

> I'm leaving, on a jet plane
> I don't know if I'll be back again
> Kiss me and smile for me
> Tell me that you'll wait for me
> Hold me, like you know I'll never go
> Even though you know I will
> I'm a travellin' man
> Moving through places
> Space and time
> But, Inshallah, I'm coming back to you
>
> Yasiin Bey, "I'm Leavin'," 2013

On August 8, 1959, Du Bois's friends were gathered at a dock with wine and flowers, giving a farewell to Du Bois and Graham, who were headed abroad. Boarding the ship, Du Bois "felt like a released prisoner" (11).[5] Not only was the trial still a painfully close memory, but he had also been on a midcentury "No Fly" list since the trial.

A result of restrictive policies instituted by the secretary of state against all peace activists, the government had denied Du Bois a passport, claiming it was not "in the best interest of the United States" for him to travel abroad. A landmark Supreme Court case challenging the constitutionality of these restrictions, *Kent v. Dulles,* had ultimately cleared the path for Du Bois to once again travel abroad. Justice William O. Douglas's majority opinion is important in its affirmation of the right of citizens to move freely and without persecution, underscoring Du Bois's, Bey's, and Black people's demands for equal access to freedom of travel and movement:

> The right to travel is a part of the "liberty" of which the citizen cannot be deprived without due process of law under the Fifth Amendment. . . . Freedom to travel is, indeed, an important aspect of the citizen's "liberty." We need not decide the extent to which it can be curtailed. We are first concerned with the extent, if any, to which Congress has authorized its

curtailment. . . . We will not readily infer that Congress gave the Secretary of State unbridled discretion to grant or withhold it. . . . We would be faced with important constitutional questions were we to hold that Congress, by § 1185 and § 211a, had given the Secretary authority to withhold passports to citizens because of their beliefs or associations. Congress has made no such provision in explicit terms, and, absent one, the Secretary may not employ that standard to restrict the citizens' right of free movement.[6]

Within months of the decision, Du Bois had his passport and booked travel to Accra, Ghana, at the invitation of President Kwame Nkrumah. The once-optimistic scholar now held an embittered coldness toward the country he had called home. In the intervening years between the trial and what would be his fifteenth trip abroad, he had expanded his criticism of the hypocrisy of American democracy, penning the now-famous "Why I Won't Vote" essay in an October 1956 issue of the *Nation*, which is widely resuscitated and circulated during every current American presidential election.

Each day he stayed in the United States was a reminder of "the certainty that thousands of innocent victims are in jail today because they had neither the money, experience nor friends to help them." "God only knows how many who were as innocent as I and my colleagues are in hell," Du Bois recoiled, thinking about how these innocent incarcerated and disproportionately Black people, this "army of the wronged . . . daily stagger out of prison doors embittered, vengeful, hopeless, ruined. There is a desperate need of nationwide organizations to oppose this national racket of railroading to jails and chain gangs the poor, friendless and black" (390). His own trial had exposed him to the very underbelly of American democracy, leaving him relieved that his innocence prevailed but also with a negative forecast for the current and future state of affairs in the United States. And so when the opportunity and means to leave the United States came, Du Bois took it. He would never live in the United States again. While in Africa, he "faced [his] lower income and lived within it" (395).

Today, just beyond the shores of Labadi Beach, Ghana, sits Du Bois's final resting place. On a compound several miles from the Slave Castles, a bust of his face stands beside his final home, 22 First Circular Road, better known as the W. E. B. Du Bois Memorial Centre for Pan African Culture. The postwar pivot toward Africa, which led to Du Bois's fervent interest in ensuring international peace and equity for maligned peoples and nations, had started an intellectual and activist journey that shattered the scholar's faith in the American democratic project. There, in a chocolate city across the Black Atlantic, Du Bois spent his last days reflecting and imagining a freedom that had not come during the near century he was on earth.

The war had heightened the stakes for Black people moving about the chocolate maps in search of freedom and solidarity with other oppressed groups. Within the United States people moved back and forth across chocolate maps, escaping danger, searching for new opportunities, returning to care for loved ones, and looking to subvert the mounting urban policies that constricted their movement in tandem with the rise of the suburbs. For those making their way across the global chocolate map in search of peace, the U.S. government took direct, explicit, and often devastating action, often tying civil rights and other antiracist causes to charges of espionage and conspiracy on behalf of the Soviet Union. As the Du Bois trial demonstrates, not even a Harvard PhD provided cover if one was targeted by the government for challenging war and imperialism with calls for peace.

There is power in movement, and restricting the movements of Black people is a central feature of anti-Black racism globally. From the physical confines of slave ship–cargo holds to fugitive slave laws to "Whites-only" signs to ghettoization and gentrification, keeping Black people in a designated place is essential to White supremacy. Black people, chocolate city traveling folk, have nonetheless pushed and moved and resisted. Migration, immigration, and within–chocolate city movement have been essential reflections of Black power and Black people asserting their rights as humans and world citizens to be where they choose without racial restrictions, domestically and abroad.

14 Seeing like a Chocolate City

> The "black-world" will see the light and Busia from Ghana,
> Birago Diop from Senegal, Hampate Ba from the Sudan
> and Saint-Clair Drake from Chicago will not hesitate to
> assert the existence of common ties and a motive power
> that is identical.
>
> Frantz Fanon, *Wretched of the Earth*, 1963

Nestled between freeways and waterways separating the chocolate cities of Greensboro and Durham, North Carolina, lies a town made of Black residents and imagination. If you look for it, you may miss it. Google Maps will lead you just west of your intended destination, taking you instead to the town of High Point, made famous by hometown hero and American Idol Fantasia Barrino. During the summer, tables of chess and spades and bid wiz and the smell of barbeque fill the air just the same. Even still, its geography is obscured; its location unspecified by the state of North Carolina.

A city within and outside of a city, a county within and outside of a county, Mebane, North Carolina, is home to a predominantly Black community. Situated within Alamance County, for more than a hundred years Mebane has been home to a long-standing critical mass of Black residents whose needs have been greatly ignored by the state. Its boundaries are treated as invisible, and thus its blocks and residents do not administratively exist. Yet when Black scholars Danielle Purifoy and Torkwase Johnson arrived, it was clear to them they were in the midst of an obscured yet vibrant chocolate city.[1]

Purifoy and Johnson interviewed Black residents, "all of whom say they're from a city called Mebane," and concluded that "most of the evidence supports their claims." "Their local grocer, public library, and post office are in Mebane," as are their addresses. The Black community center is also in Mebane. Yet, according to state administrative boundaries and the existing White geography of North Carolina, the Black residents "don't live in Mebane."[2]

In a dangerously clever attempt to obscure this chocolate city, the "city's [official] boundaries stretch around their homes and even bisect their streets, but never in the over 100 years since emancipated Blacks settled on these lands has the City of Mebane incorporated them into its polity." The result: Black Mebaners "can neither vote in municipal elections or run for public office." Meanwhile, the city "controls their land for up to three miles outside the city limits." While the city refers to Mebane's chocolate city as an extraterritorial jurisdiction, longtime resident and community activist Omega Jones "calls it feudalism."[3]

After arriving to Mebane from Tougaloo, Mississippi, where he had been a communications professor, Jones and "his family moved back to West End," opening an independent insurance agency. Given his entrepreneurial know-how and educational success, "his community wanted him to do something" about the poor housing, abandonment, and lack of infrastructure in Black Mebane. Though the city governed the land, officials "refused to provide basic services to residents, whose septic tanks were failing and whose drinking water was contaminated," commonly rejecting "requests for public funds to support renovations." It is common for residents to travel to the local stores near Mebane Oaks Road to gather cases of water for drinking and other needs.[4]

Despite being made administratively and geographically invisible by the city and state, Black Mebaners formed the West End Revitalization Association. Through this organization Black residents have been able to achieve a historic moratorium on highway construction for the past two decades. Despite death threats and opposition, Black activism defeated a 1993 plan between the city and North Carolina's Department of Transportation to build State Route 119, which would bypass through Mebane's West End.

The residents were not expendable. Black Mebane was a chocolate city created by the post-Emancipation dreams of their ancestors, and they, as the song goes, "shall not be moved." Though White North Carolinians and

Mebaners refused to see their chocolate city, Black residents in the West End saw it clearly. And though the map hasn't changed to reflect this, a road destroying it has also never been built.[5]

Black Mebane is exemplary of a kind of chocolate city obfuscation that happens often to small Black towns. Black density is not merely an outcome. Black density is a practice. It is repeated over and again, in places and nations of varying sizes. This model is not unique to the United States. Rather, it is a practice across the African diaspora, manifesting chocolate city formations in some of the most unlikely places. Thousands of miles away from Mebane, Guangzhou (China's third-largest city), for example, is home to Asia's biggest African community. There in the central districts of Yuexiu and Baiyun, Africans drawn to shipping and trading have created an entire community that has persisted for decades. A Black village nestled in Asia's largest nation; locals call it "chocolate city." Though not known to many beyond the borders of China, Guangzhou is a persisting all-black place with distinct African roots.

Despite this persistence of the chocolate city, there is erasure that draws on economic and social boundaries to render places once demographically dominated by Black people to become what sociologist Derek Hyra calls "latte" and "cappuccino" cities.[6] Washington, DC, Harlem, and Atlanta are all places where the complex processes of deindustrialization, gentrification, and neighborhood revitalization combine to push older Black residents out even as they sometimes attract younger, but fewer, Black residents.

Homeowners in historically Black communities across these chocolate cities collaborate when they can to ensure that properties that turn over because of foreclosure or sale continue to be occupied by Black residents. The return of White residents to the city center, particularly in places like Detroit, Atlanta, and Memphis, means the power of numbers that in part ensured the rise of so many chocolate cities is in jeopardy. Still, as Black people have consistently shown, the village endures through space and time, in political reality and artistic practice. And where there is a village, there is always a chocolate city.

Like political scientist Albert O. Hirschman's classic typology of "voice" and "exit" forecasts, *Chocolate Cities* shows how citizens resist and express their dismay with the status quo by leaving places and telling on racism. Black people do not simply take racism and inequality laying down, nor are they oblivious to the continuity between the traditional South and all the other Souths that make up the United States. Under the umbrella of a critical Black geography of chocolate maps and cities, Black people have used place, space, and migration to respond and anticipate enduring racist structural conditions. As Hirschman reminds us, "withdrawal or exit" is a direct "way of expressing one's unfavorable views" of the state and its institutions.[7] That is, leaving a place is an essential act of political agency.

In this way, critical Black geographies and maps, in the words of political scientist James C. Scott, make the state and power structures "legible." "Formal schemes of order are untenable without some elements of the practical knowledge that they tend to dismiss," Scott observes.[8] The state and its tools of oppression—like misogyny, glass ceilings, heteronormativity, and racism—can be hard to see.

A racially conscious mapping of the United States, then, allows what sociologist Patricia Hill Collins calls the "matrix of domination," to be demystified, as it is often covered by our attention on individuals and people who serve as agents of the state.[9] In turn, a chocolate city framework represents the practical knowledge of which Scott notes, and chocolate maps and cities provide a fruitful way to locate, understand, and analyze the interface between Black people and state-sanctioned actions, procedures, and policies. Together both form the essential contours of the "indigenous perspective" that sociologist Aldon Morris finds, for example, as a motivating synergy for the successes of the modern civil rights movement.[10]

Black maps and migrants also reveal the erasures created by White maps and explorers. The Black Lewises and Clarks presented throughout help to restore the histories, herstories, place making, and politics lost due to the dominant White logic and map. Chocolate cities help to recover voices and adventures of those whose lives serve as this book's protagonists. Zora Neale Hurston, Arthur Lee Robinson, Ida B. Wells, Duanna Johnson, Mary Sanders, Alma Burrell, and W. E. B. Du Bois are not simply Black people reacting to White supremacy; each possessed a savvy yet undervalued world and geographic view that informed their actions and attitudes especially against and within the multiple Souths. These Black explorers are also a compass, helping to navigate the multiple dangers of an ever-present and pervasive South, always with an eye North—North as freedom and equality, not necessarily always in Canada or outside of the boundaries of the United States.

BELOW THE CANADIAN CURTAIN

After a few layups and dunks, the lead had changed over the series several times. Led by point guard Kyle Lowry and shooting guard DeMar DeRozan, in 2016 the Toronto Raptors defeated the Miami Heat in seven games, earning their first appearance in the NBA Eastern Conference finals in franchise history. Lowry, a Philly native, and DeRozan, a Compton native, had successfully had found the promised land of the conference finals in the arena for Canada's only NBA team. The celebration began and the camera panned across the jubilee of pop star and Toronto-native Drake and the Raptors' bench. As the telecast broke for commercials, a poster of Lowry appeared. He is in uniform, facing forward with his eyes staring back at the viewer. Etched across is a statement near and dear to the Raptors' fans: "We The North."

Even in that highly commercial and hypermedia NBA context, certain Black truths find their way into our homes and vantage point. Though not free of its own racism and discriminatory tendencies, even in the new millennium Canada is the North—just above the persisting patterns and variations of the American South traditionally believed to be found in places like Miami or Cleveland (whose team the Raptors would play and lose to in the conference final).

Whether we follow or ease on down the chocolate brick road, we are likely to see and find peoples and places whose geographies differ from dominant maps of the United States, or from the world for that matter. Black people have clicked their collective heels and moved, stayed, and taken over places near and far. It can be hard to see this using our traditional tools, like the current U.S. map. "Dominant geographic patterns," Black feminist geographer Katherine McKittrick powerfully notes, "can often undermine complex interhuman geographies by normalizing spatial hierarchies and enacting strict rules and regulations."[11]

Our classrooms, where maps are critical tools for students to learn how to locate places and measure the American experience, often contain this back-and-forth: "Chicago is North, and Birmingham is South. California is West and New England is East." The traditional map, then, diminishes and makes invisible the persisting Black communities that have not died but endured. Recovering this race-conscious perspective is key, as "the locations of black history, selfhood, imagination, and resistance are . . . attached to the production of space through their marginality" and "bring into focuses responses to geographic domination."[12] That is, we cannot see or measure phenomena accurately if the tools themselves were not designed with the oppressed and marginalized in mind.[13]

Here the travelers and slave trade within what sociologist Paul Gilroy frames the "Black Atlantic" takes on added meaning.[14] Whether Black people are passing through the Caribbean Sea and the Atlantic Ocean as expatriates or slaves, the travel itself happens to and through their eyes, just as the Whites moving and pushing them are conjuring their own sense of the world. This geographic consciousness is racial and gendered, guided by sexual orientation, love, fame, opportunity, and oppression. The result is a doubly doubled double consciousness.

ONE NATION UNDER A GROOVE

> I can hear my neighbor crying, "I can't breathe"
> Now I'm in the struggle; I can't leave
> Calling out the violence of the racist police
> We ain't gonna stop, till people are free
>
> Queen Ifrica, "I Can't Breathe," 2015

Three years after Parliament Funkadelic sonically and politically remapped America as a network of chocolate cities, in 1978 the group offered up an anthem for these places the world over. As the song "One Nation under a Groove" took over airwaves, the complementary anthem to 1975's "Chocolate City" began its global circulation. The cover artwork, a funk-inflected flag, was a symbol to capture the enduring linked fate and experiences of Black people everywhere. A black box with the song's title in white letters sits at the left corner where the white stars of the American flag would be, with multicolored stripes of orange, black, white, red, green, and a hint of pink fluttering as though the Funkadelic-imagined flag hung at full staff in chocolate cities near and far. Though an up-tempo mashup of whistles, heavy bass, and unison singing, alongside percussive cowbells, the emphasis on *nationhood* and *groove* are not simply about a dance of Black celebration but also of Black resistance. As George Clinton's tenor narrates the song, the groove under which this nation moves is a response to the constraints on and possibilities of Blackness.

On the one hand, we have the constraints or "constrictions" on Black people; thus, the idea of nationhood includes places where Black people are gathered under intense structural supervision and disadvantage. Consider, for example, what scholar Beth Richie dubs "the prison nation," the vast network of incarceration, policing, and punishment that looms large in the lives of people of color across the world, but especially in the United States.[15] Due to a combination of racism, hyperpolicing, and backlash against the progress of the civil rights movement during the 1950s and 1960s, many sites of incarceration, jails and prisons, are consequently predominantly Black—chocolate cities of constriction.

But here's our chance to dance our way out of our constrictions. If we cut the groove the other way, a variety of possibilities emerge beyond just thinking about chocolate cities as silos of socially and spatially isolated Blackness. We can also imagine chocolate cities as examples of what Jürgen Habermas calls *lifeworlds*—social, economic, and political places of dynamism and great consequence.[16]

"South of the North, yet north of the South, lies the City of a Hundred Hills, peering out from the shadows of the past into the promise of the future," sociologist and activist W. E. B. Du Bois observed in his 1903 classic *The Souls of Black Folk*.[17] After years of traveling throughout the United States and abroad, Du Bois had discovered the Black wonderland of Atlanta, long before it became known as "the city too busy to hate," the "Black Mecca," and "the Los Angeles of the South." His geographic designation of it as a city between two imagined regions—North and South—spoke to Atlanta's status as a southern city during a time when the South was overwhelmingly rural, and the rural spaces of the Midwest and Northeast existed in the shadow of those regions' big industrial cities. A longtime professor at (Clark) Atlanta University, Du Bois would go on to look to Atlanta and its residents as a major social scientific laboratory, situating Atlanta as a representative site for understanding Black urban experiences in the twentieth and twenty-first centuries.

Like other southern cities, the racialized spatial organization of Atlanta was different in some ways from the ghettoization that occurred in metropolises of the Northeast and Midwest, and later the West. Black people made up a higher percentage of the population in southern cities, which meant they occupied larger swaths of urban America than their counterparts in other regions. Further, Black elite actors in these cities brokered bargains with White elites that maintained the regional norm of segregation, while making space for Black prosperity and resources within the separate city.

There, Black folks developed a diverse life, economy, and culture that existed beyond the White gaze, between the Depression and the major gains of the civil rights era. Yet, even within these separate Black and White spaces, competing interests and pursuits among Black residents impacted patterns of migration and urban development. Until the pressures of federal and local housing and economic policies ghettoized the "truly disadvantaged" in smaller and smaller portions of the inner city, Atlanta was a prime example of the separate city, which enabled its status as the Black Mecca and chocolate city.[18]

Chocolate cities are geographic concentrations of Black life—neighborhoods, small towns, and entire cities—where Black people make and revise place through tight-knit community networks of place makers, cultural production, and the consolidation of political and economic power. Throughout the book we use the metaphors and grooves of the village city, the soul city, and the power city to chronicle sets of characteristics present in a variety of Black places. These metaphors help us move away from the deficit frame that has dominated much of the scholarship about Black urban life.

Our approach centers Black people as strategic place makers and city makers who used the assets of size, concentration, and cultural production to create cultural and economic power that influenced the spatial organization of the American landscape. To borrow from the Parliament Funkadelic insight and song, chocolate cities like Atlanta spent most of the twentieth century "gaining on ya!," progressing so much that by the time the White House turned Black, Atlanta had surpassed Chicago in its total Black population. Atlanta's Black political establishment, coupled with its Black elite, served for a time to ensure some, though not all, Black interests were represented in the municipal establishment.

But we also know that the gains Black populations made in Atlanta and other chocolate cities were uneven and staggered at best. As soon as Black wealth, business acumen, cultural production, and population concentration rendered the city's status as Black Mecca a self-fulfilling prophecy, the marginalization of poorer Black people accelerated. From the destruction of housing projects to the displacement of Black populations in the wake of the 1996 Olympic Games, the spatial rearrangement of Atlanta had devastating effects on its most vulnerable populations. The city's transportation infrastructure reflects an inherent political desire to maintain the spatial mismatch between jobs and the people who need them.

Further, the rising costs of living in the city, coupled with the Whitening of the city, shift and deflate the meaning of the Black Mecca in the twenty-first century. When Parliament Funkadelic penned the triumphant "Chocolate City," saying that Black people were "working on Atlanta" becoming a chocolate city, they could not have foreseen the city's demographics shifting from "chocolate" to "latte," or that Black political power would not function in service of all Black people. In Atlanta, though, this reality is now glaringly evident.

For outsiders, particularly those who continue to flock to the city in search of prosperity, the idea of Atlanta as a Black Mecca will likely never recede, spurred on as it is by media representations of the city. Du Bois warned us about Atlanta and materialism, saying that the city "must not lead the South to dream of material prosperity as the touchstone of all success; already the fatal might of this idea is beginning to spread; it is replacing the finer type of Southerner with vulgar money-getters."[19]

Despite the tone of respectability in Du Bois's observation, in their animation of a particular kind of Black wealth and Black pain in a chocolate city, the long-running Bravo reality series *The Real Housewives of Atlanta* and VH-1's *Love and Hip-Hop Atlanta* both reflect, in part, his fears about the Black Mecca. Beyond respectability, though, the image of Black prosperity— from Tyler Perry's expanding Atlanta empire to the enduring success of the city's music industry and its hip-hop ambassadors—obscures the reality of rising inequality, even for middle-class African Americans, in the city. FX's award-winning series *Atlanta*, spearheaded by Donald Glover, is a much-needed examination of the other side of Black Atlanta that has always been there and for which the city's shiny Black veneer is an unreachable illusion.

If by "Black Mecca" we mean a place to which Black people will always feel the cultural and sometimes political security of large populations and concentrations of other Black people, then Atlanta will endure as a Black Mecca. But if a Black Mecca is made possible by most Black people being able to be economically and socially successful in a place, then Atlanta, like other places across the ever-evolving chocolate maps, is in danger of losing that designation. Add to this the custom of ignoring Black geographic sensibilities, and the true jeopardy of disappearing that plagues many chocolate cities, then and now, is visible.

The elders often say, "Seeing is believing." Mebane, North Carolina, and the many other peoples and places covered in this book reflect this wisdom. Black people in Philadelphia, Clarksdale, Newark, San Jose, Memphis, Detroit, Harlem, Kansas City, Tulsa, Oakland, Seattle, Los Angeles, Dallas, New Orleans, Boston, and Atlanta see a chocolate city. Even more, in cities like Miami, for instance, Black residents see many chocolate cities (e.g., Overtown, Little Haiti, Black Grove), born from the network of enclaves built by varying populations from the African diaspora. The belief in this vision motivates their actions and attitudes. This insight, then, is crucial and consequential to the ebbs and flows of race and migration.

Unfortunately, our traditional geographies do not take their attitudes and maps seriously. Extending this point, geographer Parag Khanna finds that "the biggest mistake our traditional maps make is to portray countries as unified wholes, equating political geography with sovereign authority—as if to have a country means you actually control it." Offering the idea of *connectivity*, Khanna argues that linkages and continuities are a more useful tool for mapping the world of human experience: "The arc of history is long, but it bends toward connectivity."[20]

No experience more animates this insight than that of Black people. Usually political maps are colored in red and blue to indicate the tension between conservative (Republican) and liberal (Democrat) voting states. But it is also common political wisdom and fact that Black Americans by and large lean and vote for the Democratic Party, meaning their map, the chocolate map, is politically a virtual bluesy landscape.

Even more than recoloring the political map blue, as scholar Nikhil Singh reminds us, "Black is a country," and southern racial practices pervade the United States culturally, politically, and economically. "For just as

Jim Crow subjugated blacks in the South," Singh observes, "the black migrants who came North between World War I and the 1960s had their chances curtailed and confined by racial separation violently enforced by riot, pogrom, hate strikes, restrictive covenants, urban renewal, red-lining and block-busting." Indeed, "few social groups in human history have experienced the depth and duration of residential segregation that has been imposed upon black internal migrants within the United States."[21]

More than any other recent technological innovation, social media has made connections across the chocolate maps more evident and clear, as the digital Black spaces created on Twitter, Facebook, Instagram, and other social-media platforms complement "real life" Black life. They are a virtual Black space, a collection of virtual chocolate cities that enable a range of possibilities both within and beyond Black communities.

While a significant amount of Black joy is shared across these platforms, it is also a space where Black people collectively live the trauma of being under siege. The murders of Black people by police play on an endless loop, sending numbing shock waves across the chocolate maps. That these murders go unpunished is a source of angst, stress, and grief for many Black people. News of such murders has always traveled across chocolate maps. Now it travels in seconds, and sometimes we experience it live. The list of names of Black people—cis and trans; children and adults; women, men, and nonbinary; homosexual, bisexual, and heterosexual; able-bodied and disabled—murdered by state actors or racist extrajudicial citizens grows every single day.

But Black people are responding now as they always have, by organizing in and through chocolate city spaces. The Movement for Black Lives, a collective of organizations working against anti-Black racism, has called for reinvestment in chocolate cities and a redirection of monies for policing and incarceration to rebuild Black communities devastated by disinvestment. In Chicago, Atlanta, New York, Chattanooga, Memphis, Seattle, Houston, Omaha, and stops in between, Black people are using the power of place making to organize for liberation. From suburban spaces to the central city, from tight-knit neighborhood blocks to small towns, Black resistance continues.

There are still signs of weariness, in part spurred on by the incessant spectacle of Black death, the profiting from Black death, and the unanswered questions and unpunished murderers. In July 2016 #Blaxit trended on Twitter, as Black people expressed their frustrations with ongoing violence and neglect and took an accounting of their contributions to the nation. The hashtag, sober, practical, and wishful, pointed to Black Americans' desire to explore parts of the chocolate maps throughout the world. However, Black immigrants and Black people from places outside of the United States reminded folks that anti-Blackness is global, and that diasporic chocolate cities are made of the same resistance struggles as the ones in the United States. Perhaps the South is the world for Black people as long as anti-Blackness permeates global politics.

There is hope for the future, in and through our imagination, through culture work, and through the work of organizing to create a present that can hold and fulfill those future hopes. Whether we ride on Parliament Funkadelic's Mothership, sail on Gilroy's Black Atlantic, stay awhile in Singh's Black country, escape to the Oz of *The Wiz*, or cast the first stone at the Stonewall Inn like Marsha P. Johnson, Blackness and the South have a way of overlapping in the American experiment.

Once space is involved, places are made. The chocolate city is born and reborn. Blackness contracts and expands as the ebbs and flows or as people come and go, like moving dots and stars on the map.

Black is a galaxy. Black is a planet. Black is an ocean. Black is a map. Black is a country. Black is a city. Black is a village. And its future is wrapped in chocolate.

Acknowledgments

Chocolate Cities was ten years in the making. It required endurance, patience, support, and the kindness of many. We had a vision and goal to express a Black perspective that we'd encountered both in each of our earlier works and during the research process for this book. This Black sensibility was in the music; the mouths of young children in rural and urban America; the wise eyes of big mama's, granddads, memaws, church elders, mothers, fathers, and cousins; and the work of the ancestors.

If not for the access people provided us, from librarians to interviewees to archivists to activists, these pages would be empty. Soon into the writing of the book, we were convinced that what would fill its pages would be the collective good sense of Black folk here, there, and nearly everywhere. From the moment we met and discussed this project, Naomi Schneider, our editor extraordinaire, has been an avid supporter who encouraged us to keep being as brave and bold as we could and tell the stories as they had been told to us. Many thanks to Renee Donovan, as well, for her tireless work alongside Naomi.

A wonderfully brilliant group of students, our chocolate city soldiers, gave their time and creativity to this endeavor: Justin Dior Combs, Chelsea Dormevil, Christian Green, Kyle Nelson, Lina Stepick, and Bahar Razavi. We are grateful to each of them for their belief in the project and their rigorous research and assistance with data collection. There have been so many people of all walks of life whose support and encouragement and push back has been essential to the development of this book. For their feedback, encouragement, and support along this journey, we are grateful to Luke Harris, Roger Rouse, Joe Trotter, Nicole Gonzalez Van Cleve, Mikaela Rabinowitz, Courtney Patterson, Rashida Shaw McMahon, Jean Beaman, David Johns, Paul Butler, Priscilla Ocen, Justine Bateman, Jamey Hatley, Dante Taylor, Tauheed Rahim, Malakiah "Max" Hunter, Alexandra Murphy, GerShun Avilez, Gary Fine, Sandra L. Barnes, Christopher Wildeman, Paul Lichterman, Juan Battle, Howard Winant, Alford Young, Joe Feagin, Alma Burrell, Walter Wilson, Andrew Pappachristos, Melvin Rogers, Waverly Duck, Elijah Anderson, Daniel Widener, Mary Pattillo, Davarian Baldwin, Aldon Morris, Charles Camic, Takima Darnell, and Elizabeth Alexander.

We are grateful to a brilliant combination of UCLA colleagues, especially Walter Allen, Kimberlé Crenshaw, Darnell Hunt, Devon Carbado, Gaye Theresa Johnson, Roger Waldinger, Jemima Pierre, Abigail Saguy, Cheryl Harris, Richard Yarborough, Peter Hudson, Cesar Ayala, Rogers Brubaker, Robin D.G. Kelley, C.K. Lee, Zsuzsa Berend, Juliet Williams, Edward Walker, Chris Tilly, and Karida Brown, for their generative feedback and support. We deeply appreciate the supportive intellectual and scholarly environments of UCLA's Sociology and African American Studies Departments, the Ralph J. Bunche Center for African American Studies and Research, University of Michigan's Department of Sociology and Detroit School Series, Yale University's African American Studies and Sociology Departments, Rhodes College, the American Sociological Association's Minority Fellowship Program, the National Science Foundation, Northwestern University's Sociology and African American Studies Departments, the Scholar Strategy Network, and the Association of Black Sociologists. We are eternally grateful to Frank Robinson for allowing us to use his powerful and magical art to adorn the cover. We are also grateful to Hal Leonard LLC and Bridgeport Records for help securing permissions for the music used throughout the book.

We have also had the great fortune to be able to rely on a mighty network of family whose lives and love inspired us to work harder and write better at every turn. Without our families this endeavor would have been not only impossible but also incomplete. They have heard our ideas, shared stories, and encouraged us to pursue this idea to its fullest extent. We hope that in these pages they see how much each of them helped in the creation and realization of this book. Love is the message.

Appendix

1950 CENSUS

We were unable to find county-level data for race for 1950, and the census tract-level data for race was also inconsistent. Searching by place individually in multiple sources resulted in incomplete and inconsistent data as well, so we omitted 1950 for most places, opting to wait until we could figure out a consistent methodology.

A NOTE ON VARIABLES: RACE

On the 1900 census, race is measured only for populations between the ages of five and twenty. We calculated the percentage of Black population from the total population, ages five to twenty, divided by the Black population, ages five to twenty.

Both 2000 and 2010 censuses also include the "two or more races" category, but for this report, we included only the populations of "Black" or "Black or African American alone." The 1980 census includes a section called "Race by Spanish Origin Status," but we worked under the assumption that this population would be included in the "Black" population in the "Race" section.

UNIT OF ANALYSIS: CITIES AND REGIONS

All regions were previously defined.

To account for changing cities and metropolitan areas, we decided to calculate populations based on Metropolitan Statistical Areas (MSAs) defined according to the U.S. Department of Commerce's Bureau of Economic Analysis (www.bea .gov/regional/docs/msalist.cfm). We used the current counties to determine MSA-level population statistics throughout the designated period (1900–2010) and marked any variation in parentheses.

Down South

Atlanta–Sandy Springs–Roswell, GA
  Barrow (post-1920)
  Bartow
  Butts
  Campbell (pre-1930)
  Carroll
  Cherokee
  Clayton
  Cobb
  Coweta
  Dawson
  DeKalb
  Douglas
  Fayette
  Forsyth
  Fulton
  Gwinnett
  Haralson
  Heard
  Henry
  Jasper
  Lamar (post-1930)
  Meriwether
  Milton (pre-1930)
  Morgan
  Newton
  Paulding
  Pickens
  Pike
  Rockdale
  Spalding
  Walton
Charleston–North Charleston, SC
  Berkeley
  Charleston
  Dorchester
Charlotte–Concord–Gastonia, NC
  Cabarrus, NC
  Chester, SC
  Gaston, NC
  Iredell, NC
  Lancaster, SC
  Lincoln, NC
  Mecklenburg, NC
  Rowan, NC
  Union, NC
  York, SC
Columbia, SC
  Calhoun (post-1910)
  Fairfield
  Kershaw
  Lexington
  Orangeburg (incl. 1900, due to
    Calhoun County; not part of the
    Columbia MSA)
  Richland
  Saluda
Durham–Chapel Hill, NC
  Chatham
  Durham

Orange
Person
Greensboro–High Point, NC
  Guilford
  Randolph
  Rockingham
Hilton Head Island–Bluffton–
  Beaufort, SC
  Beaufort
  Jasper (post-1920)
Jacksonville, FL
  Baker
  Clay
  Duval
  Nassau
  Saint John's
Miami–Fort Lauderdale–West Palm
  Beach, FL
  Broward (post-1920)
  Miami-Dade
  Palm Beach (post-1910)
Raleigh, NC
  Franklin
  Johnston
  Wake
Richmond, VA
  Amelia
  Caroline
  Charles City
  Chesterfield
  Dinwiddie, Colonial Heights (post-
    1960), Petersburg
  Goochland
  Hanover
  Henrico
  King William
  New Kent
  Powhatan
  Prince George, Hopewell
    (post-1920)
  Richmond (independent)

  Sussex
Savannah, GA
  Bryan
  Chatham
  Effingham
Virginia Beach–Norfolk–Newport
  News, VA
  Chesapeake, VA (Independent;
    post-1970)
  Currituck, NC
  Gates, NC
  Gloucester, VA
  Hampton, VA (independent; aka
    Elizabeth City County,
    pre-1950)
  Isle of Wight, VA
  James City, Williamsburg, VA
    (post-1930)
  Mathews, VA
  Newport News, VA (independent;
    aka Warwick County and
    Newport News City County,
    pre-1950)
  Norfolk, VA (independent; South
    Norfolk City County, pre-
    1960)
  Portsmouth, VA (independent)
  Suffolk, VA (independent;
    aka Nansemond County,
    pre-1970 and Suffolk
    [independent])
  Virginia Beach, VA (independent;
    aka Princess Anne County,
    pre-1960)
  York, Poquoson, VA (post-1980)
Winston-Salem, NC
  Davidson
  Davie
  Forsyth
  Stokes
  Yadkin

Up South

Baltimore–Columbia–Towson, MD
  Anne Arundel
  Baltimore
  Baltimore (Independent)
  Carroll
  Harford
  Howard
  Queen Anne's
Boston–Cambridge–Newton, MA
  Essex
  Middlesex
  Norfolk
  Plymouth
  Rockingham, NH
  Stafford, NH
  Suffolk
New York, NY–Newark, NJ–Jersey
  City, NJ
  Bergen, NJ
  Bronx, NY
  Dutchess, NY
  Essex, NJ
  Hudson, NJ
  Hunterdon, NJ
  Kings, NY
  Middlesex, NJ
  Monmouth, NJ
  Morris, NJ
  Nassau, NY
  New York, NY
  Ocean, NJ
  Orange, NY
  Passaic, NJ
  Pike, PA
  Putnam, NY
  Queens, NY
  Richmond, NY
  Rockland, NY
  Somerset, NJ
  Suffolk, NY
  Sussex, NJ

  Union, NJ
  Westchester, NY
Philadelphia PA–Camden, NJ–
  Wilmington, DE
  Bucks, PA
  Burlington, NJ
  Camden, NJ
  Cecil, MD
  Chester, PA
  Delaware, PA
  Gloucester, NJ
  Montgomery, PA
  New Castle, DE
  Philadelphia, PA
  Salem, NJ
Washington, DC–Arlington, VA–
  Alexandria, VA
  Alexandria, VA (independent;
    post-1910)
  Arlington, VA
  Calvert, MD
  Charles, MD
  Clarke, VA
  Culpeper, CA
  District of Columbia
  Fairfax, Fairfax City, VA (post-1970)
  Falls Church, VA (post-1960)
  Fauquier, VA
  Frederick, MD
  Jefferson, WV
  Loudoun, VA
  Montgomery, MD
  Prince George's, MD
  Prince William, Manassas (post-
    1980), Manassas Park, VA
    (post-1980)
  Rappahannock, VA
  Spotsylvania, Fredericksburg, VA
    (post-1960)
  Stafford, VA
  Warren, VA

Mid South

Chicago, IL–Naperville, IL–Elgin, IL
(includes Gary, IN)
  Cook, IL
  DeKalb, IL
  DuPage, IL
  Grundy, IL
  Jasper, IN
  Kane, IL
  Kendall, IL
  Kenosha, WI
  Lake, IL
  Lake, IN
  McHenry, IL
  Newton, IN
  Porter, IN
  Will, IL
Cincinnati, OH
  Boone, KY
  Bracken, KY
  Brown, OH
  Butler, OH
  Campbell, KY
  Clermont, OH
  Dearborn, IN
  Gallatin, KY
  Grant, KY
  Hamilton, OH
  Kenton, KY
  Ohio, IN
  Pendleton, KY
  Union, IN
  Warren, OH
Cleveland–Elyria, OH
  Cuyahoga
  Geauga
  Lake
  Lorain
  Medina
Detroit–Warren–Dearborn, MI
  Lapeer
  Livingston
  Macomb

  Oakland
  Saint Clair
  Wayne
Flint, MI
  Genesee
Indianapolis–Carmel–Anderson, IN
  Boone
  Brown
  Hamilton
  Hancock
  Hendricks
  Johnson
  Madison
  Marion
  Morgan
  Putnam
  Shelby
Kansas City, MO/KS
  Bates, MO
  Caldwell, MO
  Cass, MO
  Clay, MO
  Clinton, MO
  Jackson, MO
  Johnson, KS
  Lafayette, MO
  Leavenworth, KS
  Linn, KS
  Miami, KS
  Platte, MO
  Ray, MO
  Wyandotte, KS
Lincoln, MO
  Lancaster
  Seward
Louisville, KY/Jefferson County, IN
  Bullitt, KY
  Clark, IN
  Floyd, IN
  Harrison, IN
  Henry, KY
  Jefferson, KY

Oldham, KY
Scott, IN
Shelby, KY
Spencer, KY
Trimble, KY
Washington, IN
Milwaukee–Waukesha–West
  Allis, WI
  Milwaukee
  Ozaukee
  Washington
  Waukesha
Minneapolis–Saint Paul–Bloomington,
  MN
  Anoka, MN
  Carver, MN
  Chisago, MN
  Dakota, MN
  Hennepin, MN
  Isanti, MN
  Le Sueur, MN
  Millie Lacs, MN
  Pierce, WI
  Ramsey, MN
  Saint Croix, WI
  Scott, MN
  Sherburne, MN
  Sibley, MN
  Washington, MN
  Wright, MN
Omaha, NE–Council Bluffs, IA

Cass, NE
Douglas, NE
Harrison, IA
Mills, IA
Pottawattamie, IA
Sarpy, NE
Saunders, NE
Washington, NE
Pittsburgh, PA
  Allegheny, PA
  Armstrong, PA
  Beaver, PA
  Bond, IL
  Butler, IL
  Calhoun, IL
  Clinton, IL
  Fayette, MO
  Franklin, MO
  Jefferson, MO
  Jersey, IL
  Lincoln, MO
  Macoupin, IL
  Madison, IL
  Monroe, IL
  Saint Charles, MO
  Saint Clair, IL
  Saint Louis, MO
  Saint Louis, MO (independent)
  Warren, MO
  Washington, MO
  Westmoreland, MO

Out South

Anchorage, AK
  Anchorage Municipality
  Kenai Peninsula Borough
  Matanuska–Susitna Borough
Bend, OR
  Deschutes (in 1900 and 1910
    Deschutes is Crook County)
  Jackson

Lane
Marion
Polk
Denver–Aurora–Lakewood, CO
  Adams
  Arapahoe
  Broomfield City and County
  Clear Creek

Denver City and County
Douglas
Elbert
Gilpin
Jefferson
Park
Fargo–Moorhead, ND
Cass
Clay
Honolulu, HI
Honolulu
Portland–Vancouver–Hillsboro, OR
Clackamas
Clark
Columbia
Multnomah
Skamania
Washington
Yamhill

Sacramento–Roseville–Arden–Arcade,
CA
Douglas
El Dorado
Nevada
Placer
Sacramento
Sutter
Yolo
Yuba
San Francisco–Oakland–Hayward, CA
Alameda
Contra Costa
Marin
San Mateo
Seattle–Tacoma–Bellevue, WA
King
Pierce
Snohomish

Deep South

Baton Rouge (Parishes), LA
Ascension
East Baton Rouge
East Feliciana
Iberville
Livingston
Pointe Coupee
Saint Helena
West Baton Rouge
West Feliciana
Birmingham–Hoover MSA, AL
Bibb
Blount
Chilton
Jefferson
Saint Clair
Shelby
Walker
Chattanooga MSA, TN
Bradley

Catoosa
Dade
Hamilton
Jackson
Marion
Sequatchie
Walker
Florida Panhandle (not MSA)
Bay
Calhoun
Escambia
Gulf
Holmes
Jackson
Okaloosa
Santa Rosa
Walton
Washington
Jackson, MS
Copiah

Hinds
Madison
Rankin
Simpson
Knoxville, TN
Anderson
Blount
Campbell
Cocke
Grainger
Hamblen
Jefferson
Knox
Loudon
Morgan
Roane
Sevier
Union
Little Rock–North Little Rock–
Conway, AR
Faulkner
Grant
Lonoke
Perry
Pulaski
Saline
Memphis MSA, TN
Benton, MS
Crittenden, AR
Desoto, MS
Fayette, MS
Marshall, MS
Saint Francis, MS
Shelby, MS
Tate, MS
Tipton, MS

Tunica, MS
Mobile, AL
Baldwin
Mobile
Montgomery, AL
Autauga
Elmore
Lowndes
Nashville–Davidson–Murfreesboro–
Franklin, TN
Cannon
Cheatham
Davidson
Dickson
Hickman
Macon
Maury
Robertson
Rutherford
Smith
Sumner
Trousdale
Williamson
Wilson
New Orleans–Metairie (Parishes),
LA
Jefferson
Orleans
Plaquemines
Saint Bernard
Saint Charles
Saint John the Baptist
Saint Tammany
Selma, AL (doesn't have its own MSA,
in Dallas County)
Dallas

West South

Albuquerque, NM
Bernalillo
Sandoval

Torrance
Valencia
Austin–Round Rock, TX

Bastrop
Caldwell
Hays
Travis
Williamson
Dallas–Fort Worth–Arlington, TX
   Collin
   Dallas
   Delta
   Denton
   Ellis
   Hood
   Hunt
   Johnson
   Kaufman
   Parker
   Rockwall
   Somervell
   Tarrant
   Wise
Houston–The Woodlands–Sugarland, TX
   Austin
   Brazoria
   Chambers
   Fort Bend
   Galveston
   Harris
   Liberty
   Montgomery

Las Vegas–Henderson, NV
   Clark
   Lincoln
   Mohave
   Nye
Los Angeles–Long Beach–Anaheim, CA
   Los Angeles
   Orange
Oklahoma City, OK
   Canadian
   Cleveland
   Grady
   Lincoln
   Logan
   McClain
   Oklahoma
Phoenix–Mesa–Glendale, AZ
   Maricopa
   Pinal
San Antonio–New Braunfels, TX
   Atascosa
   Bandera
   Bexar
   Comal
   Guadalupe
   Kendall
   Medina
   Wilson
San Diego–Carlsbad, CA
   San Diego

Notes

1. As is discussed more fully in later chapters, our conception of "chocolate cities" is rooted across several fields and formats. Most notably, we find the popularized idea of the chocolate city within the major album of the legendary Funk band, Parliament Funkadelic, alongside informal and colloquial Black references to Washington, DC, due to its population being predominantly Black well through the end of the twentieth century. Our first definition springs from literary and nonfiction works and scholars, all of which point to enclaves such as Philadelphia's Black Seventh Ward, New Orleans' Tremé and Congo Square, Washington, DC's U/Shaw neighborhood, Pittsburgh's Hill District, Chicago's Bronzeville, and Seattle's Central District (to name a few). These works provide templates for early documentation and analyses of predominantly Black cities within cities, as writings on these neighborhoods indicate emergent trends or types regarding the chocolate city.

To analyze, present, explain, and expand on each type, we draw on a range of necessary sources, such as the ten-play series of Black playwright August Wilson, Gwendolyn Brook's poetic ethnographies of Chicago's Black Belt, Audre Lorde's *Zami*, and autobiographies and biographies of Jimi Hendrix, James Baldwin, Richard Wright, Ann Julia Cooper, Zora Neale Hurston, Bessie Smith, and Ida B. Wells-Barnett. We then evaluated and expanded these initial analyses and concepts, using original archival and interview data, along with the insights of social scientists and historians on these same communities.

Key in this regard, for example, are W. E. B. Du Bois, *The Philadelphia Negro: A Social Study* (Philadelphia: University of Pennsylvania, 1899); Du Bois, *Black Reconstruction in America, 1860–1880* (1935; repr., New York: Free Press, 1998); Lee Rainwater, *Behind Ghetto Walls: Black Families in a Federal Slum* (Chicago: Aldine, 1970); Carol B. Stack, *All Our Kin: Strategies for Survival in a Black Community* (New York: Harper and Row, 1974); Stack, *Call to Home: African Americans Reclaim the Rural South* (New York: Basic Books, 1996); Ulf Hannerz, *Soulside: Inquiries into Ghetto Culture and Community* (New York: Columbia University Press, 1969); Sudhir Alladi Venkatesh, *American Project* (Cambridge, MA: Harvard University Press, 2000); Elijah Anderson, *Streetwise: Race, Class and Change in an Urban Community* (Chicago: University of Chicago Press, 1990); Mary Pattillo, *Black on the Block: The Politics of Race and Class in the City* (Chicago: University of Chicago Press, 2007); Omar McRoberts, *Streets of Glory: Church and Community in a Black Urban Neighborhood* (Chicago: University of Chicago Press, 2000); Steven Gregory, *Black Corona: Race and the Politics of Place in an Urban Community* (Princeton: Princeton University Press, 1998); William Julius Wilson and Richard P. Taub, *There Goes the Neighborhood* (New York: Vintage, 2006); Gerald David Jaynes, *Branches without Roots: Genesis of the Black Working Class in the American South, 1862–1882* (New York: Oxford University Press, 1986); Karyn R. Lacy, *Blue-Chip Black: Race, Class, and Status in the New Black Middle Class* (Berkeley: University of California Press, 2007); William Julius Wilson, *Truly Disadvantaged: The Inner City, the Underclass, and Public Policy* (Chicago: University of Chicago Press, 1987); Wilson, *When Work Disappears: The World of the New Urban Poor* (New York: Knopf, 1996); Amanda Seligman, *Block by Block: Neighborhoods and Public Policy on Chicago's West Side* (Chicago: University of Chicago Press, 2005); and Kevin M. Kruse, *White Flight: Atlanta and the Making of Modern Conservatism* (Princeton: Princeton University Press, 2005).

Carol Stack, for example, notes that during her fieldwork for *All Our Kin* she noticed children leaving the community to go visit relatives in the South but did not until later grasp the full importance of this movement, some of which she details in *Call to Home*. We then aligned this and other seminal scholarship with what we were finding in the field, interviews, decennial census records, local- and state-level records, and news media. Music lyrics and performance, literary texts, photographs, images, film, and television helped to clarify types, pointing to an ongoing and persistent cognitive mapping in the United States for Black Americans over time. To this end, films from "Blaxploitation" through the contemporary rendering of the civil rights movement in the film *Selma* indicate that there were at least three versions of what might be imagined as chocolate cities— sites of Black historical and contemporary prominence and density. This typology is especially significant as it informs the politics, worldviews, and historical outcomes for Black Americans.

Our preliminary global chocolate city research, which naturally extends from the U.S.-focused one presented here, indicates that there are likely other chocolate city types that have been developed within a different context from the United States, though sharing important similarities. This contrast in context most notably includes European imperialism in Islamic nations and sub-Saharan Africa following the European nations' policies of ending the slave trade. This preliminary research indicates that colonization and globalization have generated at least two additional chocolate city types. All of the aforementioned receive further attention in the chapters that follow.

2. In addition to the more than ten thousand miles of road travel logged by each of the authors, this research is based on more than two hundred interviews, collected oral histories, ethnography in thirty-plus Black places (towns, cities, wards, districts), and an inventory of Black literature and cultural production and archives.

3. See, for example, Douglas Brinkley, *The Great Deluge: Hurricane Katrina, New Orleans, and the Mississippi Gulf Coast* (New York: Harper Perennial, 2007); Chester W. Hartman, *There Is No Such Thing as a Natural Disaster: Race, Class, and Hurricane Katrina* (New York: Taylor and Francis, 2006); Raymond J. Burby, "Hurricane Katrina and the Paradoxes of Government Disaster Policy: Bringing about Wise Governmental Decisions for Hazardous Areas," *Annals of the American Academy of Political and Social Science* 604, no. 1 (2006): 171–91; James R. Elliot and Jeremy Pais, "Race, Class, and Hurricane Katrina: Social Differences in Human Responses to Disaster," *Social Science Research* 35, no. 2 (2006): 295–321; Robert William Kates et al., "Reconstruction of New Orleans after Hurricane Katrina: A Research Perspective," *Proceedings of the National Academy of Sciences* 103, no. 40 (2006): 14653–60; Select Bipartisan Committee to Investigate the Preparation for and Response to Hurricane Katrina, *A Failure of Initiative: Final Report of the Select Bipartisan Committee to Investigate the Preparation for and Response to Hurricane Katrina,* vol. 109, no. 377 (Washington, DC: U.S. Government Printing Office, 2006); and Ron Eyerman, *Is This America? Katrina as Cultural Trauma* (Austin: University of Texas Press, 2015).

4. Nikhil Singh, *Black Is a Country* (Cambridge, MA: Harvard University Press, 2004).

5. Barbara Christian's analysis is especially impactful on ours. In her classic essay she illustrates the untapped potential of Black folk knowledge for intellectual production. See "The Race for Theory," *Cultural Critique* 6 (1987): 51–63.

6. Coined by law scholar and critical race theorist Kimberlé Crenshaw in 1989, the concept of intersectionality illustrates the simultaneity of identities while also uncovering where and how the state and legal structures obscure and diminish the freedoms of those on the margins. "Demarginalizing the Intersection of Race and Sex: A Black Feminist Critique of Antidiscrimination Doctrine,

Feminist Theory and Antiracist Politics," *University of Chicago Legal Forum* 1 (1989): 139–67. Crenshaw's use of the concept of intersectionality codified concepts forwarded by both Black feminist scholarship and the early work of African American scholar-activists such as Anna Julia Cooper, Ida B. Wells, and W. E. B. Du Bois. Intersectionality, a portable articulation of the crux of Black feminist theorizing, considers the ways in which Black women experience what Deborah K. King has called "multiple jeopardy"—simultaneously occupying disadvantaged positions in the three major systems of oppression: race, class, and gender. "Multiple Jeopardy, Multiple Consciousness: The Context of a Black Feminist Ideology," *Signs* 14, no. 1 (1988): 42–72. Sociologist Patricia Hill Collins extended this work in *Black Feminist Thought: Knowledge, Consciousness, and the Politics of Empowerment* (New York: Routledge, 1990) and ushered in a broad acceptance of the mutually reinforcing and co-occurring nature of systems of oppression.

See Kimberlé Crenshaw, "Mapping the Margins: Intersectionality, Identity Politics, and Violence against Women of Color," *Stanford Law Review* 43, no. 6 (1991): 1241–99; Crenshaw, *Critical Race Theory: The Key Writings That Formed the Movement* (New York: New Press, 1995); Crenshaw, "Demarginalizing the Intersection," 139; Patricia Hill Collins, "Intersectionality's Definitional Dilemmas," *Annual Review of Sociology* 41 (2015): 1–20; Collins, "Moving beyond Gender: Intersectionality and Scientific Knowledge," *Revisioning Gender* 2 (1999): 261–84; Leslie McCall, "The Complexity of Intersectionality," *Signs* 30, no. 3 (2005): 1771–800; and Zandria Felice Robinson, "Intersectionality," in *Handbook of Contemporary Sociological Theory*, ed. Seth Abrutyn, 477–99 (New York: Springer International, 2016).

7. Collins, *Black Feminist Thought;* Patricia Hill Collins, "The Social Construction of Black Feminist Thought," *Signs* 14, no. 4 (1989): 745–73. The impact of the matrix of domination—that is, the ability of misogyny, homophobia, racism, and ageism (among other factors) to alter the life chances and experience of marginalized and oppressed peoples—is also covered and foreshadowed in King, "Multiple Jeopardy."

8. Drawing from the representative data base, the "National Black Election Survey" (1984, 1988, 1996), Michael C. Dawson powerfully illustrates that links and connections across Black places and chocolate cities influence Black voting outcomes and turnout, as Black folk perceive their fates as linked to one another politically, economically, and socially. Data is available at ICPSR, www.icpsr .umich.edu/icpsrweb/ICPSR/studies/2029, accessed September 20, 2016. For more discussion and enriching analyses, see Dawson, *Behind the Mule: Race and Class in African-American Politics* (Princeton: Princeton University Press, 1994); Cathy J. Cohen and Michael C. Dawson, "Neighborhood Poverty and African American Politics," *American Political Science Review* 87, no. 2 (1993): 286–302; Dawson, *Black Visions: The Roots of Contemporary African-American*

Political Ideologies (Chicago: University of Chicago Press, 2003); and Cathy J. Cohen, *The Boundaries of Blackness: AIDS and the Breakdown of Black Politics* (Chicago: University of Chicago Press, 1999).

CHAPTER ONE. EVERYWHERE BELOW CANADA

1. Following his pilgrimage to Mecca, Malcolm X returned to the United States, delivering this speech and offering a new political platform he called the "Black Nationalist Party." By July Malcolm X was a consistent presence in Harlem, where he continued this line of political thought while also retaining his stance on the necessities of Black self-protection in the face of White aggression and violence. The text for X's "The Ballot or the Bullet" speech is available in Catherine Ellis and Stephen Smith, *Say It Loud: Great Speeches on Civil Rights and African American Identity* (New York: New Press, 2010) 1–18. For the transcription and additional details about the audience and the events of the day for the April 12, 1964, version of the speech, the following audio was used: Malcolm X, "The Ballot or the Bullet," *All Time Greatest Speeches*, vol. 2 (New York: Master Classics Records, Sony Music Entertainment, 2009).

Additional resources were also consulted to enrich our understanding of April 1964 and X's trajectory that led to the speech, as well as the weeks and months that followed. Theses sources include Manning Marable, *Malcolm X: A Life of Reinvention* (New York: Penguin Press, 2011); Malcolm X, *The Autobiography of Malcolm X*, with Alex Haley (New York: Ballantine Books, 1989), recently released FBI files on Malcolm X: "FBI Records: The Vault," Federal Bureau of Investigation, accessed December 1, 2014, https://vault.fbi.gov /Malcolm%20X; "Clay Talks with Malcolm X Here," *New York Times*, March 2, 1964, "Goals Changed by Malcolm X," *Los Angeles Times*, May 24, 1964, "King Views Malcolm X as Tragic," *New York Amsterdam News*, March 28, 1964; "Malcolm X Forming Own Muslim Group," *Los Angeles Times*, March 9, 1964; "Malcolm X in Brooklyn," *New York Amsterdam News*, April 25, 1964; "Malcolm X Plans a New Negro Group," *Chicago Tribune*, March 9, 1964; "Malcolm X Seeks Support for Negroes," *Washington Post and Times Herald*, July 14, 1964; "Malcolm X Tells of Death Threats," *New York Amsterdam News*, March 21, 1964; "Malcolm X to Visit Maryland," *New York Times*, April 9, 1964; "Malcolm X Warns of Violence," *Washington Post and Times Herald*, May 24, 1964; "Malcolm X's Detroit Date Sparks Battle of Ministers," *Afro-American*, April 11, 1964; "Nationalist Pleads for Malcolm X," *New York Amsterdam News*, February 29, 1964; "Negroes Need Guns, Declares Malcolm X," *Chicago Daily Defender*, March 16, 1964; "Report Clay, Malcolm X Plan[s] New Organization," *Chicago Daily Defender*, March 2, 1964; "Say Malcolm X Barred from Chicago Meeting," *Chicago Daily Defender*, February 17, 1964; "Says Malcolm X Converted Cassius

Clay," *Afro-American*, March 28, 1964; "Malcolm X Says Visit to Mecca Turned Him from Race Hatred," *Washington Post and Times Herald*, May 9, 1964; "Malcolm X Sees Rise in Violence," *New York Times*, March 13, 1964; "The Inside Outlook," *Los Angeles Sentinel*, March 5, 1964.

While Malcolm X's speech was heavily attended, many Black Christian ministers in Detroit had an internal conflict leading up to his arrival. Speaking for the dissenters, Rev. William R. Haney claimed, "we believe these separatist ideas can do nothing but set back the colored man's cause" ("Malcolm X's Detroit Date"). Despite this initial battle, the rector for King Solomon pressed on, having already paid Malcolm X for the speaking engagement. The church and the seat where Malcolm X sat at King Solomon were designated a historical landmark in June 2015. See "National Register Taps Detroit Church Where Giants Spoke," *Detroit Free Press*, June 12, 2015.

2. In fact, Detroit was not Malcolm X's first stop. He gave the same speech just a week before, on April 3, 1964, to Black Clevelanders at the Cory Methodist Church and in March to Black Harlemites. Existing reports and records indicate that the "The Ballot or the Bullet" speech was equally meaningful and impactful for Black Clevelanders and Harlemites as well, which likely provided Malcolm X a useful barometer regarding how Black Americans would receive him and his new rhetoric upon his return from Mecca. See "Malcolm X Tells Negroes to Use Ballots and Bullets," *Chicago Tribune*, March 23, 1964.

3. As indicated in historical records (including news media, FBI files, and his writings), much of his work and interviews continued to be produced under the name "Malcolm X." As such, we respectfully refer to him as Malcolm X throughout.

4. The year 1964 was an impactful year across the United States. By the time Malcolm X arrived in April, Black Detroiters had endured racial violence, high levels of unemployment, and racial residential segregation. Historians and social scientists have shown that these issues alongside many others served as the seeds of uprising and of the "urban crisis." For further historical description and political context, see Thomas J. Sugrue, *The Origins of the Urban Crisis: Race and Inequality in Postwar Detroit* (Princeton: Princeton University Press, 1996); Chris Rhomberg, *The Broken Table: The Detroit Newspaper Strike and the State of American Labor* (New York: Sage Foundation, 2012); J. Phillip Thompson III, *Double Trouble: Black Mayors, Black Communities, and the Call for a Deep Democracy* (New York: Oxford University Press, 2006).

5. Ellis and Smith, *Say It Loud*, 1–18; "Malcolm X Tells Negroes."

6. "Midnight Train to Georgia," was released in 1973 to wide acclaim as a part of the groups *Imagination* album. It reached number one on both the Hot 100 and R&B Billboard Charts and was awarded a Grammy Award in 1974 for "Best R&B vocal performance by a Group, Band or Duo."

7. Isabel Wilkerson's *The Warmth of Other Suns: The Epic Story of America's Great Migration* (New York: Vintage Books, 2011) and Nicolas Lehman's *The Promised Land: The Great Black Migration and How It Changed America* (New York: Vintage Books, 1992) both aptly illustrate the calls, pushes, and advertisements to new places Black Americans were inundated with during the bulk of the twentieth century.

8. See, for example, Joe William Trotter, *The Great Migration in Historical Perspective: New Dimensions of Race, Class, and Gender* (Bloomington: Indiana University Press, 1991); Stewart E. Tolnay, "The African American 'Great Migration' and Beyond," *Annual Review of Sociology* 29 (2003): 209–32; James R. Grossman, *Land of Hope: Chicago, Black Southerners, and the Great Migration* (Chicago: University of Chicago Press, 1991); Carole Marks, *Farewell—We're Good and Gone: The Great Black Migration* (Bloomington: Indiana University Press, 1989); Alferdteen Harrison, ed., *Black Exodus: The Great Migration of from the American South* (Jackson: University Press of Mississippi, 2012); Davarian L. Baldwin, *Chicago's New Negroes: Modernity, the Great Migration, and Black Urban Life* (Chapel Hill: University of North Carolina Press, 2007); and Alan D. DeSantis, "Selling the American Dream Myth to Black Southerners: The Chicago Defender and the Great Migration of 1915–1919," *Western Journal of Communication* 62, no. 4 (1998): 474–511.

9. Humanities and social science scholars alike have shown, through a variety of data and approaches, the influence and impact of persistent patterns of racism and anti-Blackness across the diaspora. See Derrick A. Bell, *Race, Racism, and American Law* (New York: Aspen, 2004); Eduardo Bonilla-Silva, *Racism without Racists: Color-Blind Racism and the Persistence of Racial Inequality in America*, 4th ed. (New York: Roman and Littlefield, 2013); Bell, *Faces at the Bottom of the Well: The Permanence of Racism* (New York: Basic Books, 1992); Bell, *Silent Covenants: Brown v. Board of Education and the Unfulfilled Hopes for Racial Reform* (Oxford: Oxford University Press, 2004); Devon W. Carbado, "(E)racing the Fourth Amendment," *Michigan Law Review* 100, no. 5 (2002): 946–1044; Carbado, "Black Rights, Gay Rights, Civil Rights," *UCLA Law Review* 47 (1999): 1467; Joe R. Feagin and Melvin P. Sikes, *Living with Racism: The Black Middle-Class Experience* (Boston: Beacon Press, 1994); Feagin, "The Continuing Significance of Race: Antiblack Discrimination in Public Places," *American Sociological Review* 56, no. 1 (1991): 101–16; Feagin, *Racist America: Roots, Current Realities, and Future Reparations* (New York: Routledge, 2014); and Elijah Anderson, *The Cosmopolitan Canopy: Race and Civility in Everyday Life* (Chicago: University of Chicago Press, 2011).

10. Racial residential segregation is high, persistent, and pervasive, especially in and across urban America and the conventional North. Importantly, scholars have noted how such inequality also significantly overlaps with racial disadvantages and

disparities in education, labor, and housing (just to name a few), thus constituting what sociologists Douglas Massey and Nancy Denton coined "American Apartheid."

See "Trends in the Residential Segregation of Blacks, Hispanics, and Asians: 1970–1980," *American Sociological Review* 52, no. 6 (1987): 802–25); Massey and Denton, *American Apartheid: Segregation and the Making of the Underclass* (Cambridge, MA: Harvard University Press, 1993); Massey and Denton, "The Dimensions of Residential Segregation," *Social Forces* 67, no. 2 (1988): 281–315; Massey, "American Apartheid: Segregation and the Making of the Underclass," *American Journal of Sociology* 96, no. 2 (1990): 329–57; John Dollard, *Caste and Class in a Southern Town* (1949; repr., New York: Doubleday, 1957); Baldwin, *Chicago's New Negroes;* Luther Adams, *Way Up North in Louisville: African American Migration in the Urban South, 1930–1970* (Chapel Hill: University of North Carolina Press, 2010); Sandra L. Barnes, *The Costs of Being Poor* (Albany: State University of New York Press, 2005); Sudhir Alladi Venkatesh, *American Project: The Rise and Fall of a Modern Ghetto* (Cambridge, MA: Harvard University Press, 2000); Mary Pattillo, *Black on the Block: The Politics of Race and Class in the City* (Chicago: University of Chicago Press, 2007); Patrick Sharkey, *Stuck in Place: Urban Neighborhoods and the End of Progress toward Racial Equality* (Chicago: University of Chicago Press, 2013); Carla Shedd, *Unequal City: Race, Schools, and Perceptions of Injustice* (New York: Sage Foundation, 2015); Waverly Duck, *No Way Out: Precarious Living in the Shadow of Poverty and Drug Dealing* (Chicago: University of Chicago Press, 2015); and Christopher Silver and John V. Moeser, *The Separate City: Black Communities in the Urban South, 1940–1968* (Lexington: University of Kentucky Press, 1995).

11. In recent decades scholarship has exploded time and again, showing how the prison industrial complex pervades and interrupts the lives of poor and minority communities, especially for Black Americans. It is also important to see incarceration as an extension and reflection of state strategies of oppression that can be traced back in one fashion or another to enslavement and the juridical and legislative missteps and missed opportunities in the undoing of legalized slavery.

See Angela Y. Davis, *Are Prisons Obsolete?* (New York: Seven Stories Press, 2011); Davis, *Women, Race, and Class* (New York: Vintage, 2011); Megan Comfort, *Doing Time Together: Love and Family in the Shadow of the Prison* (Chicago: University of Chicago Press, 2009); Sara Wakefield and Christopher Wildeman, *Children of the Prison Boom: Mass Incarceration and the Future of American Inequality* (New York: Oxford University Press, 2014); Amy E. Lerman and Vesla M. Weaver, *Arresting Citizenship: The Democratic Consequences of American Crime Control* (Chicago: University of Chicago Press, 2014); Michelle Alexander, *The New Jim Crow: Mass Incarceration in the Age of Colorblindness* (New York: New Press, 2012); Todd R. Clear, *Imprisoning Communi-*

ties: How Mass Incarceration Makes Disadvantaged Neighborhoods Worse (New York: Oxford University Press, 2009); Devah Pager, *Marked: Race, Crime, and Finding Work in an Era of Mass Incarceration* (Chicago: University of Chicago Press, 2008); Dorothy E. Roberts, "The Social and Moral Cost of Mass Incarceration in African American Communities," *Stanford Law Review* 56, no. 5 (2004): 1271–305); Bruce Western and Christopher Wildeman, "The Black Family and Mass Incarceration," *Annals of the American Academy of Political and Social Science* 621, no. 1 (2009): 221–42; Mary Pattillo, Bruce Western, and David Weiman, eds., *Imprisoning America: The Social Effects of Mass Incarceration* (New York: Sage Foundation, 2004); Robert J. Sampson and Charles Loeffler, "Punishment's Place: The Local Concentration of Mass Incarceration," *Daedalus* 139, no. 3 (2010): 20–31; Nicole Gonzalez Van Cleve, *Crook County: Racism and Injustice in America's Largest Criminal Court* (Stanford: Stanford University Press, 2016); Paul Butler, "Racially Based Jury Nullification: Black Power in the Criminal Justice System," *Yale Law Journal* 105, no. 3 (1995): 677–725; Butler, *Let's Get Free: A Hip-Hop Theory of Justice* (New York: New Press, 2010); Marie Gottschalk, *The Prison and the Gallows: The Politics of Mass Incarceration in America* (New York: Cambridge University Press, 2006); John Hagan, *Who Are the Criminals? The Politics of Crime Policy from the Age of Roosevelt to the Age of Reagan* (Princeton: Princeton University Press, 2012); Holly Foster and John Hagan, "The Mass Incarceration of Parents in America: Issues of Race/Ethnicity, Collateral Damage to Children, and Prisoner Reentry," *Annals of the American Academy of Political and Social Science* 623, no. 1 (2009): 179–94; Christopher Wildeman, "Parental Incarceration, Child Homelessness, and the Invisible Consequences of Mass Imprisonment," *Annals of the American Academy of Political and Social Science* 651, no. 1 (2014): 74–96; Jeffrey D. Morenoff and David J. Harding, "Incarceration, Prisoner Reentry, and Communities," *Annual Review of Sociology* 40 (2014): 411; David J. Harding, *Living the Drama: Community, Conflict, and Culture among Inner-City Boys* (Chicago: University of Chicago Press, 2010); Jason Schnittker and Andrea John, "Enduring Stigma: The Long-Term Effects of Incarceration on Health," *Journal of Health and Social Behavior* 48, no. 2 (2007): 115–30; Loïc Wacquant, "Deadly Symbiosis When Ghetto and Prison Meet and Mesh," *Punishment and Society* 3, no. 1 (2001): 95–133; Wacquant, "The Penalisation of Poverty and the Rise of Neo-liberalism," *European Journal on Criminal Policy and Research* 9, no. 4 (2001): 401–12; Wacquant, "The Curious Eclipse of Prison Ethnography in the Age of Mass Incarceration," *Ethnography* 3, no. 4 (2002): 371–97; Cleve, *Crook County;* and Becky Pettit, *Invisible Men: Mass Incarceration and the Myth of Black Progress* (New York: Sage Foundation, 2012).

12. There is a long history and deep tradition of scholarship that has demonstrated the overwhelming and enduring connection between race and poverty in America. In addition to aforementioned resources, see, for example, William

Julius Wilson, *The Truly Disadvantaged: The Inner City, the Underclass, and Public Policy* (Chicago: University of Chicago Press, 1987); Wilson, "Studying Inner-City Social Dislocations: The Challenge of Public Agenda Research: 1990 Presidential Address," *American Sociological Review* 56, no. 1 (1991): 1–14; William Julius Wilson and Robert Aponte, "Urban Poverty," *Annual Review of Sociology* 11 (1985): 231–58; and Carole Marks, "The Urban Underclass," *Annual Review of Sociology* 17 (1991): 445–66.

13. See Harding, *Living the Drama;* Andrew V. Papachristos, Tracey L. Meares, and Jeffrey Fagan, "Attention Felons: Evaluating Project Safe Neighborhoods in Chicago," *Journal of Empirical Legal Studies* 4, no. 2 (2007): 223–72; Khalil Gibran Muhammad, *The Condemnation of Blackness: Race, Crime, and the Making of Modern Urban America* (Cambridge, MA: Harvard University Press, 2011); Wilson, *Truly Disadvantaged;* Elijah Anderson, *Code of the Street: Decency, Violence, and the Moral Life of the Inner City* (New York: Norton, 2000); Lauren J. Krivo and Ruth D. Peterson, "Extremely Disadvantaged Neighborhoods and Urban Crime," *Social Forces* 75, no. 2 (1996): 619–48; Krivo and Peterson, "The Structural Context of Homicide: Accounting for Racial Differences in Process," *American Sociological Review* 65, no. 4 (2000): 547–59; Peterson and Krivo, *Divergent Social Worlds: Neighborhood Crime and the Racial-Spatial Divide* (New York: Sage Foundation, 2010); Muhammad, *Condemnation of Blackness;* Kali N. Gross, *Colored Amazons: Crime, Violence, and Black Women in the City of Brotherly Love, 1880–1910* (Durham: Duke University Press, 2006); and Elijah Anderson, *Streetwise: Race, Class, and Change in an Urban Community* (Chicago: University of Chicago Press, 1990).

14. Bell, *Faces at the Bottom;* Bell, *Silent Covenants;* Elijah Anderson, "The White Space," *Sociology of Race and Ethnicity* 1, no. 1 (2014): 10–21; Anderson et al., "The Legacy of Racial Caste: An Exploratory Ethnography," *Annals of the American Academy of Political and Social Science* 642, no. 1 (2012): 25–42; Feagin, "Continuing Significance of Race"; Feagin, *Racist America;* Alexander, *New Jim Crow;* Muhammad, *Condemnation of Blackness;* Eric Foner, *The Story of American Freedom* (New York: Norton, 1999); Harvard Sitkoff and Eric Foner, *The Struggle for Black Equality, 1954–1992* (New York: Macmillan, 1993); Foner, *Nothing but Freedom: Emancipation and Its Legacy* (Baton Rouge: Louisiana State University Press, 2007); Foner, *Politics and Ideology in the Age of the Civil War* (New York: Oxford University Press, 1980); Foner, *Freedom's Lawmakers: A Directory of Black Officeholders during Reconstruction* (New York: Oxford University Press, 1993); Darlene Clark Hine, "Rape and the Inner Lives of Black Women in the Middle West," *Signs* 14, no. 4 (1989): 912–20; Hine, *Hine Sight: Black Women and the Re-construction of American History* (Bloomington: Indiana University Press, 1994); Sugrue, *Urban Crisis;* Thomas J. Sugrue, *Sweet Land of Liberty: The Forgotten Struggle for Civil Rights in the North* (New York: Random House, 2008); Sugrue, "Affirmative Action from Below: Civil Rights,

the Building Trades, and the Politics of Racial Equality in the Urban North, 1945–1969," *Journal of American History* 91, no. 1 (2004): 145–73; Glenda Gilmore and Thomas Sugrue, *These United States: A Nation in the Making, 1890 to the Present* (New York: Norton, 2015); Jonathan Scott Holloway, *Confronting the Veil: Abram Harris Jr., E. Franklin Frazier, and Ralph Bunche, 1919–1941* (Chapel Hill: University of North Carolina Press, 2003); Holloway, *Jim Crow Wisdom: Memory and Identity in Black America since 1940* (Chapel Hill: University of North Carolina Press, 2013).

See also Saidiya V. Hartman, *Scenes of Subjection: Terror, Slavery, and Self-Making in Nineteenth-Century America* (New York: Oxford University Press, 1997); Deborah Gray White, *Ar'n't I a Woman? Female Slaves in the Plantation South* (New York: Norton, 1999); Tera Hunter, *To 'Joy My Freedom: Southern Black Women's Lives and Labors after the Civil War* (Cambridge, MA: Harvard University Press, 1997); and Michael Omi and Howard Winant, *Racial Formation in the United States* (New York: Routledge, 2014).

15. Daphne A. Brooks, "'All That You Can't Leave Behind': Black Female Soul Singing and the Politics of Surrogation in the Age of Catastrophe," *Meridians* 8, no. 1 (2008): 180–204; Brooks, "'Bring the Pain': Post-soul Memory, Neo-soul Affect, and Lauryn Hill in the Black Public Sphere," in *Taking It to the Bridge: Music as Performance*, ed. Nicholas Cook and Richard Pettengill, 180–203 (Ann Arbor: University of Michigan Press, 2013); Brooks, *Bodies in Dissent: Spectacular Performances of Race and Freedom, 1850–1910* (Durham: Duke University Press, 2006); Aldon D. Morris, *The Origins of the Civil Rights Movement* (New York: Free Press, 1986); Morris, "Political Consciousness and Collective Action," in *Frontiers in Social Movement Theory*, ed. Carol McClurg Mueller and Aldon D. Morris, 351–73 (New Haven: Yale University Press, 1992); Morris, *The Scholar Denied: W. E. B. Du Bois and the Birth of Modern Sociology* (Berkeley: University of California Press, 2015); Manning Marable, *How Capitalism Underdeveloped Black America: Problems in Race, Political Economy, and Society* (Chicago: Haymarket Books, 2015); Marable, *W. E. B. Du Bois: Black Radical Democrat* (New York: Routledge, 2015); Marable, *Beyond Black and White: Transforming African-American Politics* (New York: Verso, 1995); Marable, *Black Leadership* (New York: Columbia University Press, 2013); Robin D. G. Kelley, *Yo' Mama's Disfunktional! Fighting the Culture Wars in Urban America* (Boston: Beacon, 2001); Kelley, *Freedom Dreams: The Black Radical Imagination* (Boston: Beacon, 2002); Kelley, *Race Rebels: Culture, Politics, and the Black Working Class* (New York: Simon and Schuster, 1996); Walter Rodney, *How Europe Underdeveloped Africa* (London: Bogle-L'Ouverture, 1972); Hortense J. Spillers, *Black, White, and in Color: Essays on American Literature and Culture* (Chicago: University of Chicago Press, 2003); Spillers, "Mama's Baby, Papa's Maybe: An American Grammar Book," *Diacritics* 17, no. 2 (1987): 65–81; Gaye Theresa Johnson, *Spaces of Conflict, Sounds of Solidarity: Music, Race, and Spatial Entitlement*

in Los Angeles (Berkeley: University of California Press, 2013); Mark Anthony Neal, *What the Music Said: Black Popular Music and Black Public Culture* (New York: Routledge, 2013); Neal, *Songs in the Key of Black Life: A Rhythm and Blues Nation* (New York: Routledge, 2014); Neal, *Soul Babies: Black Popular Culture and the Post-soul Aesthetic* (New York: Routledge, 2002). See also bell hooks, *Talking Back: Thinking Feminist, Thinking Black* (Boston: South End, 1989).

16. Alan Spear, *Black Chicago: The Making of a Negro Ghetto, 1890-1920* (Chicago: University of Chicago Press, 1967), 174-75.

17. This second major thesis of the book is especially influenced by scholarship that has illustrated how soul music has traveled and been shaped and transformed over time and across place. In particular, we take great stock in the examples of scholars across a range of disciplines whose analyses explore how Black cultural production gives insight into the intersections of freedom, expression, place, and the American experiment. See GerShun Avilez, "Cartographies of Desire: Mapping Queer Space in the Fiction of Samuel Delany and Darieck Scott," *Callaloo* 34, no. 1 (2011): 126-42, Avilez, *Radical Aesthetics and Modern Black Nationalism* (Urbana: University of Illinois Press, 2016); Brooks, "You Can't Leave Behind"; Brooks, "Bring the Pain"; Brooks, *Bodies in Dissent;* Daphne A. Brooks, "'This Voice Which Is Not One': Amy Winehouse Sings the Ballad of Sonic Blue(s) Face Culture," *Women and Performance: A Journal of Feminist Theory* 20, no. 1 (2010): 37-60; Morris, *Civil Rights Movement;* Morris, "Political Consciousness"; Neal, *What the Music Said;* Neal, *Key of Black Life;* Neal, *Soul Babies;* Kelley, *Yo' Mama's Disfunktional;* Kelley, *Freedom Dreams;* Patricia A. Turner, *I Heard It through the Grapevine: Rumor in African-American Culture* (Berkeley: University of California Press, 1993); and Makani Themba Nixon and Nan Rubin, "Speaking for Ourselves: A Movement Led by People of Color Seeks Media Justice Not Just Media Reform," *Nation* 277, no. 16 (2003): 17-19.

18. The chocolate maps draw on scholarship across several fields. In particular, the intersections of critical race theory and critical geography are especially significant, as each points to the importance of master narratives and master histories monopolizing who gets counted, how phenomena get names, and for whom systems of power will work and will not work. See, for example, Madhu Dubey, "Postmodern Geographies of the U.S. South," *Nepantla: Views from South* 3, no. 2 (2002): 351-71; Anderson, "White Space"; Karyn R. Lacy, "Black Spaces, Black Places: Strategic Assimilation and Identity Construction in Middle-Class Suburbia," *Ethnic and Racial Studies* 27, no. 6 (2004): 908-30; Marcus Anthony Hunter, *Black Citymakers: How "The Philadelphia Negro" Changed Urban America* (New York: Oxford University Press, 2013); Joe R. Feagin, *The New Urban Paradigm: Critical Perspectives on the City* (New York: Rowman and Littlefield, 1998); Mark Gottdiener and Chris G. Pickvance, *Urban Life in Transition* (Newbury, CA: Sage, 1991); Mary Pattillo-McCoy, *Black Picket Fences: Privilege and Peril among the Black Middle Class* (Chicago: University of Chicago Press, 1999);

Pattillo, *Black on the Block;* Cathy J. Cohen, *The Boundaries of Blackness: AIDS and the Breakdown of Black Politics* (Chicago: University of Chicago Press, 1999); Arnold R. Hirsch, *Making the Second Ghetto: Race and Housing in Chicago, 1940–1960* (Chicago: University of Chicago Press, 1983); W. E. B. Du Bois, *Black Reconstruction in America, 1860–1880* (1935; repr., New York: Free Press, 1998); Morris, *Civil Rights Movement;* Paul Gilroy, *Black Atlantic: Modernity and Double-Consciousness* (Cambridge, MA: Harvard University Press, 1993); Baldwin, *Chicago's New Negroes;* Nikhil Singh, *Black Is a Country* (Cambridge, MA: Harvard University Press, 2004); Clyde Woods, *Development Arrested: Race, Power and the Blues in the Mississippi Delta* (New York: Verso, 1998); and Katherine McKittrick, *Demonic Grounds: Black Women and the Cartographies of Struggle* (Minneapolis: University of Minnesota Press, 2006).

See also Michael B. Preston, Lenneal J. Henderson Jr., and Paul L. Puryear, eds., *The New Black Politics: The Search For Political Power,* 2nd ed. (New York: Longman, 1987); Katherine Tate, *From Protest to Politics: The New Black Voters in American Elections* (New York: Sage Foundation, 1993); Albert K. Karnig and Susan Welch, *Black Representation and Urban Policy* (Chicago: University of Chicago Press, 1980); Carol M. Swain, *Black Faces, Black Interests: The Representation of African Americans in Congress* (Cambridge, MA: Harvard University Press, 1995); Melissa V. Harris-Lacewell, *Barbershops, Bibles, and BET: Everyday Talk and Black Political Thought* (Princeton: Princeton University Press, 2006); Thompson, *Double Trouble;* and St. Clair Drake and Horace Cayton, *Black Metropolis: A Study of Negro Life in a Northern City* (Chicago: University of Chicago Press, 1993).

See also James Weldon Johnson, *Black Manhattan* (New York: Atheneum, 1968); and Blair Ruble, *Washington's U-Street* (Baltimore: Johns Hopkins University Press, 2010). In his analysis Johnson also characterizes Black Harlem as a distinct area unto itself. Scholars of the urban South have also extended this characterization, arguing that in southern Black communities, what emerges as a result of the racial geography and racial history of the South are Black communities that constitute separate cities. For further discussion of this concept and southern Black communities, see Silver and Moeser, *Separate City.* Historian David Goldfield argues that three factors unique to the South—race, ruralism, and colonialism—shaped and continue to shape the evolution of the region from slavery to present. *Black, White and Southern: Race Relations and Southern Culture, 1940 to the Present* (Baton Rouge: Louisiana State University Press, 1991). The particular formulation of racial and spatial relationships in the South informs enduring struggles over power and values, from funding for public education to the structure and ideology of southern politics. Sociologist John S. Reed has consistently found evidence of a relatively uniform southern White identity that endures in attitudes and public culture, despite changes in the South's social, ethnic, and political landscape. *The Enduring South: Subcultural Persistence in*

Mass Society (Chapel Hill: University of North Carolina Press, 1986); *One South: An Ethnic Approach to Regional Culture* (Baton Rouge: Louisiana State University Press, 1982). Further, historian James Cobb's examination of regional identity firmly roots the most signified-on instantiation of southern identity—Mississippi Delta identity—in sets of cultural practices and products that sprang from the unique conditions of the plantation, agrarian South. *The Selling of the South: The Southern Crusade for Industrial Development, 1936–1990* (Urbana: University of Illinois Press, 1993); *The Most Southern Place on Earth: The Mississippi Delta and the Roots of Regional Identity* (Oxford: Oxford University Press, 1994); *Away Down South: A History of Southern Identity* (Oxford: Oxford University Press, 2007). Finally, sociologist Clyde Woods documents the distinctive racial and regional epistemology, which he termed *blues epistemology,* that arose from the experiences of Black folks in the Delta that laid important groundwork for our understanding of marginalized Black communities throughout the South. *Development Arrested;* Katherine McKittrick and Clyde Adrian Woods, eds., *Black Geographies and the Politics of Place* (Toronto: Between the Lines, 2007).

19. Our consideration here is also informed by Antonio Gramsci's distinction between "common sense" and "good sense." Where common sense is a logic of false consciousness that upholds and maintains the status quo (e.g., the argument that someone is in constant poverty because of laziness and should just get a job), good sense, as Gramsci reminds us, is guided by an elevated consciousness wherein logics of capitalism, moralism, and imperialism do not easily obscure the shared humanity of the "other" (e.g., the argument that someone is in constant poverty because the state would have it be so). See Gramsci and Joseph A. Buttigieg, *Prison Notebooks,* vol. 2 (New York: Columbia University Press, 1992).

20. This moment in Malcolm X's life is perhaps best captured visually in the 1992 Oscar-nominated Spike Lee film *Malcolm X.* See also Marable, *Malcolm X;* Malcolm X, *Autobiography of Malcolm X,* and "FBI Records."

21. Dapper Dan, interview, New York, April 20, 2016. We are grateful to each of the Harlemites who agreed to be interviewed as a part of this book, and especially to Justin Dior Combs for his tenacity and diligence in gathering these exclusive and original interviews. Indeed, what is presented here is a mere slice of a range of lengthy and rich interviews conducted with Faheem Muhammad, Kelvin Mensah, Jojo Brim, Mike B., and Troy Webstar, producer of the cult classic "Chicken Noodle Soup." Each of these individuals offered varying but similar accounts emphasizing Harlem's importance. Webstar, for instance, offered his sincere assessment:

> In my opinion [Harlem] changed the whole country. Harlem is very small, and for it to have such an effect on the whole world is beautiful and shows how powerful the culture in Harlem is. The Harlem Renaissance changed perspectives on how people lived and thought about things. It enlightened people. People understood

the power of their voice, and the power that they had, and how culturally rich they really were. . . . Harlem influenced America from the way you dressed. I sat down one day with the head of Nike, and he said the highest-selling Nike shoe is the low-cut Air Force One, and Harlem started that trend and the whole world started buying the sneaker. This is a fact, and I really sat down with the head of Nike when I had the whole "Chicken Noodle Soup" movement going, and he wanted me to design a shoe because he was like, "Harlem, ya'll are trend setters." Dam[on] Dash told me this one time, "The whole United States follow[s] New York, and the whole New York follows Harlem."

22. Jai Hudson, interview, Los Angeles, March 12, 2016.

23. Sean Combs, interview, Los Angeles, May 1, 2016.

24. Janice Combs, interview, New York, April 22, 2016.

CHAPTER TWO. DUST TRACKS ON THE CHOCOLATE MAP

1. Zora Neale Hurston, *Dust Tracks on a Road: An Autobiography* (1942; repr., New York: Harper Perennial, 1991), 1.

2. Ibid., 7.

3. W. E. B. Du Bois, *Black Reconstruction in America, 1860–1880* (1935; repr., New York: Free Press, 1998); Stephen Ellis, *The Mask of Anarchy: The Destruction of Liberia and the Religious Dimension of an African Civil War* (New York: New York University Press, 2007); Jean-Germain Gros, "Towards a Taxonomy of Failed States in the New World Order: Decaying Somalia, Liberia, Rwanda and Haiti," *Third World Quarterly* 17, no. 3 (1996): 455–72; J. Gus Liebenow, *Liberia: The Quest for Democracy* (Bloomington: Indiana University Press, 1987).

4. Norman Crockett, *The Black Towns* (Topeka: University Press of Kansas, 1979).

5. Hurston, *Dust Tracks*, 11. See also Robert E. Hemenway, *Zora Neale Hurston: A Literary Biography* (Urbana: University of Illinois Press, 1977); Lillie P. Howard, *Zora Neale Hurston* (Boston: Twayne, 1980); and Valerie Boyd, *Wrapped in Rainbows: The Life of Zora Neale Hurston* (New York: Simon and Schuster, 2003).

6. Hurston, *Dust Tracks*, 128, 213.

7. For David Harvey, see *Spaces of Capital: Towards a Critical Geography* (New York: Routledge, 2001); David Harvey and Bruce Braun, *Justice, Nature and the Geography of Difference* (Cambridge, MA: Blackwell, 1996); Harvey, *The Urban Experience* (Baltimore: Johns Hopkins University Press, 1989); Harvey, "On the History and Present Condition of Geography: An Historical Materialist Manifesto," *Professional Geographer* 36, no. 1 (1984): 1–11; and Harvey, "What Kind of Geography for What Kind of Public Policy?" *Transactions of the Institute of British Geographers*, no. 63 (1974): 18–24. See also Camilo Arturo Leslie,

"Territoriality, Map-Mindedness, and the Politics of Place, *Theory and Society* 45, no. 2 (2016): 169–201.

For Katherine McKittrick, see *Demonic Grounds: Black Women and the Cartographies of Struggle* (Minneapolis: University of Minnesota Press, 2006); Katherine McKittrick and Clyde Adrian Woods, eds., *Black Geographies and the Politics of Place* (Toronto: Between the Lines, 2007); McKittrick, "'Black and 'Cause I'm Black I'm Blue': Transverse Racial Geographies in Toni Morrison's *The Bluest Eye*," *Gender, Place and Culture: A Journal of Feminist Geography* 7, no. 2 (2000): 125–42; McKittrick, "'Who Do You Talk to, When a Body's in Trouble?': M. Nourbese Philip's (Un)silencing of Black Bodies in the Diaspora," *Social and Cultural Geography* 1, no. 2 (2000): 223–36; and McKittrick, ed., *Sylvia Wynter: On Being Human as Praxis* (Durham: Duke University Press, 2014).

For Paul Gilroy, see *The Black Atlantic: Modernity and Double Consciousness* (Cambridge, MA: Harvard University Press, 1993); and Gilroy, *Darker Than Blue: On the Moral Economies of Black Atlantic Culture* (Cambridge, MA: Harvard University Press, 2010).

For Neil Smith, see "Neo-critical Geography; or, The Flat Pluralist World of Business Class," *Antipode* 37, no. 5 (2005): 887–99.

For Rinaldo Walcott, see "Caribbean Pop Culture in Canada; or, The Impossibility of Belonging to the Nation," *Small Axe* 5, no. 1 (2001): 123–39; Walcott, *Black Like Who? Writing Black Canada* (Toronto: Insomniac, 2003); Walcott, *Performing the Postmodern: Black Atlantic Rap and Identity in North America* (Toronto: University of Toronto, 1996); Walcott, "Homopoetics: Queer Space and the Black Queer Diaspora," in McKittrick and Woods, *Black Geographies*, 233–45; Walcott, "Lament for a Nation: The Racial Geography of the Oh! Canada Project," *Fuse Magazine* 19 (1996): 15–23; and Walcott, "'A Tough Geography': Towards a Poetics of Black Space(s) in Canada," in *Unhomely States: Theorizing English-Canadian Postcolonialism*, ed. Cynthia Sugars, 277–88 (Peterborough, Ontario: Broadview, 2004).

8. Julia Coates, *Trail of Tears* (New York: Wiley and Sons, 2014); William G. McLoughlin, *After the Trail of Tears: The Cherokees' Struggle for Sovereignty, 1839–1880* (Chapel Hill: University of North Carolina Press, 2014); Gloria Jahoda, *The Trail of Tears* (New York: Holt, 1975).

9. Jerry Stanley, *I Am an American: A True Story of Japanese Internment* (New York: Crown, 1994); Cheryl Greenberg, "Black and Jewish Responses to Japanese Internment," *Journal of American Ethnic History* 14, no. 2 (1995): 3–37; Maisie Conrat and Richard Conrat, *Executive Order 9066: The Internment of 110,000 Japanese Americans* (Los Angeles: UCLA Asian American Studies Center Press, 1972).

10. Albert Camarillo, *Chicanos in a Changing Society: From Mexican Pueblos to American Barrios in Santa Barbara and Southern California, 1848–1930* (Dallas: Southern Methodist University Press, 2005); Edward M. Telles and

Vilma Ortiz, *Generations of Exclusion: Mexican-Americans, Assimilation, and Race* (New York: Sage Foundation, 2008); and Cecilia Menjívar, *Fragmented Ties: Salvadoran Immigrant Networks in America* (Berkeley: University of California Press, 2000).

11. Animating the geographic dimensions and consequences of oppression from the perspective of Black social, political, and economic experience and research, we look through new windows to gauge the intersections of American history, urbanization, politics, and enduring patterns of inequality.

12. Mapping is, of course, tricky. As in all maps, lines are informed by local, national, and administrative differences. For our part, we outline the array of data and materials we consulted and incorporated as a means of generating our map conceptually and geographically. We begin with the Black American experience, not to privilege or center the lives of this particular group, but rather to use it as one starting point, an *ideal type* or hermeneutic, to go back in time and remap, narrate, and analyze the urban America based on new and existing data from the Black American experience.

13. On the return migration of southern-born Black women, see Robert M. Adelman, Chris Morett, and Stewart E. Tolnay, "Homeward Bound: The Return Migration of Southern-Born Black Women, 1940 to 1990," *Sociological Spectrum* 20 (2000): 433–63.

14. Our contention is not that Black migration is not happening but that existing terms elide some key points. "Reverse migration" is meant to highlight that continued and recent Black migration *reverses* or inverts the spatial shifts of the Great Migration. Scholars along this vein use the idea of reverse migration to make this intervention, often showing that the racism and White domination Black Americans found and endure in the Great Migration destinations has compelled recent generations to migrate south. Also key here are the increased costs of living in the urban North relative to the urban South. Barry Bluestone and Bennett Harrison, *The Deindustrialization of America* (New York: Basic Books, 1982); John Kasarda, "Industrial Restructuring and the Changing Location of Jobs," in *State of the Union: America in the 1990s*, vol. 1, *Economic Trends*, ed. Reynolds Farley, 215–67 (New York: Sage Foundation, 1995).

Also important are increased job opportunities in the urban South relative to the urban North; see Kyle D. Crowder, Stewart E. Tolnay, and Robert M. Adelman, "Intermetropolitan Migration and Locational Improvement for African American Males, 1970–1990," *Social Science Research*, 30 no. 3 (2001): 449–72. This research shows that most all-Black reverse migrants are of recent generations, sometimes several generations removed from their family's Great Migrant(s). Further, the research indicates that Black reverse migrants do not always *return* South (in the manner the term implies, à la a southern home) but migrate within the American South more generally and may also return North at a moment's notice. In agreement with the sentiment and research about the push-and-pull factors as motivating recent Black migration, we offer the idea of *long migration*, to convey what we see in the research: that the aspirations, experiences, grapevines, and media campaigns calling recent Black migrants south share key similarities with the Great Migration because freedom and civil and social rights struggles, while in changing contexts, persists.

See W. E. B. Du Bois, "The Migration of Negroes," *Crisis* 142, no. 2 (1917): 63–66; Du Bois, *The Philadelphia Negro: A Social Study* (Philadelphia: University of Pennsylvania, 1899); Carol B. Stack, *Call to Home: African Americans Reclaim the Rural South* (New York: Basic Books, 1996); Stewart E. Tolnay, "The African American 'Great Migration' and Beyond," *Annual Review of Sociology* 29 (2003): 209–32; Stewart E. Tolnay and E. M. Beck, "Racial Violence and Black Migration in the American South, 1910 to 1930," *American Sociological Review* 57, no. 1 (1992): 103–16; Joe William Trotter, *The Great Migration in Historical Perspective: New Dimensions of Race, Class, and Gender* (Bloomington: Indiana University Press, 1991); Steven Tuch and Jack K. Martin, "Regional Differences in Whites' Racial Policy Attitudes," in *Racial Attitudes in the 1990s: Continuity and Change*, ed. Steven Tuch and Jack K. Martin, 165–74 (Westport, CT: Greenwood, 1997); Townsand Price-Spratlen, "Urban Destination Selection among African Americans during the 1950s Great Migration," *Social Science History* 32, no. 3 (2008): 437–69; Sabrina Pendergrass, "Perceptions of Race and Region in the Black Reverse Migration South," *Du Bois Review* 10, no. 1 (2013): 155–78; George Gmelch, "Return Migration," *Annual Review of Anthropology* 9 (1980): 135–59; Russell King, "Return Migration: A Neglected Aspect of Population Geography," *Area* 10, no. 3 (1978): 175–82; Larry H. Long and Kristin A. Hansen, "Trends in Return Migration to the South," *Demography* 12, no. 4 (1975): 601–14; and Rex R. Campbell, Daniel M. Johnson, and Gary J. Stangler, "Return Migration of Black People to the South," *Rural Sociology* 39 (1974): 514–29.

Our use of the term *long* extends from the important insights of historians suggesting that the civil rights movement was a *long* northern and southern movement. See Jacquelyn Dowd Hall, "The Long Civil Rights Movement and the Political Uses of the Past," *Journal of American History* 91, no. 4 (2005): 1233–63; Belinda Robnett, *How Long? How Long? African-American Women in the Struggle for Civil Rights* (New York: Oxford University Press, 1997); Sara Evans, *Personal Politics: The Roots of Women's Liberation in the Civil Rights Movement and the New Left* (New York: Vintage, 1979); Kenneth T. Andrews, *Freedom Is a Constant Struggle: The Mississippi Civil Rights Movement and Its Legacy* (Chicago: University of Chicago Press, 2004); Martha Biondi, *To Stand and Fight: The Struggle for Civil Rights in Postwar New York City* (Cambridge, MA: Harvard University Press, 2009); and Matthew J. Countryman, *Up South: Civil Rights and Black Power in Philadelphia* (Philadelphia: University of Pennsylvania Press, 2007). Scholars have also shown that, when it pertains to racial violence and injustices endured, Black folks have *long memories*. See Mary Frances

Berry and John W. Blassingame, *Long Memory: The Black Experience in America* (New York: Oxford University Press, 1982).

Reflecting on Black perceptions and experiences in the United States is foremost an exercise in Black geography that draws on multiple sources to delineate and center a Black cognitive cartography. It challenges the master narrative of geographies of the United States, which includes ideas about westward expansion, urban growth, and American global dominance without considering how these processes were enabled by genocide, slavery, land appropriation, and the subjugation of groups of color. Just as histories written from the perspectives of winners are being exposed as epistemologies of supremacy, with the chocolate maps we offer geography from the other's side. On chocolate maps, time, space, place, and sound converge to highlight the connectedness of transhistorical and transatlantic experiences of Black folks in the diaspora.

15. Lauryn Hill, "Every Ghetto, Every City," *The Miseducation of Lauryn Hill* (New York: Columbia Records, 1998), emphasis added to chorus to identify for the reader its role and occurrence in the song. The lyrics have been edited also to capture the narrative and residential logic within them. The chorus and ten other bars have been removed from this version for analytic purposes.

16. Mary Pattillo, *Black on the Block: The Politics of Race and Class in the City* (Chicago: University of Chicago Press, 2007), 3.

17. C. L. R. James, *The Black Jacobins: Toussaint L'Ouverture and the San Domingo Revolution* (New York: Random House, 1963), 17. During 2015 we began to witness the lasting effects of the slavery on the island formerly known as Hispaniola. Recent policy shifts in the Dominican Republic have formally given power to the persistent animus across the two countries sharing the larger island. Dominican officials' institutionalization of a massive deportation policy of Haitians from the Republic, is in large part due to the continued competition over minimal resources, poor health outcomes, and limited educational opportunities in two underdeveloped former colonies. Walter Rodney's *How Europe Underdeveloped Africa* (London: Bogle-L'Ouverture, 1972) is especially instructive.

18. Mary Waters, *Black Identities* (New York: Sage Foundation, 1999), 25. Fast-forward and these shared contexts have outcomes that include unequal access to employment, harsher treatment in the criminal justice system, lower life expectancy and overall quality of life; structural outcomes like these in the United States, serve as socioeconomic and political context for our research, through which we especially hone in on how Black people have mapped the world in response to and independent of institutional discrimination. See, for example, Anthony Marx, *Making Race and Nation: A Comparison of the United States, South Africa and Brazil* (New York: Cambridge University Press, 1998); Richard Iton, *In Search of the Black Fantastic: Politics and Popular Culture in the Post–Civil Rights Era* (New York: Oxford University Press, 2008); Christina Greer,

Black Ethnics: Race, Immigration and the Pursuit of the American Dream (New York: Oxford University Press, 2013); and Michael George Hanchard, *Orpheus and Power: The "Movimento Negro" of Rio de Janeiro and São Paulo, Brazil, 1945–1988* (Princeton: Princeton University Press, 1998).

19. The violence of slavery and White supremacy that was so consistent across the Black American experience connects two major American literary forms: the slave narrative and the migration narrative. See Farah Jasmine Griffin, *Who Set You Flowin': The African American Migration Narrative* (New York: Oxford University Press, 1995). Moreover, social scientists and historians have also indicated enslavement as a central and defining component of the Black American experience and identity. See Orlando Patterson, *Rituals of Blood: Consequences of Slavery in Two American Centuries* (New York: Basic Civitas Books, 1998); Ira Berlin et al., eds., *Free at Last: A Documentary History of Slavery, Freedom, and the Civil War* (New York: New Press, 1992); Albert J. Raboteau, *Slave Religion: The "Invisible Institution" in the Antebellum South* (New York: Oxford University Press, 1980); and Aldon D. Morris, *Origins of the Civil Rights Movements* (New York: Free Press, 1986).

20. Waters, *Black Identities;* Greer, *Black Ethnics;* Iton, *Black Fantastic.*

21. Iton, *Black Fantastic,* 200.

22. Michael Angelo Gomez, *Exchanging Our Country Marks: The Transformation of African Identities in the Colonial and Antebellum South* (Chapel Hill: University of North Carolina Press, 1998).

23. Michael C. Dawson, *Behind the Mule: Race and Class in African-American Politics* (Princeton: Princeton University Press, 1994); Cathy J. Cohen, *The Boundaries of Blackness: AIDS and the Breakdown of Black Politics* (Chicago: University of Chicago Press, 1999). See also Charles P. Henry, *Culture and African American Politics* (Bloomington: Indiana University Press, 1990).

Inquiry in this area has focused on the political attitudes of Blacks in the period of "new Black politics," an era of postsegregation and increased Black electoral representation. In this research scholars have focused particularly on the prominence of what political scientist Dawson refers to as the *linked fate* perspective, a political framework that presumes that Black people share a common fate. The linked-fate perspective has been shown to influence voting behaviors, particularly the strong support of the Democratic Party among Black Americans, while also impacting mobilization efforts and the creation and maintenance of a Black political community. Dawson, *Behind the Mule.*

As scholars have shown, however, the pervasiveness of such a perspective does not mean that Black attitudes are homogeneous, as the operationalization of the perspective varies among Black people dramatically. Acknowledging that the mobilization of indigenous resources often occurs under the guise of a linked-fate perspective, scholars have uncovered the intraracial processes involved in mobilizing a Black political constituency. Political scientist Cathy J. Cohen, for example, complicates the notion of linked fate by demonstrating that within Black political agendas segments of the population are further marginalized for the sake of a supposed consensus, constituting what she refers to as *secondary marginalization*. As we see in the story of the Black Seventh Ward, Black political attitudes are tied to the mobilization of resources, particularly indigenous resources such as the Black press, churches, schools, and social clubs, influencing voting practices and outcomes. Applying Dawson's and Cohen's insights to the local context, Black neighborhoods, such as the Black Seventh Ward, are perhaps best understood as linked to one another.

24. Fred Landon, "The Negro Migration to Canada after the Passing of the Fugitive Slave Act," *Journal of Negro History* 5, no. 1 (1920): 22–36; Philip Sheldon Foner, *History of Black Americans*, vol. 3 (Westport, CT: Greenwood, 1983); Allen Johnson, "The Constitutionality of the Fugitive Slave Acts," *Yale Law Journal* 31, no. 2 (1921): 161–82; Solomon Northup, *Twelve Years a Slave* (New York: Norton, 2016); Stanley W. Campbell, *The Slave Catchers: Enforcement of the Fugitive Slave Law, 1850–1860* (Chapel Hill: University of North Carolina Press, 1970); Julius Yanuck, "The Garner Fugitive Slave Case," *Mississippi Valley Historical Review* (1953): 47–66; United States v. Costello, 666 F.3d 1040 (7th Cir. 2012); State v. Short, 851 N.W.2d 474 (Iowa 2014). It is also important to note that scholars of Black Canadian life have demonstrated that racism and anti-Blackness are pervasive in Canada as well. See, for example, Katherine McKittrick, "Freedom Is a Secret," in McKittrick and Woods, *Black Geographies*, 97–114.

25. Griffin, *Who Set You Flowin'*. In the book Griffin marks that the commonality of Black migration produced its own literary genre and approach, sharing "with slave narratives notions of ascent from the South into a 'freer' North" and "is marked by an exploration of urbanism, an explication of sophisticated modern power, and, in some instances, a return South," taking "shape in a variety of art forms: autobiography, fiction, music, poetry, photography, and painting" (3–4).

26. Du Bois, "Migration of Negroes"; Du Bois, *Philadelphia Negro;* Stack, *Call to Home;* Tolnay, "Great Migration"; Tolnay and Beck, "Racial Violence"; Trotter, *Great Migration;* Price-Spratlen, "Urban Destination."

27. Du Bois, *Black Reconstruction*.

28. Isabel Wilkerson, *The Warmth of Other Suns: The Epic Story of America's Great Migration* (New York: Vintage Books, 2011), 35.

29. Farrah Griffin, *"Who Set You Flowin'?" The African-American Migration Narrative,* (Oxford: Oxford University Press, 1995), 30.

30. Elise Watson, interview, Philadelphia, October 15, 2013. In some cases names have been altered at the request of and out of respect for the individuals who agreed to be interviewed and share their stories for free.

31. Griffin, *Who Set You Flowin'*, 30.

32. Christopher Silver and John V. Moeser, *The Separate City: Black Communities in the Urban South, 1940–1968* (Lexington: University of Kentucky Press, 1995), x. This trend is also found and explained in St. Clair Drake and Horace Cayton, *Black Metropolis: A Study of Negro Life in a Northern City* (Chicago: University of Chicago Press, 1993); and Du Bois, *Philadelphia Negro.* See also James Weldon Johnson, *Black Manhattan* (New York: Atheneum, 1968).

33. Wilkerson, *Warmth of Other Suns*, 31.

34. Du Bois, *Philadelphia Negro*, 44, 25, 76.

35. William Julius Wilson, *When Work Disappears: The World of the New Urban Poor* (New York: Knopf, 1996), 29–30.

36. William Julius Wilson, *Truly Disadvantaged: The Inner City, the Underclass, and Public Policy* (Chicago: University of Chicago Press, 1987); Wilson, *When Work Disappears.*

37. Douglas S. Massey and Nancy A. Denton, *American Apartheid: Segregation and the Making of the Underclass* (Cambridge, MA: Harvard University Press, 1993); Wilson, *When Work Disappears;* Patrick Sharkey, *Stuck in Place: Urban Neighborhoods and the End of Progress toward Racial Equality* (Chicago: University of Chicago Press, 2013); Devah Pager, *Marked: Race, Crime, and Finding Work in an Era of Mass Incarceration* (Chicago: University of Chicago Press, 2008).

38. For Brixton, see Gilroy, *Black Atlantic;* Paul Gilroy, *Black Britain: A Photographic History* (London: Al Saqi, 2007); and Alex Wheatle, *The Dirty South* (London: Serpent's Tale Books, 2008). For Saint-Denis, see Jean Beaman, "But Madame, We Are French Also," *Contexts* 11, no. 3 (2012): 46–51; Beaman, "Boundaries of Frenchness: Cultural Citizenship and France's Middle-Class North African Second-Generation," *Identities* 22, no. 1 (2015): 36–52; and Beaman, "As French as Anyone Else: Islam and the North African Second Generation in France," *International Migration Review*, no. 1 (2015): 1–29. For Soweto, see Marx, *Making Race and Nation.*

39. Ruth D. Peterson and Lauren J. Krivo, "Racial Segregation and Black Urban Homicide," *Social Forces* 71, no. 4 (1993): 1001–26; Krivo and Peterson, "Extremely Disadvantaged Neighborhoods and Urban Crime," *Social Forces* 75, no. 2 (1996): 619–48; Ruth D. Peterson, Lauren J. Krivo, and Mark A. Harris, "Disadvantage and Neighborhood Violent Crime: Do Local Institutions Matter?," *Journal of Research in Crime and Delinquency* 37, no. 1 (2000): 31–63; Massey and Denton, *American Apartheid*, 150. See also Camille Zubrinksy Charles, *Won't You Be My Neighbor: Race, Class, and Residence in Los Angeles* (New York: Sage Foundation, 2006); Wilson, *When Work Disappears;* and Sharkey, *Stuck in Place.*

40. Massey and Denton, *American Apartheid*, 150. See also Charles, *Be My Neighbor;* Wilson, *When Work Disappears;* and Sharkey, *Stuck in Place.*

41. The key is how the changes from industrial labor to service-based employment have led to persistent patterns of Black unemployment and underemploy-

ment. As a result, there has been persistent Black poverty at individual and neighborhood levels in the post–civil rights era. William Julius Wilson, *The Truly Disadvantaged: The Inner City, the Underclass, and Public Policy* (Chicago: University of Chicago Press, 1987); Wilson, *When Work Disappears: The World of the New Urban Poor* (New York: Knopf, 1996); Mary Pattillo-McCoy, *Black Picket Fences: Privilege and Peril among the Black Middle Class* (Chicago: University of Chicago Press, 1999); Mario Luis Small and Katherine Newman, "Urban Poverty after *The Truly Disadvantaged:* The Rediscovery of the Family, the Neighborhood, and Culture," *Annual Review of Sociology* 27 (2001): 23–45; Amanda Seligman, *Block by Block: Neighborhoods and Public Policy on Chicago's West Side* (Chicago: University of Chicago Press, 2005).

Today regional distinctions between spaces normally considered as "The South" and "The North" are still marked by evidence of the separate city. For example, southern cities such as Memphis and New Orleans consistently have larger Black-to-White population ratios. The largely Black-White racial demographics of many southern cities generate different political and social outcomes for Black people in the South. Still, chocolate cities across the nation have striking similarities.

42. Toni Morrison continues, "There will be nothing left of the Bottom (a footbridge that crossed the river is already gone), but perhaps it is just as well, since it wasn't a town anyway: just a neighborhood where on quiet days people in valley houses could hear singing sometimes, banjos sometimes, and if a valley man happened to have business up in those hills—collecting rent or insurance payments—he might see a dark woman in a flowered dress doing a bit of a cakewalk, a bit of black bottom, a bit of 'messing around' to the lively notes of a mouth organ." *Sula* (New York: Vintage Books, 1973), 3–4.

43. Elijah Anderson, *Streetwise: Race, Class, and Change in an Urban Community* (Chicago: University of Chicago Press, 1990); Christopher Mele, *Selling the Lower East Side: Culture, Real Estate and Resistance in New York City* (Minneapolis: University of Minnesota Press, 2000); Pattillo-McCoy, *Black Picket Fences;* Pattillo, *Black on the Block;* Sudhir Alladi Venkatesh, *American Project: The Rise and Fall of a Modern Ghetto* (Cambridge, MA: Harvard University Press, 2000); Venkatesh, *Off the Books: The Underground Economy of the Urban Poor* (Cambridge, MA: Harvard University Press, 2006).

44. This broad field of social scientific research on Black communities has significantly shaped the way we think about race and urban change since the early studies of the pioneering Chicago School of Sociology. Patterns of the residential mobility of Black and White middle-class residents and the displacement of poor and working-class Blacks have been posited as integral to not only an understanding of current neighborhood change but also future possibilities and migration patterns for Black residents across cities.

45. As John Logan and Harvey Molotch convincingly show, these broad structural shifts mean that "poor people are double losers" in urban change because

"they have the least to gain from the infrastructural development and much to lose by the choice of its location." *Urban Fortunes: The Political Economy of Place* (Berkeley: University of California Press, 2007), 114.

46. However, much of this research has placed disproportionate emphasis on the decisions of White stakeholders and officials rather than decisions made by their Black counterparts. Further, focusing primarily on external forces to explain changes in Black neighborhoods diminishes the important role of Black residents as city makers and place makers. We instead focus our analysis on Black actors, geographic perspectives, stakeholders, and residents through different locales and histories during the twentieth century, offering a new perspective on enduring urban and racial inequalities. Although scholars have studied locales similar to that covered in this book, our development of the chocolate map, with its explicit attention to racial history, intraracial relations, and Black cultural production, provides a much needed exploration into the active role Black residents play in patterns of change and progress. Massey and Denton, *American Apartheid;* Pattillo-McCoy, *Black Picket Fences;* Kevin Fox Gotham, *Race, Real Estate, and Uneven Development: The Kansas City Experience, 1900–2000* (Albany: State University of New York Press, 2002); Sharkey, *Stuck in Place.*

47. Stuart Hall continues,

> Popular culture always has its base in the experiences, the pleasures, the memories, [and] the traditions of people. It has connections with local hopes and local aspirations, local tragedies, and local scenarios that are the everyday practices and the everyday experiences of ordinary folks. . . . That is why it has always been counterpoised to high or elite culture, and is thus a site of alternative traditions. . . . By definition, black popular culture is . . . a site of strategic contestation. . . . In its expressivity, its musicality, its orality, in its rich, deep, and varied attention to speech, in its inflections toward the vernacular and the local, in its rich production of counternarratives, and above all, in its metaphorical use of the musical vocabulary, black popular culture has enabled the surfacing, inside the mixed and contradictory modes even of some mainstream popular culture, of elements of a discourse that is different—other forms of life, other traditions of representation.

Stuart Hall, "What Is This 'Black' in Black Popular Culture?," *Social Justice* 20, no. 1 (1993): 106–9. Hall rightly locates the potential of Black popular culture as a site of data on Black resistive practices, invention, and artistic and political representation. As Hall recalls for us, Black public culture—including music, writings, speeches, radio, and news—is data that can allow us to gauge how Black people understood the varied similarities and differences in the various chocolate cities across the United States.

48. James Baldwin is especially apt here because he provides two major autobiographies, *Notes of a Native Son* (New York: Beacon, 1955) and later *Nobody Knows My Name* (New York: Vintage, 1961), where we can measure and see his

evolving conception of the similarities and differences between "The North" and "The South." Written immediately after a long stint abroad, the former book, in detailing Baldwin's southward journey and tour, offers especially key insights. Baldwin does this research and observation by amplifying the "special attitude" of Black Americans—the "special place in this scheme" called America. *Nobody Knows My Name*, 7.

49. For our research we also include Alaska and Hawaii (the last two of the fifty states) within the existing region paradigm we developed within the chocolate maps. However, we anticipate that there are likely to be some exceptions and slipperiness, given the recent inclusion of these two states in 1959 within the differing context of the Cold War.

CHAPTER THREE. MULTIPLYING THE SOUTH

1. James Baldwin, *Notes of a Native Son* (New York: Beacon, 1955), 3, 4.

2. Ibid., 6, 7 (emphasis added).

3. Ibid., 7, 4.

4. James Baldwin, "Of the Sorrow Songs: The Cross Redemption," *Views on Black Music*, no. 2 (1984–85): 12.

5. James Baldwin, *Nobody Knows My Name* (New York: Vintage, 1961), 2.

6. Ibid., 93.

7. Ibid.

8. Ibid., 70–71.

9. Ibid., 84.

10. Ibid., 65–66.

11. *Take This Hammer* was produced by Richard Moore for local network KQED TV and National Educational Television. The documentary premiered locally in the Bay Area on February 4, 1964, just five months after the Birmingham church bombing. Baldwin and Moore's relationship would become strained after the airing of the documentary, as the televised version had removed a significant chunk of his visit. Many of the comments of Black youth were deemed by the KQED board as too controversial for White audiences and were thus edited out from the original documentary and its television airing. This editing occurred despite Baldwin's desire and request to center these perspectives, especially because he was himself taken with and surprised by their insights and commentary on race in America. In subsequent years the film was readjusted to include these comments, though it never aired in full on television.

12. Baldwin, *Take This Hammer*.

13. Ibid. Baldwin's use of the word *incident* here should be understood as especially purposeful and likely linked to Harriet Ann Jacobs's 1861 autobiography, *Incidents in the Life of Slave Girl*. Much like Baldwin's use of the term, the

notion of *incidents* in Jacobs's tale involves episodes of racial and sexual violence and White supremacy and domination, among other racialized events.

14. Ibid.

CHAPTER FOUR. SUPER LOU'S CHITLIN' CIRCUIT

1. Chitlin' Circuit is a popular reference for the network of Black performance places and sites across the United States. See, for example, Henry Louis Gates Jr., "The Chitlin Circuit," *New Yorker* 3 (1997): 44–55; Mark Anthony Neal, "Sold Out on Soul: The Corporate Annexation of Black Popular Music," *Popular Music and Society* 21, no. 3 (1997): 117–35; Lewis Walker, *Black Eden: The Idlewild Community* (Jackson: Mississippi State University Press, 2002); and Rashida Z. Shaw, "Insert [Chitlin Circuit] Here: Teaching an Inclusive African American Theatre Course," *Theatre Topics* 19, no. 1 (2009): 67–76.

2. Rawls's narrative was transcribed by the authors, using the commercial release of the album *Lou Rawls: LIVE! in 1966* (New Orleans: Blue Note Records, 2005). The medley occurs on track 2, "Southside Blues/Tobacco Road," 7:56.

3. Ibid.

4. Melvin L. Oliver and Thomas M. Shapiro, *Black Wealth/White Wealth: A New Perspective on Racial Inequality* (New York: Routledge, 1997). See also Khalil Gibran Muhammad, *The Condemnation of Blackness: Race, Crime, and the Making of Modern Urban America* (Cambridge, MA: Harvard University Press, 2011); Joe R. Feagin and Melvin P. Sikes, *Living with Racism: The Black Middle-Class Experience* (Boston: Beacon Press, 1994); and Dalton Conley, *Being Black, Living in the Red* (Berkeley: University of California Press, 1999).

For discussions of Black wealth and racial differences in wealth accumulation, see Andrew F. Brimmer, "Income, Wealth, and Investment Behavior in the Black Community," *American Economic Review* 78, no. 2 (1988): 151–55; Robert L. Boyd, "Residential Segregation by Race and the Black Merchants of Northern Cities during the Early Twentieth Century," *Sociological Forum* 13, no. 4 (1998): 595–609; Frances K. Goldscheider and Calvin Goldscheider, "The Intergenerational Flow of Income: Family Structure and the Status of Black Americans," *Journal of Marriage and Family* 23, no. 2 (1991): 499–508; Ivan Light, "Gambling among Blacks: A Financial Institution," *American Sociological Review* 42, no. 6 (1977): 892–904; A. Wade Smith and Joan V. Moore, "East-West Differences in Black Economic Development," *Journal of Black Studies* 16, no. 2 (1985): 131–54; Maury Gittleman and Edward N. Wolff, "Racial Differences in Patterns of Wealth Accumulation," *Journal of Human Resources* 39, no. 1 (2004): 193–227; Kyle Crowder, Scott J. South, and Erick Chavez, "Wealth, Race, and Interneighborhood Migration," *American Sociological Review* 71, no. 1 (2006): 72–94;

and Albert Karnig, "Black Economic, Political, and Cultural Development: Does City Size Make a Difference?," *Social Forces* 57, no. 4 (1979): 1194–211.

5. Our conception of chocolate maps draws inspiration and insight from the instructive works of several key scholars. This is more fully addressed in the subsequent chapter, but it is worth noting here the pioneering blueprints for our critical race geography. First, in the classic *The Philadelphia Negro: A Social Study* (Philadelphia: University of Pennsylvania, 1899), we see that W. E. B. Du Bois found it more precise to draw the mapping of the Seventh Ward based on interviews and surveys of Black households in the neighborhood. From these sources Du Bois developed an unprecedented and refined mapping of the neighborhood that better aligned with the facts, evidence, histories, and spatial arrangements he observed. See also Du Bois, *The Black North: A Social Study* (New York: New York Times Magazine Supplement, 1901).

We also take much guidance from the tremendous insights of the anthropologist and African historian Cheikh Anta Diop. In some of his most major work, Diop retraces the origins of human history through a rereading of the African continent and reestablishes its prominence as the origin for humanity. He thus recalibrates conventional and Eurocentric notions of history that place western Europeans nations as the epicenters and drivers of world history. Diop powerfully uses his own "Black Map" to trace the underrecognized contributions of the various African empires and intellectual traditions. We draw specifically on Diop's following works: *The African Origin of Civilization: Myth or Reality*, trans. Mercer Cook (Westport, CT: Lawrence Hill Books, 1974); *Black Africa: The Economic and Cultural Basis for a Federated State*, trans. Harold Salemson (Westport, CT: Lawrence Hill Books, 1978); *Civilization or Barbarism: An Authentic Anthropology*, trans. Yaa-Lengi Meema Ngemi (Brooklyn: Lawrence Hill Books, 1991); *Precolonial Black Africa: A Comparative Study of the Political and Social Systems of Europe and Black Africa, from Antiquity to the Formation of Modern States*, trans. Harold J. Salemson (Westport, CT: Lawrence Hill Books, 1987); and *Towards the African Renaissance: Essays in African Culture and Development, 1940–1960*, trans. Egbuna P. Modum (London: Karnak House, 1996).

Detailing the role and impact of the slave trade and Black intellectual and cultural production from western Europe to the Caribbean to the United States, Paul Gilroy, *Black Atlantic: Modernity and Double-Consciousness* (Cambridge, MA: Harvard University Press, 1993), demonstrates that there is a Black landscape of this oceanic and continental geography that is distinctively Black and hugely consequential for the larger ebbs and flows of socioeconomic and political history and cultural and artistic production.

We also draw on an ongoing endeavor, best exemplified in the works of Clyde Woods and Katherine McKittrick, whose critical geographies of Black life in the Mississippi Delta took into consideration the intersection of Black culture and political economy. See Woods, *Development Arrested: Race, Power and the Blues in the Mississippi Delta* (New York: Verso, 1998); and McKittrick, *Demonic Grounds: Black Women and the Cartographies of Struggle* (Minneapolis: University of Minnesota Press, 2006).

Furthermore, our notion of a racial cartography for the United States is grounded by and emergent from the intersections of the fields of critical geography and critical race theory. That the intersections of master statuses and master narratives have measurable and lasting consequences is clearest in maps. Because maps inform ideas and policies regarding citizenship, statehood, politics, and capital, the development of a map reflecting new narratives and new perspectives opens new and fruitful avenues of inquiry and knowledge.

The following especially inform our thinking at this critical philosophical intersection: David Harvey, *Spaces of Capital: Towards a Critical Geography* (New York: Routledge, 2001), Nicholas Blomley, "Uncritical Critical Geography?," *Progress in Human Geography* 30, no. 1 (2006): 87; Henri Lefebvre, *The Production of Space*, vol. 142 (Oxford: Blackwell, 1991); Gloria Ladson-Billings and William Tate IV, "Toward a Critical Race Theory of Education," *Teachers College Record* 97, no. 1 (1995): 47–68; Kimberlé Crenshaw, *Critical Race Theory: The Key Writings That Formed the Movement* (New York: New Press, 1995); McKittrick, *Demonic Grounds;*

6. McKittrick, *Demonic Grounds*, xii. McKittrick's follow-up to this important point provides further inspiration and guidance for our use of racially conscious and Black feminist cartographic logics:

> And while we all produce, know, and negotiate space—albeit on different terms—geographies in the diaspora are accentuated by racial paradigms of the past and their ongoing hierarchical patterns. I have turned to geography and black geographic subjects not to provide a corrective story, nor to "find" and "discover" lost geographies. Rather, I want to suggest that space and place give black lives meaning in a world that has, for the most part, incorrectly deemed black population and their attendant geographies as "ungeographic" and/or philosophically undeveloped. That black lives are necessarily geographic, but also struggle with discourses that erase and despatialize their sense of place, is where I begin to conceptualize geography. (xii–xiii)

See also Patricia Hill Collins, *Black Feminist Thought: Knowledge, Consciousness, and the Politics of Empowerment* (New York: Routledge, 1990); Dorothy E. Smith, The Everyday World as Problematic: A Feminist Sociology (Toronto: University of Toronto Press, 1987); Kimberlé Crenshaw, "Mapping the Margins: Intersectionality, Identity Politics, and Violence against Women of Color," Stanford Law Review 43, no. 6 (1991): 1241–99; and Beverly Guy-Sheftall, *Words of Fire: An Anthology of African-American Feminist Thought* (New York: New Press, 1995).

7. Christopher Silver and John V. Moeser, *The Separate City: Black Communities in the Urban South, 1940–1968* (Lexington: University of Kentucky Press,

1995), x. See also St. Clair Drake and Horace Cayton, *Black Metropolis: A Study of Negro Life in a Northern City* (Chicago: University of Chicago Press, 1993); and James Weldon Johnson, *Black Manhattan* (New York: Atheneum, 1968). We find the "city within a city" concept used to describe urban Black neighborhoods and communities as early as Du Bois's *Philadelphia Negro*. For a deeper look into the consequences and use of this concept by Du Bois, see Marcus Anthony Hunter, "A Bridge over Troubled Urban Waters: W. E. B. Du Bois's *The Philadelphia Negro* and the Ecological Conundrum," *Du Bois Review: Social Science Research on Race* 10, no. 1 (2013): 7–27.

8. Elijah Anderson, "The White Space," *Sociology of Race and Ethnicity* 1, no. 1 (2014): 10–21); Karyn R. Lacy, "Black Spaces, Black Places: Strategic Assimilation and Identity Construction in Middle-Class Suburbia," *Ethnic and Racial Studies* 27, no. 6 (2004): 908–30.

9. Marcus Anthony Hunter, *Black Citymakers: How "The Philadelphia Negro" Changed Urban America* (New York: Oxford University Press, 2013); Marcus Anthony Hunter and Zandria F. Robinson, "The Sociology of Urban Black America," *Annual Review of Sociology* 42 (2016): 385–405; Joe R. Feagin, *The New Urban Paradigm: Critical Perspectives on the City* (New York: Rowman and Littlefield, 1998); M. Gottdiener and Chris G. Pickvance, *Urban Life in Transition* (Newbury, CA: Sage, 1991). All these authors demonstrate that there has been a real absence of focus on Black civic engagement and actors in broader policies of urbanization and local change. This is in many ways a challenge to existing scholarship, such as John Logan and Harvey Molotch, *Urban Fortunes: The Political Economy of Place* (Berkeley: University of California Press, 2007); John Mollenkopf, *The Contested City* (Princeton: Princeton University Press, 1983); Mollenkopf, *Power, Culture, and Place: Essays on New York City* (New York: Russell Sage Foundation, 1988); and John Walton, "Urban Sociology: Contributions and Limits of Political Economy," *Annual Review of Sociology* 19 (1993): 301–20.

Any discussion of neighborhood change and the social realities of urban Blacks would be incomplete without a discussion of the local sociopolitical landscape. People live locally. People's lives are shaped by events and processes of change at the local level, such as gentrification, urban renewal, and the rise and decline of public and affordable housing. One basic question has been central to research in this area: how and why do cities grow? Usually invoking the concept of *community* to distinguish such discussions of local politics and urban development from that occurring at the national level, scholars have emphasized multiple lines of argument, often highlighting the importance of local economies and power brokers.

While for some a conception of urban development is tied to the principles of a free-market economy, others have emphasized a Marxist-informed conception, critiquing the inequality inherent to local capitalist enterprises. Notwithstanding such differing dispositions, research thus far has emphasized the importance of competition, particularly over urban land. Some of the most notable research demarcating the difference between local- and national-level politics and growth include Floyd Hunter, *Community Power Structure: A Study of Decisions Makers* (Chapel Hill: University of North Carolina Press, 1953); Robert Dahl, *Who Governs?* (New Haven, CT: Yale University Press, 1961); Charles M. Bonjean, Terry N. Clark, and Robert L. Lineberry, eds., *Community Politics: A Behavioral Approach* (New York: Free Press, 1971); Rufus P. Browning, Dale Rogers Marshall, and David H. Tabb, *Protest Is Not Enough* (Berkeley: University of California Press, 1984); and Floyd Hunter, Ruth Connor Schaffer, and Cecil G. Sheps, *Community Organization: Action and Inaction* (Chapel Hill: University of North Carolina Press, 1956).

For arguments asserting a free-enterprise perspective of urban development in which local political advances and shifts in representation reflect a continual process of change within cities, see Robert Park, Ernest Burgess, and Roderick D. McKenzie, eds., *The City*, 2nd ed. (Chicago: University of Chicago Press, 1924).

Others have contended, however, that free-market conceptions elide the inequality emergent in urban capitalistic regimes; see, for example, Manuel Castells, *The City and the Grassroots* (Berkeley: University of California Press, 1983); and Robert Bailey Jr., *Radicals in Urban Politics: The Alinsky Approach* (Chicago: University of Chicago Press, 1974). See also Manuel Castells, *The Urban Question: A Marxist Approach* (Cambridge, MA: MIT Press, 1977); David Harvey, "Government Policies, Financial Institutions and Neighborhood Change in United States Cities," in *Captive Cities*, ed. Michael Harloe (London: Wiley, 1977), 123–40; Kevin Cox, ed., *Urbanization and Conflict in Market Societies* (Chicago: Methuen, 1978); and William K. Tabb and Larry Sanders, eds., *Marxism and the Metropolis: New Perspectives in Urban Political Economy* (New York: Oxford University Press, 1984).

Arguments about the importance of networks for understanding urban development are furthered in other works, particularly Barry Wellman's discussion of the "community liberated" perspective. Accounting for the shifts in local social urban relationships, Wellman suggests that advances in mass transit, technology, and communication have shifted social networks so that they are no longer rooted in singular neighborhoods but are instead ramified across a series of neighborhoods and cities. "The Community Question: Intimate Networks of East New Yorkers," *American Journal of Sociology* 84, no. 5 (1979): 1201–21. See also Wellman, ed., *Networks in the Global Village: Life in Contemporary Communities* (Boulder, CO: Westview, 1999); Barry Wellman and Barry Leighton, "Networks, Neighborhoods, and Communities: Approaches to the Study of the Community Question," *Urban Affairs Quarterly* 14, no. 3 (1979): 363–90; Claude Fischer, *The Urban Experience* (New York: Harcourt, Brace, Jovanovich, 1976); and Louis Wirth, "Urbanism as a Way of Life," *American Journal of Sociology* 44, no. 1 (1938): 1–24.

Additional notable exceptions to this larger trend include Mary Pattillo, *Black on the Block: The Politics of Race and Class in the City* (Chicago: University of

Chicago Press, 2007), 3; Katherine Tate, *From Protest to Politics: The New Black Voters in American Elections* (New York: Sage Foundation, 1993); Michael B. Preston, Lenneal J. Henderson Jr., and Paul L. Puryear, *The New Black Politics: The Search for Political Power*, 2nd ed. (New York: Longman, 1987); Carol M. Swain, *Black Faces, Black Interests: The Representation of African Americans in Congress* (Cambridge, MA: Harvard University Press, 1995); Browning, Marshall, and Tabb, *Protest Is Not Enough;* Robin D. G. Kelley, *Race Rebels: Culture, Politics, and the Black Working Class* (New York: The Free Press, 1996); Kelley, *Yo Mama's Disfunktional! Fighting the Culture Wars in Urban America* (Boston: Beacon, 2001); Cathy J. Cohen, *Democracy Remixed: Black Youth and the Future of American Politics* (New York: Oxford University Press, 2010); and Marcus Anthony Hunter, "The Nightly Round: Space, Social Capital and Urban Black Nightlife," *City and Community* 9, no. 2 (2010): 165–86.

For a discussion of the larger rise of Black mayors in the post–civil rights era, see J. Phillip Thompson III, *Double Trouble: Black Mayors, Black Communities, and the Call for a Deep Democracy* (New York, NY: Oxford University Press, 2006).

10. The literature on agency is quite rich and vast. However, there have been two major strands in this area, that is, agency as a form of delegation, and agency as a sense of free will vis-à-vis Protestantism. Perhaps heavily influenced the most by sociologist Max Weber, *Economy and Society: An Outline of Interpretive Sociology* (Berkeley: University of California Press, 1978), the work on agency has revealed that the actions and attitudes of "everyday" men and women have both an empirical and theoretical significance, especially in understanding structure and structural change. Here we also mean to invoke the notion of *political agency* as offered by Hunter, *Black Citymakers*, and cultural accomplishment as indicated by Zandria Felice Robinson, *This Ain't Chicago: Race, Class, and Regional Identity in the Post-soul South* (Chapel Hill: University of North Carolina Press, 2014). As Hunter shows, political agency includes the ability of citizens to develop political frames for issues, mobilize, migrate, and vote.

See also, for example, Margaret Archer, *Being Human: The Problem of Agency* (New York: Cambridge University Press, 2001); James S. Coleman, *Foundations of Social Theory* (Cambridge, MA: Harvard University Press, 1990); Max Weber, *The Theory of Social and Economic Organization* (New York: Free Press, 1964); Weber, *The Protestant Ethic and the Spirit of Capitalism* (New York: Routledge, 2002); Erving Goffman, *The Presentation of Self in Everyday Life* (New York: Doubleday, 1959); Arlie Hochschild, *The Managed Heart: The Commercialization of Human Feeling*, 2nd ed. (Berkeley: University of California Press, 2003); Hans Joas, *The Creativity of Action* (Chicago: University of Chicago Press, 1996); Talcott Parsons, *The Structure of Social Action: A Study in Social Theory with Special Reference to a Group of Recent European Writers*, vol. 1 (New York: Free Press, 1968); Charles Taylor, *Human Agency and Language: Philosophical Papers I* (New York: Cambridge University Press, 1985); Linda M. G. Zerilli, *Feminism and the Abyss of Freedom* (Chicago: University of Chicago Press, 2005); Jeffrey C. Alexander, *The Civil Sphere* (New York: Oxford University Press, 2006); Albert O. Hirschman, *Exit, Voice and Loyalty: Responses to Decline in Firms, Organizations, and States* (Cambridge, MA: Harvard University Press, 1970); Mustafa Emirbayer and Ann Mische, "What Is Agency?," *American Journal of Sociology* 103, no. 4 (1998): 962–1023; Susan P. Shapiro, "Agency Theory," *Annual Review of Sociology* 31 (2005): 263–84; Julia Adams, "Principals and Agents, Colonialists and Company Men: The Decay of Colonial Control in the Dutch East Indies," *American Sociological Review* 61 (1996): 12–28; Adams, "1-800-How-Am-I-Driving? Agency in Social Science History," *Social Science History* 35, no. 1 (2011): 1–17; Hunter, "Nightly Round"; James Scott, *Weapons of the Weak: Everyday Forms of Peasant Resistance* (New Haven, CT: Yale University Press, 2008); Scott, *Seeing Like a State: How Certain Schemes for Improving the Human Condition Have Failed* (New Haven, CT: Yale University Press, 1999); and Frances Fox Piven and Richard A. Cloward, *Poor People's Movements: Why They Succeed, How They Fail* (New York: Pantheon Books, 1977).

As relates to Black politics, we also draw on the key ideas about Black voters, institutions, and politics. See Adolph Reed, *Race, Politics, and Culture* (New York: Greenwood, 1986); Aldon D. Morris, *The Origins of the Civil Rights Movement: Black Communities Organizing for Change* (New York: Free Press, 1986); Preston, Henderson, and Puryear, *New Black Politics;* Tate, *From Protest to Politics;* Albert K. Karnig and Susan Welch, *Black Representation and Urban Policy* (Chicago: University of Chicago Press, 1980); Thompson, *Double Trouble.* See also Michael C. Dawson, *Behind the Mule: Race and Class in African-American Politics* (Princeton: Princeton University Press, 1994); Charles P. Henry, *Culture and African American Politics* (Bloomington: Indiana University Press, 1990); and Cathy J. Cohen, *The Boundaries of Blackness: AIDS and the Breakdown of Black Politics* (Chicago: University of Chicago Press, 1999).

11. Pattillo, *Black on the Block;* Robinson, *This Ain't Chicago;* Du Bois, *Philadelphia Negro;* Hunter, *Black Citymakers;* Cohen, *Democracy Remixed;* Drake and Cayton, *Black Metropolis;* Thomas Sugrue, *The Origins of Urban Crisis: Race and Inequality in Postwar Detroit* (Princeton: Princeton University Press, 1996); Raymond A. Mohl, "Making the Second Ghetto in Metropolitan Miami, 1940–1960," *Journal of Urban History* 21 (1995): 395–427; Michael B. Katz, ed., *The "Underclass" Debate: Views from History* (Princeton: Princeton University Press, 1993); Arnold Hirsch and Raymond Mohl, eds., *Urban Policy in Twentieth-Century America* (New Brunswick: Rutgers University Press, 1993); Charles F. Casey-Leininger, "Making the Second Ghetto in Cincinnati: Avondale, 1925–1970," in *Race and the City: Work, Community, and Protest in Cincinnati, 1820–1970,* ed., Henry Louis Taylor Jr. (Urbana: University of Illinois Press, 1993), 232–57; William Julius Wilson, *Truly Disadvantaged: The Inner City, the Underclass, and Public Policy* (Chicago: University of Chicago Press, 1987); and

Wilson, *When Work Disappears: The World of the New Urban Poor* (New York: Knopf, 1996).

For some of the most notable discussions and studies of the "initial" ghetto, see Gilbert Osofky, *Harlem: The Making of a Ghetto, 1890–1930* (New York: Harper and Row, 1963); Allan Spear, *Black Chicago: The Making of a Negro Ghetto, 1890–1920* (Chicago: University of Chicago Press, 1967); Kenneth L. Kusmer, *A Ghetto Takes Shape: Black Cleveland, 1870–1930* (Urbana: University of Illinois Press, 1976); Mitchell Duneier, *Ghetto: The Invention of a Place, the History of an Idea* (New York: Macmillan, 2016); and Robert J. Sampson, *Great American City: Chicago and the Enduring Neighborhood Effect* (Chicago: University of Chicago Press, 2013).

12. See, for example, Michelle Alexander, *The New Jim Crow: Mass Incarceration in the Age of Colorblindness* (New York: New Press, 2012); Isabel Wilkerson, *The Warmth of Other Suns: The Epic Story of America's Great Migration* (New York: Vintage Books, 2011); and James Baldwin, *Notes of a Native Son* (New York: Beacon, 1955).

13. Much of this discussion occurs in an analysis of the deterioration of urban Black neighborhoods in the wake of deindustrialization. With the increasing social isolation of urban Black poor and working-class residents, scholars have stressed the critical role that middle-class Blacks played as social and political buffers between Whites and poor Blacks. In these analyses researchers often emphasize the out-migration and disappearance of the urban Black middle class to explain the general dilapidation and decline of urban Black neighborhoods in the post–civil rights context. For a more detailed discussion of this topic, see Wilson, *When Work Disappears;* Elijah Anderson, *Streetwise: Race, Class and Change in an Urban Community* (Chicago: University of Chicago Press, 1990); Conley, *Being Black;* and Patrick Sharkey, *Stuck in Place: Urban Neighborhoods and the End of Progress toward Racial Equality* (Chicago: University of Chicago Press, 2013).

There has been debate, however, about the role and disappearance of the Black middle class claimed in existing scholarship such as the aforementioned research. Recent research has not only suggested that the Black middle class continues to reside in urban Black neighborhoods but also points to a reciprocal relationship between poor and middle-class Blacks. The most notable works in this regard include Mary Pattillo-McCoy, *Black Picket Fences: Privilege and Peril among the Black Middle Class* (Chicago: University of Chicago Press, 1999); Pattillo, *Black on the Block;* Cohen, *Boundaries of Blackness;* and Arnold R. Hirsch, *Making the Second Ghetto: Race and Housing in Chicago, 1940–1960* (Chicago: University of Chicago Press, 1983).

For further elaboration of the concept of a *second ghetto,* see Douglas S. Massey and Nancy A. Denton, *American Apartheid: Segregation and the Making of the Underclass* (Cambridge, MA: Harvard University Press, 1993); and June Manning Thomas and Marsha Ritzdorf, eds., *Urban Planning and the African*

American Community (Thousand Oaks, CA: Sage, 1996). See also Lee Rainwater, *Behind Ghetto Walls: Black Families in a Federal Slum* (Chicago: Aldine, 1970); Carol B. Stack, *All Our Kin: Strategies for Survival in a Black Community* (New York: Harper and Row, 1974); Ulf Hannerz, *Soulside: Inquiries into Ghetto Culture and Community* (New York: Columbia University Press, 1969); Massey and Denton, *American Apartheid;* Camille Zubrinsky Charles, "The Dynamics of Racial Residential Segregation," *Annual Review of Sociology* 29 (2003): 167–207; and David Harding, "Cultural Context, Sexual Behavior, and Romantic Relationships in Disadvantaged Neighborhoods," *American Sociological Review* 72, no. 3 (2007): 341–64.

Some notable examples of this work include Anderson, *Streetwise;* Sudhir Alladi Venkatesh, *Off the Books: The Underground Economy of the Urban Poor* (Cambridge, MA: Harvard University Press, 2006); Venkatesh, *American Project: The Rise and Fall of a Modern Ghetto* (Cambridge, MA: Harvard University Press, 2000); Mitchell Duneier, *Sidewalk* (New York: Farrar, Strauss, and Giroux, 1999); Pattillo, *Black on the Block;* Pattillo-McCoy, *Black Picket Fences;* Steven Gregory, *Black Corona: Race and the Politics of Place in an Urban Community* (Princeton: Princeton University Press, 1998); Hannerz, *Soulside;* William G. Hawkeswood, *One of the Children: Gay Black Men in Harlem* (Berkeley: University of California Press, 1992); John L. Jackson, *Harlemworld: Doing Race and Class in Contemporary Black America* (Chicago: University of Chicago Press, 2001); Jane Jacobs, *The Death and Life of Great American Cities* (New York: Random House, 1981); Elliot Liebow, *Tally's Corner* (Boston: Little, Brown, 1967); Herbert Gans, *The Urban Villagers: Group and Class in the Life of Italian-Americans* (New York: Free Press, 1962); and Jay MacLeod, *Ain't No Makin' It: Aspirations and Attainment in a Low-Income Neighborhood* (Boulder, CO: Westview, 1987).

14. Within those regions, we also highlight distinctions based on the movement of Black folks between and across spaces. While we emphasize the contiguous United States, our data does include major locales in Hawaii and Alaska. Due to the imprecision of the 1950 U.S. census data that coincides with both states' entry into the union, we acknowledge the limits this posed for our analysis. As a result, we have made necessary adjustments and are sensitive in our analysis and language to the special cases that Hawaii, Alaska, the Virgin Islands, Guam, and Puerto Rico have relative to the U.S. census data we access and examine here.

15. Carol Stack writes that during her fieldwork for *All Our Kin,* she noticed children leaving the community to go visit relatives Down South, but did not until later grasp the full importance of this movement, some of which she details in *Call to Home: African Americans Reclaim the Rural South* (New York: Basic Books, 1996). However, for children already Down South, as it were, in Memphis, Louisville, Charlotte, or Atlanta, Down South may have meant being sent to the country for the summer—down to the Delta, to rural Georgia, or to small-town North Carolina. Down South is also reflective of tensions around where one is located on chocolate maps. That is, the South is only "down" to folks who

reside in the geographic and discursive North. For people on Chicago's South Side, Down South may mean the Mississippi Delta. For people in Philadelphia, Down South may mean the Georgia Piedmont, the Virginia Chesapeake, or Carolina Hills. Still, regardless of one's location on the chocolate maps, Down South is always representative of a relation between places, low and high, Black Bottoms and Beverly Hills, South Sides and North Sides, and thus captures how Black people think about their geographic and cultural relationship to the region and place. Thus, Down South is both a relative geography from the traditional North to the traditional South, as well as a mapping of the diversity of space in the South, for instance, from urban to rural.

CHAPTER FIVE. THE BLACKER THE VILLAGE, THE SWEETER THE JUICE

1. Solomon Northup, *Twelve Years a Slave* (New York: Norton, 2016). Recently, Northup's experience has received more popular attention, best evidenced in the Oscar-winning film *Twelve Years a Slave* (2014). For more, see also James Olney, "'I Was Born': Slave Narratives, Their Status as Autobiography and as Literature," *Callaloo* 20 (1984): 46–73; Joyce Ladner, *Tomorrow's Tomorrow: The Black Woman* (Garden City, NY: Doubleday, 1971); Robert B. Stepto, *From behind the Veil: A Study of Afro-American Narrative* (Urbana: University of Illinois Press, 1991); Marcus Wood, *Blind Memory: Visual Representations of Slavery in England and America, 1780–1865* (Manchester: Manchester University Press, 2000); and Frances Smith Foster, *Witnessing Slavery: The Development of Ante-bellum Slave Narratives* (Madison: University of Wisconsin Press, 1979).

2. Du Bois, *Black Reconstruction in America, 1860–1880* (1935; repr., New York: Free Press, 1998), 13.

3. Our reference here is of course to Douglas S. Massey and Nancy A. Denton, *American Apartheid: Segregation and the Making of the Underclass* (Cambridge, MA: Harvard University Press, 1993), wherein they demonstrate significant patterns of racial residential segregation across urban America, particularly in Great Migration destinations and the conventional North.

4. For more on the yellow fever epidemic in Memphis and the South, see Margaret Humphreys, *Yellow Fever and the South* (Baltimore: Johns Hopkins University Press, 1999); John H. Ellis, *Yellow Fever and Public Health in the New South* (Lexington: University Press of Kentucky, 2015); David K. Patterson, "Yellow Fever Epidemics and Mortality in the United States, 1693–1905," *Social Science and Medicine* 34, no. 8 (1992): 855–65; and Khaled J. Bloom, *The Mississippi Valley's Great Yellow Fever Epidemic of 1878* (Baton Rouge: Louisiana State University Press, 1993).

5. W. E. B Du Bois, *The Souls of Black Folk* (Oxford: Oxford University Press, 1903), 100.

6. Ibid., 119.

7. Ibid. Du Bois continues this important point: "All this segregation by color is largely independent of that natural clustering by social grades common to all communities. . . . One thing, however, seldom occurs: the best of the whites and the best of the Negroes almost never live in anything like close proximity. . . . This is a vast change from the situation in the past, when, through the close contact of master and house-servant in the patriarchal big house, one found the best of both races in close contact and sympathy" (119).

8. Ida B. Wells, *Crusade for Justice: The Autobiography of Ida B. Wells* (Chicago: University of Chicago Press, 2013).

9. Ibid. See also Jacqueline Jones Royster, ed. *Southern Horrors and Other Writings: The Anti-lynching Campaign of Ida B. Wells, 1892-1900* (Boston: Bedford Books, 1997).

10. Ida B. Wells, editorial, *Free Speech*, May 21, 1892.

11. Ibid. See also Ida B. Wells-Barnett, *Southern Horrors: Lynch Law in All Its Phases* (New York: New York Age Print, 1892-94), 3.

12. Wells-Barnett, *Southern Horrors*.

13. Ibid., 19.

14. Wells, *Crusade for Justice*, 230.

15. Jacqueline Jones Royster, "To Call a Thing by Its True Name: The Rhetoric of Ida B. Wells," *Reclaiming Rhetorica: Women in the Rhetorical Tradition*, no. 1 (1995): 167-84.

16. Wells, *Crusade for Justice*, 240.

17. St. Clair Drake and Horace Cayton, *Black Metropolis: A Study of Negro Life in a Northern City.* Chicago: University of Chicago Press, 1993.

18. Wells, *Crusade for Justice*, 240.

CHAPTER SIX. THE TWO MS. JOHNSONS

1. Evelyn Brooks Higginbotham, *Righteous Discontent: The Women's Movement in the Black Baptist Church, 1880-1920* (Cambridge, MA: Harvard University Press, 1993).

2. Michael Kasino, dir., *Pay It No Mind: The Life and Times of Marsha P. Johnson* (New York: Redux Pictures, 2012), YouTube video, 55:30, posted by Michael Kasino, October 15, 2012, www.youtube.com/watch?v=rjN9W2KstqE.

3. Deborah K. King "Multiple Jeopardy, Multiple Consciousness: The Context of a Black Feminist Ideology," *Signs* 14, no. 1 (1988): 42-72.

4. Kimberlé Crenshaw, "Mapping the Margins: Intersectionality, Identity Politics, and Violence against Women of Color," *Stanford Law Review* 43, no. 6 (1991): 1241-99.

5. Kasino, *Pay It No Mind.*

6. Ibid.; Tyler Born, "Marsha 'Pay It No Mind' Johnson," accessed September 20, 2016, http://outhistory.org/exhibits/show/tgi-bios/marsha-p-johnson; Reina Gossett and Sasha Wortzel, *Happy Birthday Marsha*, official trailer, accessed September 20, 2016, www.happybirthdaymarsha.com/; Blake Bakkila, "The Transgender Heroines Who Started a Revolution," *People*, August 1, 2016, www.people.com/article/weve-been-around-transgender-docuseries-marsha-johnson-sylvia-rivera; Jessi Gan, "'Still at the Back of the Bus': Sylvia Rivera's Struggle," *CENTRO: Journal of the Center for Puerto Rican Studies* 19, no. 1 (2007): 124–40; and David Carter, *Stonewall: The Riots That Sparked the Gay Revolution* (New York: St. Martin's Press, 2004).

7. Kasino, *Pay It No Mind.* See also Leslie Feinberg, *Transgender Warriors: Making History from Joan of Arc to Dennis Rodman* (Boston: Beacon, 1996).

8. Kasino, *Pay It No Mind.*

9. Ibid.

10. Ibid.; Kate Bornstein and S. Bear Bergman, *Gender Outlaws: The Next Generation* (Berkeley, CA: Seal, 2010); Eva Hayward, "Lessons from a Starfish," in *Queering the Non/Human*, ed. Myra Hird (New York: Routledge, 2008), 249–63.

11. "Police Beating a Trans Woman Who Was Later Murdered," YouTube video, 8:26, posted by ehipassiko, November 24, 2008, www.youtube.com/watch?v=-IAPTk69XPo. See also Robbie Brown, "Murder of Transgender Woman Revives Scrutiny," *New York Times*, November 17, 2008; Japhy Grant, "Duanna Johnson Murdered 'Execution Style' in Memphis," *Queerty*, November 11, 2008, www.queerty.com/duanna-johnson-murdered-execution-style-in-memphis-20081111; Mik Kinkead, "Remembering Duanna Johnson," *GLAAD*, November 14, 2008, www.glaad.org/2008/11/14/remembering-duanna-johnson; and "Memphis Police Officer Caught on Tape Beating Transsexual," *Huffington Post*, May 25, 2011, www.huffingtonpost.com/2008/06/18/memphis-police-officer-ca_n_107797.html (video removed).

12. "Police Beating."

13. See "Police Beating"; and Brown, "Murder of Transgender Woman."

14. "Police Beating"; Brown, "Murder of Transgender Woman."

15. See Cathy J. Cohen, *The Boundaries of Blackness: AIDS and the Breakdown of Black Politics* (Chicago: University of Chicago Press, 1999).

16. Kimberlé Crenshaw, "The Girls Obama Forgot," *New York Times*, July 29, 2014.

17. The idea of "say her name" is drawn from a set of initiatives at the African American Policy Forum; see "Initiatives: #SayHerName," AAPF, accessed September 20, 2016, www.aapf.org/sayhername/.

CHAPTER SEVEN. MAKING NEGROTOWN

1. Richard Wright, *Native Son* (New York: Random House, 2000); Richard Wright *Black Boy: A Record of Childhood and Youth* (New York: Random House, 2000); Cheryl Higashida, "Aunt Sue's Children: Re-viewing the Gender(ed) Politics of Richard Wright's Radicalism," *American Literature* 75, no. 2 (2003): 395–425.

2. Carol B. Stack, *Call to Home: African Americans Reclaim the Rural South* (New York: Basic Books, 1996).

3. Kiese Laymon, *Long Division* (Chicago: Agate, 2013).

4. Malcolm D. Lee, dir., *Welcome Home, Roscoe Jenkins* (Universal City, CA: Universal Studios, 2008).

5. Data for this chapter is drawn from a combination of field notes, interviews, oral histories, and family archives from and with the Robinson family, collected over 2010–16.

6. Clyde Woods, *Development Arrested: Race, Power and the Blues in the Mississippi Delta* (New York: Verso, 1998), 17.

7. Keith Wailoo, *Dying in the City of the Blues: Sickle Cell Anemia and the Politics of Race and Health* (Chapel Hill: University of North Carolina Press, 2014). See also Wailoo, *Drawing Blood: Technology and Disease Identity in Twentieth-Century America* (Baltimore: Johns Hopkins University Press, 1999).

8. The 2016 Emmy winner for Best Variety Show, *Key and Peele* commonly takes on issues of race in America. Here we draw on the season 4 finale episode, wherein the "Negro Town" sketch appears. Peter Atencio, dir., "Negro Town," *Key and Peele* (New York: Comedy Central, 2015).

9. Zora Neale Hurston, *Dust Tracks on a Road: An Autobiography* (1942; repr., New York: Harper Perennial, 1991), 1.

10. Adolph Reed Jr, "Romancing Jim Crow: Black Nostalgia for a Segregated Past," *Village Voice*, April 16, 1996, 24–29.

CHAPTER EIGHT. WHEN AND WHERE THE SPIRIT MOVES YOU

1. This chapter draws heavily from the autobiography Aretha Franklin, *Aretha: From These Roots* (New York: Villard Books, 1999). See also Mark Bego, *Aretha Franklin: The Queen of Soul* (New York: Skyhorse, 2013).

2. "Abandoned Birthplace of Aretha Franklin," *Roadside America*, accessed September 20, 2016, www.roadsideamerica.com/story/34301; Alex Coleman, "Memphis-Born Aretha Franklin's Old Home Deserves Some R-E-S-P-E-C-T," *WREG Memphis News Channel 3*, May 12, 2014, http://wreg.com/2014/05/12/memphis-born-aretha-franklins-old-home-deserves-some-r-e-s-p-e-c-t/;

"Judge Orders Aretha Franklin's Childhood Home in Tennessee to Be Torn Down," *Fox 8,* accessed September 20, 2016, http://myfox8.com/2016/06/15/judge-orders-aretha-franklins-childhood-home-in-tenessee-to-be-torn-down/.

3. George Davis and O. Fred Donaldson, *Blacks in the United States: A Geographic Perspective* (Boston: Houghton Mifflin, 1975), 44–47.

4. Franklin, *Aretha;* Bego, *Aretha Franklin.*

5. Ibid.

6. Franklin, *Aretha.*

7. Aretha Franklin, "God Bless the Child," *The Tender, the Moving, the Swinging Aretha Franklin* (New York: Columbia Records, 1962); Franklin, "Bridge over Troubled Waters," *Amazing Grace* (Los Angeles: Atlantic Records, 1972).

8. *Amazing Grace* would go on to double-platinum status based on domestic sales, and earn Franklin a Grammy Award in 1973 for Best Soul Gospel Performance.

9. Aretha Franklin, "Mary, Don't You Weep," *Amazing Grace* (Los Angeles: Atlantic Records, 1972).

10. Ibid.

11. Aretha Franklin, "Dr. Feelgood," *I Never Loved a Man the Way I Love You* (Los Angeles: Atlantic Records, 1967).

12. Aretha Franklin, "Respect," *I Never Loved a Man the Way I Love You* (Los Angeles: Atlantic Records, 1967).

13. Mark Anthony Neal, *Soul Babies: Black Popular Culture and the Post-soul Aesthetic.* (New York: Routledge, 2002).

CHAPTER NINE. HOW BRENDA'S BABY
GOT CALIFORNIA LOVE

1. "Spanish Harlem" was originally recorded by Ben E. King in 1960, but Franklin's 1971 cover remains its most popular version. In her rendition Franklin reconfigures the song's opening, adding the descriptor "black" into the song. In the original version the rose is red. Infusing black into the song is thus not an accident but an important gesture toward and foreshadowing of the urban Black experience and the "concrete jungle" that would come to serve as a major driver of the hip-hop genre and aesthetic.

2. The role of Motown as a sight for the construction and production of popular Black culture and music cannot be overstated. Led by the pioneering vision of Berry Gordy, Motown would produce legendary acts, including Michael Jackson, Diana Ross, Stevie Wonder, Mary Wells, Smokey Robinson, Rick James, and the Temptations, just to name a few. Though no longer the powerhouse it once was in its 1960–80s heyday, by the 1990s Motown saw resurgence under Kedar Massenberg's leadership through the neo-soul music scene, with artists such as

Erykah Badu. For a fuller discussion of Motown and Detroit, see Nelson George, *Where Did Our Love Go? The Rise and Fall of the Motown Sound* (Urbana: University of Illinois Press, 2007); Suzanne E. Smith, *Dancing in the Street: Motown and the Cultural Politics of Detroit* (Cambridge, MA: Harvard University Press, 2009); David Morse, *Motown and the Arrival of Black Music* (New York: Macmillan, 1971); Gerald Lyn Early, *One Nation under a Groove: Motown and American Culture* (Ann Arbor: University of Michigan Press, 2004); and Berry Gordy, *To Be Loved: The Music, the Magic, the Memories of Motown* (New York: Warner Books, 2013).

One of the triumvirates of Black soul music, along with Motown and Philadelphia International, Stax proved to be a major sonic safe space for iconic artists such as Aretha Franklin, Gladys Knight, and Al Green. Now historicized in the city of Memphis, though on a slightly different land and location, the museum offers tours and historical information about the life and legacy of this significant Black music house. In recent years Stax has witnessed a modest return through current artists such as Angie Stone. For a richer understanding, see the following: Rob Bowman, *Soulsville, USA: The Story of Stax Records* (New York: Schirmer Trade Books, 1997); Bowman, "The Stax Sound: A Musicological Analysis," *Popular Music* 14, no. 3 (1995): 285–320; Larry Nager, *Memphis Beat: The Lives and Times of America's Musical Crossroads* (New York: St. Martin's Press, 1998); and Robert Gordon, *Respect Yourself: Stax Records and the Soul Explosion* (New York: Bloomsbury, 2013). For example, Chris Gibson, "Recording Studios: Relational Spaces of Creativity in the City," *Built Environment* 31, no. 3 (2005): 192–207, is especially generative and comfirmable of the importance and spatial intersectionality of soul and chocolate cities.

Under the leadership of Black music producers and entrepreneurs Kenny Gamble and Arthur Huff, Philadelphia International would emerge over the 1960s to the 1980s as a major Black music house. Producing hits and classics for artists such as the Jacksons, the O'Jays, Patti Labelle, Phyllis Hyman, Lou Rawls, and Teddy Pendergrass, Gamble and Huff remain pioneers in Black music. Later years would see the company in a long transition, eventually with more recent iterations coming through music projects with contemporary R&B artist Ledisi. For a fuller discussion and examination, see the thorough study John A. Jackson, *A House on Fire: The Rise and Fall of Philadelphia Soul* (New York: Oxford University Press, 2004).

3. Dave Mays, qtd. in Paul Cantor, "How the 1995 Source Awards Changed Rap Forever," *Complex Magazine*, August 3, 2015. Clips of the awards show are also scattered across YouTube, as the digital version for mass release has never occurred.

4. Cantor, "Source Awards."

5. Though the footage and remarks provided here are from an original home recording, the scene clip can also be found here: "Suge Knight Disses Puff

Daddy," *Source Awards,* YouTube video, 1:04, posted by Felix Montana, August 3, 1995, www.youtube.com/watch?v=mv2OMXngkEs. More footage includes a reaction later that evening from Snoop Dogg: "Death Row Diss," YouTube video, 1:22, posted by LokoSamoan, April 11, 2006, www.youtube.com/watch?v=JpgpS3ogvMM; and from Puffy: "The Notorious B I G Ft Puff Daddy and Lil Kim Live at Source Awards, 1995," YouTube video, 4:59, posted by Pablo Granja, July 8, 2011, www.youtube.com/watch?v=zvA56qWhMME&list=RDzvA 56qWhMME.

6. Imani Perry, *Prophets of the Hood: Politics and Poetics in Hip Hop* (Durham: Duke University Press, 2004); Tricia Rose, *Black Noise: Rap Music and Black Culture in Contemporary America* (Middletown, CT: Wesleyan University Press, 1994); H. Samy Alim, *Roc the Mic Right: The Language of Hip Hop Culture* (New York: Routledge, 2006).

7. Nelson George, *The Death of Rhythm and Blues* (New York: Penguin, 2003); see also George, *Hip Hop America* (New York: Penguin, 2005).

8. See Charles Earl Jones, *The Black Panther Party (Reconsidered)* (Baltimore: Black Classic Press, 1998).

9. Afeni Shakur, "Tupac Amaru Shakur Foundation Mission Statement," unpublished papers, Stone Mountain, CA, 2000). See also Afeni Shakur's keynote address at Vanderbilt University; the audio is available free here: "Lecture: Afeni Shakur Delivers Keynote Address of Vanderbilt University's Black History Month Commemoration," *Discover Archive,* February 9, 2007, http://discoverarchive.vanderbilt.edu/handle/1803/878.

10. Our discussion and understanding of Shakur are informed especially by the following: Tupac Shakur, *The Rose That Grew from Concrete* (New York: Simon and Schuster, 2009); Tupac Shakur et al., *Tupac: Resurrection, 1971–1996* (New York: Simon and Schuster, 2003); and Academy Award–nominated documentary *Tupac: Resurrection,* dir. Lauren Lazin (Los Angeles: Paramount Pictures, 2003). See also "Tupac Shakur: The Lost Interview," *Vibe,* YouTube video, 24:17, posted by TheDarkAssassins1511, October 14, 2013, www.youtube.com/watch?v=NPP3Up4pdVE.

11. Lazin, *Tupac,* 16:00–20:00. The authors transcribed the quotations from this film.

12. "Same Song" was recorded by the Digital Underground (featuring 2pac) in 1990 and appeared in 1991 on the movie soundtrack *Nothing but Trouble.* Produced by Shock G, the record was released through Tommy Boy Records (New York, 1991).

13. Lazin, *Tupac.*

14. Ibid., 25:00–30:00.

15. Ibid.

16. Ibid.

17. Ibid., 42:00–47:00.

18. Shakur, *Rose That Grew;* Shakur et al., *Tupac;* Lazin, *Tupac.* See also "Tupac Shakur."

19. Lazin, *Tupac,* 61:00–80:00.

20. Kendrick Lamar, "Mortal Man," *To Pimp a Butterfly* (Los Angeles: Top Dawg Entertainment/Santa Monica: Aftermath Entertainment; Interscope Records, 2015). Transcription by the authors.

21. The scene clip can be seen here: "Outkast Winning Best New Rap Group at the Source Awards, 1995," YouTube video, 5:36, posted by TheMaxTrailers, October 12, 2014, www.youtube.com/watch?v=vwLG7aSYM3w. See also Cantor, "Source Awards"; and Zandria Felice Robinson, *This Ain't Chicago: Race, Class, and Regional Identity in the Post-soul South* (Chapel Hill: University of North Carolina Press, 2014).

CHAPTER TEN. BOUNCE TO THE CHOCOLATE CITY FUTURE

1. On Big Freedia, see, for example, Holly Hobbs, "'I Used That Katrina Water to Master My Flow': Rap Performance, Disaster, and Recovery in New Orleans," *SouthernSpaces,*May6,2015,https://southernspaces.org/2015/i-used-katrina-water-master-my-flow-rap-performance-disaster-and-recovery-new-orleans; and Big Freedia's autobiography, *God Save the Queen Diva,* with Nicole Balin (New York: Gallery Books, 2015).

2. See, for example, "VLOG: Throw Back Thursday //Twerking in the Supermarket," YouTube video, 8:32, posted by GrowWithNiki Gaga, December 3, 2015, www.youtube.com/watch?v=T7DHSzLGCgY; and Kyra D. Gaunt, "YouTube, Twerking and You: Context Collapse and the Handheld Co-presence of Black Girls and Miley Cyrus," *Journal of Popular Music Studies* 27, no. 3 (2015): 244–73.

3. Kim Marie Vaz, *The "Baby Dolls": Breaking the Race and Gender Barriers of the New Orleans Mardi Gras Tradition* (Baton Rouge: Louisiana State University Press, 2013), 13. See also Matt Miller, *Bounce: Rap Music and Local Identity in New Orleans* (Amherst: University of Massachusetts Press, 2012); Farah Jasmine Griffin, "Children of Omar Resistance and Reliance in the Expressive Cultures of Black New Orleans Cultures," *Journal of Urban History* 35, no. 5 (2009): 656–67; and Michael Patrick Welch et al., *New Orleans: The Underground Guide* (Baton Rouge: Louisiana State University Press, 2014).

4. Big Freedia, *God Save the Queen Diva.*

5. Beyoncé, "Formation," *Lemonade* (Los Angeles: Parkwood Entertainment, 2016). For a rich analysis of the album and accompanying aesthetic, see Zandria Felice Robinson, "Beyonce's Black Southern Formation," *Rolling Stone,* February 8, 2016; and Robinson, "How Beyonce's 'Lemonade' Exposes the Inner Lives of Black Women," *Rolling Stone,* April 28, 2016.

6. Big Freedia, *God Save the Queen Diva*. See also, for example, Matt Sledge, "Bounce Star Big Freedia Pleads Guilty to Theft of Nearly $35k in Section 8 Housing Vouchers," *Advocate*, March 18, 2016.

CHAPTER ELEVEN. THE HOUSE THAT JANE BUILT

1. Steven Lukes, *Power* (New York: New York University Press, 1986), 79.

2. James C. Scott, *Seeing Like a State: How Certain Schemes to Improve the Human Condition Have Failed* (New Haven, CT: Yale University Press, 2008), 197. Scott's deeply important insight also conjures his notion of infrapolitics, or the politics of below, that further guides our perspective and analysis. For a fuller understanding, see Scott, *Weapons of the Weak: Everyday Forms of Peasant Resistance* (New Haven, CT: Yale University Press, 2008); Robin D. G. Kelley, *Race Rebels: Culture, Politics, and the Black Working Class* (New York: Simon and Schuster, 1996); Michael Omi and Howard Winant, *Racial Formation in the United States* (New York: Routledge, 2014); George Lipsitz, *The Possessive Investment in Whiteness: How White People Profit from Identity Politics* (Philadelphia: Temple University Press, 2006); David Croteau and William Hoynes, *Media/Society: Industries, Images, and Audiences* (Thousand Oaks, CA: Sage, 2013); and Joe R. Feagin, *Racist America: Roots, Current Realities, and Future Reparations* (New York: Routledge, 2014).

3. Scott, *Weapons of the Weak*.

4. For a fuller discussion see, for example, Natalie Hopkinson, *Go-Go Live: The Musical Life and Death of a Chocolate City* (Durham: Duke University Press, 2012); Audrey Elisa Kerr, *The Paper Bag Principle: Class, Colorism, and Rumor and the Case of Black Washington* (Knoxville: University of Tennessee Press, 2006); and Steven Mintz, "A Historical Ethnography of Black Washington, D.C.," *Records of the Columbia Historical Society, Washington, DC* 52 (1989): 235–53.

5. Cary being her married name, in the chapter we return to her given name and shift after her marriage to her full name, to keep the chronology clear.

6. Our understanding and basis for Mary Ann Shadd Cary's narrative derive from several sources, including Shadd, *A Plea for Emigration; or, Notes of Canada West, in Its Moral, Social, and Political Aspect: With Suggestions Respecting Mexico, W. Indies and Vancouver's Island, for the Information of Colored Emigrants*, no. 47542 (Detroit: Pattison, 1852); and her newspaper, the *Provincial Freeman*. See, for example, the following: Jane Rhodes, *Mary Ann Shadd Cary: The Black Press and Protest in the Nineteenth Century* (Urbana: University of Illinois Press, 1998); Shirley J. Yee, "Finding a Place: Mary Ann Shadd Cary and the Dilemmas of Black Migration to Canada, 1850–1870," *Frontiers: A Journal of Women Studies* 18, no. 3 (1997): 1–16; Rinaldo Walcott, "'Who Is She and What Is She to You?' Mary Ann Shadd Cary and the (Im)possibility of Black/Canadian

Studies," *Atlantis: Critical Studies in Gender, Culture and Social Justice* 24, no. 2 (2000): 137–46; Lana F. Rakow, ed., *Women Making Meaning: New Feminist Directions in Communication* (New York: Routledge, 2015); Richard Almonte, introd. to *A Plea for Emigration; or, Notes of Canada West* (Toronto: Mercury, 1998); Shirley J. Yee, *Black Women Abolitionists: A Study in Activism, 1828–1860* (Knoxville: University of Tennessee Press, 1992); Daniel G. Hill, *The Freedom-Seekers: Blacks in Early Canada* (1981; repr., Toronto: Stoddard, 1992); and Jim Bearden and Linda Jean Butler, *The Life and Times of Mary Shadd Cary* (Toronto: NC Press, 1977). For more on Washington, DC's U-Street Shaw Corridor, see Blair Ruble, *Washington's U-Street* (Baltimore: Johns Hopkins University Press, 2010).

7. Bearden and Butler, *Life and Times;* Shadd, *Plea for Emigration.*

8. Virginia Legislature, 1849–50, session minutes, 246. Full files can be found at the digital archive, *Hathi Trust Digital Library,* accessed September 20, 2016, https://babel.hathitrust.org/cgi/pt?id=njp.32101073363291;view=1up;seq=252.

9. Ibid.

10. See W. E. B. Du Bois, *Black Reconstruction in America, 1860–1880* (1935; repr., New York: Free Press, 1998).

11. Shadd, *Plea for Emigration,* iii.

12. Ibid., iv.

13. Ibid., 10, 26.

14. Mary Ann Shadd, *Provincial Freeman,* March 25, 1854.

15. Ibid.

16. Bearden and Butler, *Life and Times.*

17. Ibid. See also Martin R. Delany, *The Condition, Elevation, Emigration, and Destiny of the Colored People of the United States* (New York: Black Classic, 1852).

18. Shadd, *Provincial Freeman,* April 19, 1856.

19. Rhodes, *Mary Ann Shadd Cary;* Yee, "Finding a Place"; Walcott, "Who Is She?"; Bearden and Butler, *Life and Times.*

20. Among the many accounts of the Harpers Ferry Raid, W. E. B. Du Bois's *John Brown* (Philadelphia: Jacobs, 1909) is especially insightful and informs our detailing of this historic era.

21. Emancipation Proclamation, January 1, 1863, Presidential Proclamations, 1791–1991, RG 11, General Records of the United States Government, National Archives, Washington, DC.

22. The proclamation goes on to also include the following: "Arkansas, Texas, Louisiana, (except the Parishes of St. Bernard, Plaquemines, Jefferson, St. John, St. Charles, St. James Ascension, Assumption, Terrebonne, Lafourche, St. Mary, St. Martin, and Orleans, including the City of New Orleans), Mississippi, Alabama, Florida, Georgia, South Carolina, North Carolina, and Virginia, (except the forty-eight counties designated as West Virginia, and also the counties of

Berkley, Accomac, Northampton, Elizabeth City, York, Princess Ann, and Norfolk, including the cities of Norfolk and Portsmouth[)], and which excepted parts, are, for the present, left precisely as if this proclamation were not issued." Emancipation Proclamation, National Archives.

23. Rhodes, *Mary Ann Shadd Cary;* Yee, "Finding a Place"; Walcott, "Who Is She?"; Bearden and Butler, *Life and Times.*

24. Bearden and Butler, *Life and Times.*

CHAPTER TWELVE. MARY, DIONNE, AND ALMA

1. Data for this chapter's discussion of Mary Hill Sanders is drawn from a combination of field notes, interviews, oral histories, and family archives from and with the Sanders and Parker family, collected from 2010 to 2016.

2. See "About Us," United Community Corporation, accessed February 7, 2017, www.uccnewark.org/about-us/.

3. Dionne Warwick, "Do You Know the Way to San Jose," *Dionne Warwick in Valley of the Dolls* (New York: Scepter Records, 1968).

4. See, for example, Cyrus S. Keller Moore, "African Americans in California and Our Pioneer Churches," *Age* 4 (1902): 194–97; Douglas Flamming, *Bound for Freedom: Black Los Angeles in Jim Crow America* (Berkeley: University of California Press, 2005); Raphael Sonenshein, *Politics in Black and White: Race and Power in Los Angeles* (Princeton: Princeton University Press, 1993); Laura Pulido, *Black, Brown, Yellow, and Left: Radical Activism in Los Angeles* (Berkeley: University of California Press, 2006); Lawrence B. De Graaf, "The City of Black Angels: Emergence of the Los Angeles Ghetto, 1890–1930," *Pacific Historical Review* 39, no. 3 (1970): 323–52; Scott Kurashige, *The Shifting Grounds of Race: Black and Japanese Americans in the Making of Multiethnic Los Angeles* (Princeton: Princeton University Press, 2010); Darnell Hunt, *Screening the Los Angeles "Riots": Race, Seeing, and Resistance* (New York: Cambridge University Press, 1997); and Darnell Hunt and Ana-Christina Ramón, eds., *Black Los Angeles: American Dreams and Racial Realities* (New York: New York University Press, 2010).

5. Hans Johnson, "Just the Facts: California's Population," *Public Policy Institute of California,* accessed September 20, 2016, www.ppic.org/main/publication_show.asp?i=259.

6. Victor H. Green, *The Negro-Motorist Green Book* (New York: Green, 1949), 1–3.

7. Wendell P. Alston, "The Green Book Helps Solve Travel Problems," in Green, *Negro-Motorist Green Book,* 3.

8. Byron Hurt, *Soul Food Junkies* (New York: PBS Films, 2012).

9. Warwick, "Way to San Jose."

10. Alma Burrell v. County of Santa Clara, May 6, 2013, Official Court Records, 158; Alma Burrell, interview and oral history, San Jose, CA, July 8, 2014.

11. *Burrell*, 1:159.

12. Ibid., 160.

13. Ibid., 164, 165.

14. Ibid., 166.

15. Alma Burrell, Vickye Hayter, Margaret Headd v. County of Santa Clara, Dan Peddycord, Rae Wedel, Marty Fenstersheib and Does 1 through 50, inclusive, original claim, September 14, 2011, 2, 22.

16. Alma Burrell, reflection statement and oral history, San Jose, CA, September 20, 2011.

17. *Burrell, Hayter, Headd*, 13.

18. Ibid., 17; Burrell, interview and oral history, July 8, 2014.

19. *Burrell, Hayter, Headd*, 17.

20. Ibid.

21. Ibid.

22. *Burrell, Hayter, Headd*, 10.

23. Ibid.

24. Ibid.

25. Burrell, interview and oral history, July 8, 2014.

CHAPTER THIRTEEN. LEAVING ON A JET PLANE

1. This episode received global news coverage, some of which can be found here: Sandra E. Garcia, "Yasiin Bey Gives World Passport Visibility," *New York Times*, February 4, 2016; "'The World Is My Country': Shows Origin of Yasiin Bey's World Passport," Vimeo video, 8:37, posted by Arthur Kanegis, accessed September 20, 2016, https://vimeo.com/153306229; and "Mos Def on Why He Left the U.S.: 'America's a Very Challenging Place for Me,'" *Radio.com, May 4, 2015*, http://radio.com/2015/05/04/mos-def-leaving-america-interview/.

2. See also Garry Davis and Greg Guma, *Passport to Freedom: A Guide to World Citizenship* (Arlington, VA: Seven Locks Press, 1992).

3. W. E. B. Du Bois, *The Autobiography of W. E. B. Du Bois: A Soliloquy on Viewing My Life from the Last Decade of Its First Century* (New York: International, 1968), 61. Hereafter cited in the text.

4. See also "Text of the Acheson Statement," *New York Times*, July 13, 1950.

5. See also Manning Marable, *W. E. B. Du Bois: Black Radical Democrat* (New York: Routledge, 2015); Adolph L. Reed Jr., *W. E. B. Du Bois and American Political Thought: Fabianism and the Color Line* (New York: Oxford University Press, 1997); Aldon D. Morris, *The Scholar Denied: W. E. B. Du Bois and the Birth of American Sociology* (Berkeley: University of California Press, 2015).

6. Majority opinion, Kent v. Dulles, 357 U.S. 116 (1958), *Legal Information Institute*, accessed September 20, 2016, www.law.cornell.edu/supremecourt /text/357/116; *Kent v. Dulles, Justia*, accessed September 20, 2016, https:// supreme.justia.com/cases/federal/us/357/116/case.html.

CHAPTER FOURTEEN. SEEING LIKE A CHOCOLATE CITY

1. Danielle Purifoy and Torkwase Johnson, "A Place Called Mebane," *Scalawag*, August 8, 2016, www.scalawagmagazine.org/in-conditions-of-fresh-water /a-place-called-mebane. See also Purifoy, "Finding Black Independence in Mebane," *Scalawag*, August 15, 2016, www.scalawagmagazine.org/in-conditions-of-fresh-water/finding-black-independence-in-mebane.

2. Purifoy, "Place Called Mebane."

3. Ibid.

4. Ibid.

5. Ibid.

6. Derek S. Hyra, *Race, Class, and Politics in the Cappuccino City* (Chicago: University of Chicago Press, 2016).

7. Albert O. Hirschman, *Exit, Voice and Loyalty: Responses to Decline in Firms, Organizations, and States* (Cambridge, MA: Harvard University Press, 1970), 17.

8. James C. Scott, *Seeing Like a State: How Certain Schemes to Improve the Human Condition Have Failed* (New Haven, CT: Yale University Press, 1998), 6–8.

9. Patricia Hill Collins, "The Social Construction of Black Feminist Thought," *Signs* 14, no. 4 (1989): 745–73; Collins, *Black Feminist Thought: Knowledge, Consciousness, and the Politics of Empowerment* (New York: Routledge, 1990).

10. Aldon D. Morris, *The Origins of the Civil Rights Movement* (New York: Simon and Schuster, 1986).

11. Katherine McKittrick, *Demonic Grounds: Black Women and the Cartographies of Struggle* (Minneapolis: University of Minnesota Press, 2006), 145.

12. Ibid., 6.

13. This idea also extends from scholarship that has demonstrated that the inherent design of many tools of scientific measurement and analysis are influenced by racism and the notion of Whiteness as the norm. For a rich and fuller discussion, see Tukufu Zuberi and Eduardo Bonilla-Silva, eds., *White Logic, White Methods: Racism and Methodology* (New York: Rowman and Littlefield, 2008).

14. Paul Gilroy, *The Black Atlantic: Modernity and Double Consciousness* (Cambridge, MA: Harvard University Press, 1993).

15. Beth Richie, *Arrested Justice: Black Women, Violence, and America's Prison Nation* (New York: New York University Press, 2012).

16. Jürgen Habermas, *The Theory of Communicative Action*, vol. 2, *A Critique of Functional Reason*, trans. Thomas A. McCarthy (Boston: Beacon, 1987).

17. W. E. B. Du Bois, *The Souls of Black Folk* (Oxford: Oxford University Press, 1903), 58.

18. William Julius Wilson, *The Truly Disadvantaged: The Inner City, the Underclass, and Public Policy.* Chicago: University of Chicago Press, 1987.

19. Du Bois, *Souls of Black Folk*, 60–61.

20. Parag Khanna, *Connectography: Mapping the Future of Global Civilization* (New York: Random House, 2016), 45, 6.

21. Nikhil Singh, *Black Is a Country* (Cambridge, MA: Harvard University Press, 2004), 222.

Bibliography

"Abandoned Birthplace of Aretha Franklin." *Roadside America*. Accessed September 20, 2016. www.roadsideamerica.com/story/34301.

"About Us." United Community Corporation. Accessed February 10, 2017. www .uccnewark.org/about-us/.

Adams, Julia. "1-800-How-Am-I-Driving? Agency in Social Science History." *Social Science History* 35, no. 1 (2011): 1–17.

———. "Principals and Agents, Colonialists and Company Men: The Decay of Colonial Control in the Dutch East Indies." *American Sociological Review* 61 (1996): 12–28.

Adams, Luther. *Way Up North in Louisville: African American Migration in the Urban South, 1930–1970.* Chapel Hill: University of North Carolina Press, 2010.

Adelman, Robert M., Chris Morett, and Stewart E. Tolnay. "Homeward Bound: The Return Migration of Southern-Born Black Women, 1940 to 1990." *Sociological Spectrum* 20 (2000): 433–63.

Alexander, Jeffrey C. *The Civil Sphere.* New York: Oxford University Press, 2006.

Alexander, Michelle. *The New Jim Crow: Mass Incarceration in the Age of Colorblindness.* New York: New Press, 2012.

Alim, H. Samy. *Roc the Mic Right: The Language of Hip Hop Culture.* New York: Routledge, 2006.

Allen, Walter. "The Color of Success: African-American College Student Outcomes at Predominantly White and Historically Black Public Colleges and Universities." *Harvard Educational Review* 62, no. 1 (1992): 26–45.

Almonte, Richard. Introduction to *A Plea for Emigration; or, Notes of Canada West*. Toronto: Mercury, 1998.

Anderson, Elijah. *Code of the Street: Decency, Violence, and the Moral Life of the Inner City*. New York: Norton, 2000.

———. *The Cosmopolitan Canopy: Race and Civility in Everyday Life*. Chicago: University of Chicago Press, 2011.

———. "The Ideologically Driven Critique." *American Journal of Sociology* 107, no. 6 (2002): 1533–50.

———. *A Place on the Corner*. 1978. Reprint, Chicago: University of Chicago Press, 2003.

———. *Streetwise: Race, Class and Change in an Urban Community*. Chicago: University of Chicago Press, 1990.

———. "The White Space." *Sociology of Race and Ethnicity* 1, no. 1 (2014): 10–21.

Anderson, Elijah, Duke W. Austin, Craig Lapriece Holloway, and Vani S. Kulkarni. "The Legacy of Racial Caste: An Exploratory Ethnography." *Annals of the American Academy of Political and Social Science* 642, no. 1 (2012): 25–42.

Andrews, Kenneth T. *Freedom Is a Constant Struggle: The Mississippi Civil Rights Movement and Its Legacy*. Chicago: University of Chicago Press, 2004.

Archer, Margaret. *Being Human: The Problem of Agency*. New York: Cambridge University Press, 2001.

Atencio, Peter, dir. "Negro Town." *Key and Peele*. New York: Comedy Central, 2015.

Avilez, GerShun. "Cartographies of Desire: Mapping Queer Space in the Fiction of Samuel Delany and Darieck Scott." *Callaloo* 34, no. 1 (2011): 126–42.

———. *Radical Aesthetics and Modern Black Nationalism*. Urbana: University of Illinois Press, 2016.

Bailey, Robert, Jr. *Radicals in Urban Politics: The Alinsky Approach*. Chicago: University of Chicago Press, 1974.

Bakkila, Blake. "The Transgender Heroines Who Started a Revolution." *People*, August 1, 2016. www.people.com/article/weve-been-around-transgender-docuseries-marsha-johnson-sylvia-rivera.

Baldwin, Davarian L. "Black Belts and Ivory Towers: The Place of Race in U.S. Social Thought, 1892–1948." *Critical Sociology* 30, no. (2004): 397–450.

———. *Chicago's New Negroes: Modernity, the Great Migration, and Black Urban Life*. Chapel Hill: University of North Carolina Press, 2007.

Baldwin, James. "Of the Sorrow Songs: The Cross Redemption." *Views on Black Music*, no. 2 (1984–85): 7–12.

———. *Nobody Knows My Name*. New York: Vintage, 1961.

———. *Notes of a Native Son*. New York: Beacon, 1955.

———. *Take This Hammer*. Documentary. San Francisco: KQED TV, 1964.

Barnes, Sandra L. *The Costs of Being Poor*. Albany: State University of New York Press, 2005.

Beaman, Jean. "As French as Anyone Else: Islam and the North African Second Generation in France." *International Migration Review*, no. 1 (2015): 1–29.

———. "Boundaries of Frenchness: Cultural Citizenship and France's Middle-Class North African Second-Generation." *Identities* 22, no. 1 (2015): 36–52.

———. "But Madame, We Are French Also." *Contexts* 11, no. 3 (2012): 46–51.

Bearden, Jim, and Linda Jean Butler. *The Life and Times of Mary Shadd Cary*. Toronto: NC Press, 1977.

Bego, Mark. *Aretha Franklin: The Queen of Soul*. New York: Skyhorse, 2013.

Bell, Derrick A. *Faces at the Bottom of the Well: The Permanence of Racism*. New York: Basic Books, 1992.

———. *Race, Racism, and American Law*. New York: Aspen, 2004.

———. *Silent Covenants: Brown v. Board of Education and the Unfulfilled Hopes for Racial Reform*. Oxford: Oxford University Press, 2004.

Berlin, Ira, Barbara J. Fields, Steven F. Miller, Joseph P. Reidy, and Leslie S. Rowland, eds., *Free at Last: A Documentary History of Slavery, Freedom, and the Civil War*. New York: New Press, 1992.

Berry, Mary Frances, and John W. Blassingame, *Long Memory: The Black Experience in America*. New York: Oxford University Press, 1982.

Beyoncé. "Formation." *Lemonade*. Los Angeles: Parkwood Entertainment, 2016.

Biondi, Martha. *To Stand and Fight: The Struggle for Civil Rights in Postwar New York City*. Cambridge, MA: Harvard University Press, 2009.

Blomley, Nicholas. "Uncritical Critical Geography?" *Progress in Human Geography* 30, no. 1 (2006): 87–94.

Bloom, Khaled J. *The Mississippi Valley's Great Yellow Fever Epidemic of 1878*. Baton Rouge: Louisiana State University Press, 1993.

Bluestone, Barry, and Bennett Harrison. *The Deindustrialization of America*. New York: Basic Books, 1982.

Bonilla-Silva, Eduardo. *Racism without Racists: Color-Blind Racism and the Persistence of Racial Inequality in America*. 4th ed. New York: Roman and Littlefield, 2013.

Bonjean, Charles M., Terry N. Clark, and Robert L. Lineberry, eds. *Community Politics: A Behavioral Approach*. New York: Free Press, 1971.

Born, Tyler. "Marsha 'Pay It No Mind' Johnson." Accessed September 20, 2016. http://outhistory.org/exhibits/show/tgi-bios/marsha-p-johnson.

Bornstein, Kate, and S. Bear Bergman. *Gender Outlaws: The Next Generation*. Berkeley, CA: Seal, 2010.

Bowman, Rob. *Soulsville, USA: The Story of Stax Records*. New York: Schirmer Trade Books, 1997.

———. "The Stax Sound: A Musicological Analysis." *Popular Music* 14, no. 3 (1995): 285–320.

Boyd, Michelle R. *Jim Crow Nostalgia: Reconstructing Race in Bronzeville*. Minneapolis: University of Minnesota Press, 2008.

Boyd, Robert L. "Residential Segregation by Race and the Black Merchants of Northern Cities during the Early Twentieth Century." *Sociological Forum* 13, no. 4 (1998): 595–609.

Boyd, Valerie. *Wrapped in Rainbows: The Life of Zora Neale Hurston*. New York: Simon and Schuster, 2003.

Brimmer, Andrew F. "Income, Wealth, and Investment Behavior in the Black Community." *American Economic Review* 78, no. 2 (1988): 151–55.

Brinkley, Douglas. *The Great Deluge: Hurricane Katrina, New Orleans, and the Mississippi Gulf Coast*. New York: Harper Perennial, 2007.

Brooks, Daphne A. "'All That You Can't Leave Behind': Black Female Soul Singing and the Politics of Surrogation in the Age of Catastrophe." *Meridians* 8, no. 1 (2008): 180–204.

———. *Bodies in Dissent: Spectacular Performances of Race and Freedom, 1850–1910*. Durham: Duke University Press, 2006.

———. "'Bring the Pain': Post-soul Memory, Neo-soul Affect, and Lauryn Hill in the Black Public Sphere." *Taking It to the Bridge: Music as Performance*, edited by Nicholas Cook and Richard Pettengill, 180–203. Ann Arbor: University of Michigan Press, 2013.

———. "'This Voice Which Is Not One': Amy Winehouse Sings the Ballad of Sonic Blue(s) Face Culture." *Women and Performance: A Journal of Feminist Theory* 20, no. 1 (2010): 37–60.

Browning, Rufus P., Dale Rogers Marshall, and David H. Tabb. *Protest Is Not Enough*. Berkeley: University of California Press, 1984.

Bullard, Robert D., ed. *In Search of the New South: The Black Urban Experience in the 1970s and 1980s*. Tuscaloosa: University of Alabama Press, 1989.

———. *Invisible Houston: The Black Experience in Boom and Bust*. College Station: Texas A&M University Press, 2000.

Burawoy, Michael. "Revisits: An Outline of a Theory of Reflexive Ethnography." *American Sociological Review* 68, no. 5 (2003): 645–79.

Burby, Raymond J. "Hurricane Katrina and the Paradoxes of Government Disaster Policy: Bringing about Wise Governmental Decisions for Hazardous Areas." *Annals of the American Academy of Political and Social Science* 604, no. 1 (2006): 171–91.

Burgess, Ernest W. "The Growth of the City." In *The City*, edited by Robert E. Park, Ernest W. Burgess, and Roderick D. McKenzie, 35–41. Chicago: University of Chicago Press, 1925.

Butler, Paul. *Let's Get Free: A Hip-Hop Theory of Justice.* New York: New Press, 2010.

———. "Racially Based Jury Nullification: Black Power in the Criminal Justice System." *Yale Law Journal* 105, no. 3 (1995): 677–725.

California Department of Education. "Demographics and Statistics: Education in the State of California." *DataQuest, 2012–2013.* Accessed June 12, 2017. http://data1.cde.ca.gov/dataquest/.

Camarillo, Albert. *Chicanos in a Changing Society: From Mexican Pueblos to American Barrios in Santa Barbara and Southern California, 1848–1930.* Dallas: Southern Methodist University Press, 2005.

Campbell, Anne. *The Girls in the Gang.* Cambridge: Basil Blackwell, 1991.

Campbell, Rex R., Daniel M. Johnson, and Gary J. Stangler. "Return Migration of Black People to the South." *Rural Sociology* 39 (1974): 514–29.

Campbell, Stanley W. *The Slave Catchers: Enforcement of the Fugitive Slave Law, 1850–1860.* Chapel Hill: University of North Carolina Press, 1970.

Cantor, Paul. "How the 1995 Source Awards Changed Rap Forever." *Complex Magazine,* August, 3, 2015.

Carbado, Devon W. "Black Rights, Gay Rights, Civil Rights." *UCLA Law Review* 47 (1999): 1467–520.

———. "(E)racing the Fourth Amendment." *Michigan Law Review* 100, no. 5 (2002): 946–1044.

Carter, David. *Stonewall: The Riots That Sparked the Gay Revolution.* New York: St. Martin's Press, 2004.

Casey-Leininger, Charles F. "Making the Second Ghetto in Cincinnati: Avondale, 1925–1970." In *Race and the City: Work, Community, and Protest in Cincinnati, 1820–1970,* edited by Henry Louis Taylor Jr., 232–57. Urbana: University of Illinois Press, 1993.

Castells, Manuel. *The City and the Grassroots.* Berkeley: University of California Press, 1983.

———. *The Urban Question: A Marxist Approach.* Cambridge, MA: MIT Press, 1977.

Charles, Camille Zubrinsky. "The Dynamics of Racial Residential Segregation." *Annual Review of Sociology* 29 (2003): 167–207.

———. *Won't You Be My Neighbor: Race, Class, and Residence in Los Angeles.* New York: Sage Foundation, 2006.

Christian, Barbara. "The Race for Theory." *Cultural Critique* 6 (1987): 51–63.

Clark, Kenneth B. *Dark Ghetto: Dilemmas of Social Power.* Middletown, CT: Wesleyan University Press, 1965.

Clear, Todd R. *Imprisoning Communities: How Mass Incarceration Makes Disadvantaged Neighborhoods Worse.* New York: Oxford University Press, 2009.

Cleve, Nicole Gonzalez Van. *Crook County: Racism and Injustice in America's Largest Criminal Court.* Stanford: Stanford University Press, 2016.

Coates, Julia. *Trail of Tears.* New York: Wiley and Sons, 2014.

Cobb, James. *Away Down South: A History of Southern Identity.* Oxford: Oxford University Press, 2007.

———. *The Most Southern Place on Earth: The Mississippi Delta and the Roots of Regional Identity.* Oxford: Oxford University Press, 1994.

———. *The Selling of the South: The Southern Crusade for Industrial Development, 1936–1990.* Urbana: University of Illinois Press, 1993.

Cohen, Albert K. *Delinquent Boys.* New York: Free Press, 1955.

Cohen, Cathy J. *The Boundaries of Blackness: AIDS and the Breakdown of Black Politics.* Chicago: University of Chicago Press, 1999.

———. *Democracy Remixed: Black Youth and the Future of American Politics.* New York: Oxford University Press, 2010.

Cohen, Cathy J., Juan Battle, Dorian Warren, Gerard Fergerson, and Suzette Audam. *Say It Loud, I'm Black and I'm Proud: Black Pride Survey 2000.* New York: Policy Institute of the National Gay and Lesbian Task Force, 2002.

Cohen, Cathy J., and Michael C. Dawson. "Neighborhood Poverty and African American Politics." *American Political Science Review* 87, no. 2 (1993): 286–302.

Coleman, Alex. "Memphis-Born Aretha Franklin's Old Home Deserves Some R-E-S-P-E-C-T." *WREG Memphis News Channel 3.* May 12, 2014. http://wreg.com/2014/05/12/memphis-born-aretha-franklins-old-home-deserves-some-r-e-s-p-e-c-t/.

Coleman, James S. *Foundations of Social Theory.* Cambridge, MA: Harvard University Press, 1990.

Collins, Patricia Hill. *Black Feminist Thought: Knowledge, Consciousness, and the Politics of Empowerment.* New York: Routledge, 1990.

———. "Intersectionality's Definitional Dilemmas." *Annual Review of Sociology* 41 (2015): 1–20.

———. "Moving beyond Gender: Intersectionality and Scientific Knowledge." *Revisioning Gender* 2 (1999): 261–84.

———. "The Social Construction of Black Feminist Thought." *Signs* 14, no. 4 (1989): 745–73.

Comfort, Megan. *Doing Time Together: Love and Family in the Shadow of the Prison.* Chicago: University of Chicago Press, 2009.

Conley, Dalton. *Being Black, Living in the Red.* Berkeley: University of California Press, 1999.

Conrat, Maisie, and Richard Conrat. *Executive Order 9066: The Internment of 110,000 Japanese Americans.* Los Angeles: UCLA Asian American Studies Center Press, 1972.

Cooper, Anna J. *A Voice from the South: By a Black Woman of the South.* Xenia: Aldine, 1892.

Countryman, Matthew J. *Up South: Civil Rights and Black Power in Philadelphia.* Philadelphia: University of Pennsylvania Press, 2007.

Cox, Kevin, ed. *Urbanization and Conflict in Market Societies.* Chicago: Methuen, 1978.

Crenshaw, Kimberlé. *Critical Race Theory: The Key Writings That Formed the Movement.* New York: New Press, 1995.

———. "Demarginalizing the Intersection of Race and Sex: A Black Feminist Critique of Antidiscrimination Doctrine, Feminist Theory and Antiracist Politics." *University of Chicago Legal Forum* 1 (1989): 139–67.

———. "Mapping the Margins: Intersectionality, Identity Politics, and Violence against Women of Color." *Stanford Law Review* 43, no. 6 (1991): 1241–99.

Cressey, Paul G. *The Taxi-Dance Hall.* Chicago: University of Chicago Press, 1932.

Crichlow, Wesley. *Buller Men and Batty Bwoys: Hidden Men in Toronto and Halifax Black Communities.* Toronto: University of Toronto Press, 2004.

Crockett, Norman. *The Black Towns.* Topeka: University Press of Kansas, 1979.

Crosby, Faye J. *Relative Deprivation and Working Women.* New York: Oxford University Press, 1982.

Cross, Malcolm, and Michael Keith, eds. *Racism, the City, and the State.* London: Routledge, 1993.

Croteau, David, and William Hoynes. *Media/Society: Industries, Images, and Audiences.* Thousand Oaks, CA: Sage, 2013.

Crowder, Kyle, Scott J. South, and Erick Chavez. "Wealth, Race, and Inter-Neighborhood Migration." *American Sociological Review* 71, no. 1 (2006): 72–94.

Crowder, Kyle D., Stewart E. Tolnay, and Robert M. Adelman. "Intermetropolitan Migration and Locational Improvement for African American Males, 1970–1990." *Social Science Research,* 30 no. 3 (2001): 449–72.

Dahl, Robert. *Who Governs?* New Haven, CT: Yale University Press, 1961.

Davis, Allison, Burleigh B. Gardner, and Mary R. Gardner. *Deep South: A Social Anthropological Study of Caste and Class.* 1941. Reprint, Columbia: University of South Carolina Press, 2009.

Davis, Angela Y. *Are Prisons Obsolete?* New York: Seven Stories Press, 2011.

———. *Women, Race, and Class.* New York: Vintage, 2011.

Davis, Garry, and Greg Guma. *Passport to Freedom: A Guide to World Citizenship.* Arlington, VA: Seven Locks Press, 1992.

Davis, George, and O. Fred Donaldson. *Blacks in the United States: A Geographic Perspective.* Boston: Houghton Mifflin, 1975.

Davis, Mike. *City of Quartz: Excavating the Future in Los Angeles.* London: Verso, 1990.

Dawson, Michael C. *Behind the Mule: Race and Class in African-American Politics*. Princeton: Princeton University Press, 1994.

———. *Black Visions: The Roots of Contemporary African-American Political Ideologies*. Chicago: University of Chicago Press, 2003.

———. "National Black Election Survey." ICPSR. Accessed September 20, 2016. www.icpsr.umich.edu/icpsrweb/ICPSR/studies/2029.

Dear, Michael. "Los Angeles and the Chicago School: Invitation to a Debate." *City and Community* 1, no. 1 (2002): 5–32.

"Death Row Diss." YouTube video, 1:22. Posted by LokoSamoan. April 11, 2006. www.youtube.com/watch?v=JpgpS3ogvMM.

De Graaf, Lawrence B. "The City of Black Angels: Emergence of the Los Angeles Ghetto, 1890–1930." *Pacific Historical Review* 39, no. 3 (1970): 323–52.

Delany, Martin R. *The Condition, Elevation, Emigration, and Destiny of the Colored People of the United States*. New York: Black Classic, 1852.

DeSantis, Alan D. "Selling the American Dream Myth to Black Southerners: The Chicago Defender and the Great Migration of 1915–1919." *Western Journal of Communication* 62, no. 4 (1998): 474–511.

Desmond, Matthew. "Eviction and the Reproduction of Urban Poverty." *American Journal of Sociology* 118 (2012): 88–133.

Digital Underground. "Same Song." *Nothing but Trouble*. New York: Tommy Boy Records, 1991.

DiMaggio, Paul, and Filiz Garip. "Network Effects and Social Inequality." *Annual Review of Sociology* 38 (2012): 93–118.

Diop, Cheikh Anta. *The African Origin of Civilization: Myth or Reality*. Translated by Mercer Cook. Westport, CT: Lawrence Hill Books, 1974.

———. *Black Africa: The Economic and Cultural Basis for a Federated State*. Translated by Harold Salemson. Westport, CT: Lawrence Hill Books, 1978.

———. *Civilization or Barbarism: An Authentic Anthropology*. Translated by Yaa-Lengi Meema Ngemi. Brooklyn: Lawrence Hill Books, 1991.

———. *Precolonial Black Africa: A Comparative Study of the Political and Social Systems of Europe and Black Africa, from Antiquity to the Formation of Modern States*. Translated by Harold J. Salemson. Westport, CT: Lawrence Hill Books, 1987.

———. *Towards the African Renaissance: Essays in African Culture and Development, 1940–1960*. Translated by Egbuna P. Modum. London: Karnak House, 1996.

Dollard, John. *Caste and Class in a Southern Town*. 1949. Reprint, New York: Doubleday, 1957.

Douglass, Frederick. *The Life and Times of Frederick Douglass*. Hartford, CT: Park, 1881.

Drake, St. Clair, and Horace Cayton. *Black Metropolis: A Study of Negro Life in a Northern City*. Chicago: University of Chicago Press, 1993.

Dubey, Madhu. "Postmodern Geographies of the U.S. South." *Nepantla: Views from South* 3, no. 2 (2002): 351–71.

Du Bois, W. E. B. *The Autobiography of W. E. B. Du Bois: A Soliloquy on Viewing My Life from the Last Decade of Its First Century.* New York: International, 1968.

———. *The Black North: A Social Study.* New York: New York Times Magazine Supplement, 1901.

———. *Black Reconstruction in America, 1860–1880.* 1935. Reprint, New York: Free Press, 1998.

———. *John Brown.* Philadelphia: Jacobs, 1909.

———. "The Migration of Negroes." *Crisis* 142, no. 2 (1917): 63–66.

———. *The Philadelphia Negro: A Social Study.* Philadelphia: University of Pennsylvania, 1899.

———. *The Souls of Black Folk.* Oxford: Oxford University Press, 1903.

———. "Why I Won't Vote." *Nation,* October 20, 1956.

———. *The World and Africa: An Inquiry into the Part Which Africa Has Played in World History.* New York: Viking, 1947.

Duck, Waverly. *No Way Out: Precarious Living in the Shadow of Poverty and Drug Dealing.* Chicago: University of Chicago Press, 2015.

Duneier, Mitchell. *Ghetto: The Invention of a Place, the History of an Idea.* New York: Macmillan, 2016.

———. *Sidewalk.* New York: Farrar, Strauss, and Giroux, 1999.

———. *Slim's Table: Race, Respectability, and Masculinity.* Chicago: University of Chicago Press, 1992.

———. "What Kind of Combat Sport Is Sociology?" *American Journal of Sociology* 107, no. 6 (2002): 1551–76.

Duneier, Mitchell, and Harvey Molotch. "Talking City Trouble: Interactional Vandalism, Social Inequality, and the 'Urban Interaction Problem.'" *American Journal of Sociology* 104, no. 5 (1999): 1263–95.

Early, Gerald Lyn. *One Nation under a Groove: Motown and American Culture.* Ann Arbor: University of Michigan Press, 2004.

Edin, Kathryn, and Maria Kefalas. *Promises I Can Keep: Why Poor Women Put Motherhood before Marriage.* Berkeley: University of California Press, 2005.

Edin, Kathryn, and Laura Lein. *Making Ends Meet: How Single Mothers Survive Welfare and Low-Wage Work.* New York: Sage Foundation, 1997.

Eichenlaub, Suzanne C., Stewart E. Tolnay, and J. Trent Alexander. "Moving Out but Not Up: Economic Outcomes in the Great Migration." *American Sociological Review* 75, no. 1 (2010): 101–25.

Elliot, James R., and Jeremy Pais. "Race, Class, and Hurricane Katrina: Social Differences in Human Responses to Disaster." *Social Science Research* 35, no. 2 (2006): 295–321.

Ellis, Catherine, and Stephen Smith. *Say It Loud: Great Speeches on Civil Rights and African American Identity*. New York: New Press, 2010.

Ellis, John H. *Yellow Fever and Public Health in the New South*. Lexington: University Press of Kentucky, 2015.

Ellis, Stephen. *The Mask of Anarchy: The Destruction of Liberia and the Religious Dimension of an African Civil War*. New York: New York University Press, 2007.

Emirbayer, Mustafa, and Ann Mische. "What Is Agency?" *American Journal of Sociology* 103, no. 4 (1998): 962–1023.

Evans, Sara. *Personal Politics: The Roots of Women's Liberation in the Civil Rights Movement and the New Left*. New York: Vintage, 1979.

Eyerman, Ron. *Is This America? Katrina as Cultural Trauma*. Austin: University of Texas Press, 2015.

Falk, William W., Larry L. Hunt, and Matthew O. Hunt. "Return Migrations of African Americans to the South: Reclaiming a Land of Promise, Going Home, or Both?" *Rural Sociology* 69 (2004): 490–509.

"FBI Records: The Vault." Federal Bureau of Investigation. Accessed December 1, 2014. https://vault.fbi.gov/Malcolm%20X.

Feagin, Joe R. "The Continuing Significance of Race: Antiblack Discrimination in Public Places." *American Sociological Review* 56, no. 1 (1991): 101–16.

———. *How Blacks Built America: Labor, Culture, Freedom and Democracy*. New York: Routledge, 2015.

———. *The New Urban Paradigm: Critical Perspectives on the City*. New York: Rowman and Littlefield, 1998.

———. *Racist America: Roots, Current Realities, and Future Reparations*. New York: Routledge, 2014.

Feagin, Joe R., and Melvin P. Sikes. *Living with Racism: The Black Middle-Class Experience*. Boston: Beacon, 1994.

Feinberg, Leslie. *Transgender Warriors: Making History from Joan of Arc to Dennis Rodman*. Boston: Beacon, 1996.

Ferguson, Ann Arnett. *Bad Boys: Public School in the Making of Black Masculinity*. Ann Arbor: University of Michigan Press, 2001.

Fischer, Claude. *The Urban Experience*. New York: Harcourt, Brace, Jovanovich, 1976.

Flamming, Douglas. *Bound for Freedom: Black Los Angeles in Jim Crow America*. Berkeley: University of California Press, 2005.

Foner, Eric. *Freedom's Lawmakers: A Directory of Black Officeholders during Reconstruction*. New York: Oxford University Press, 1993.

———. *Nothing but Freedom: Emancipation and Its Legacy*. Baton Rouge: Louisiana State University Press, 2007.

———. *Politics and Ideology in the Age of the Civil War*. Oxford: Oxford University Press, 1980.

———. *The Story of American Freedom*. New York: Norton, 1999.

Foner, Philip Sheldon. *History of Black Americans*. Vol. 3. Westport, CT: Greenwood, 1983.

Foster, Frances Smith. *Witnessing Slavery: The Development of Ante-bellum Slave Narratives*. Madison: University of Wisconsin Press, 1979.

Foster, Holly, and John Hagan. "The Mass Incarceration of Parents in America: Issues of Race/Ethnicity, Collateral Damage to Children, and Prisoner Reentry." *Annals of the American Academy of Political and Social Science* 623, no. 1 (2009): 179–94.

Franklin, Aretha. *Aretha: From These Roots*. New York: Villard Books, 1999.

———. "Bridge over Troubled Waters." *Amazing Grace*. Los Angeles: Atlantic Records, 1972.

———. "Dr. Feelgood." *I Never Loved a Man the Way I Love You*. Los Angeles: Atlantic Records, 1967.

———. "God Bless the Child." *The Tender, the Moving, the Swinging Aretha Franklin*. New York: Columbia Records, 1962.

———. "Mary, Don't You Weep," *Amazing Grace*. Los Angeles: Atlantic Records, 1972.

———. "Respect." *I Never Loved a Man the Way I Love You*. Los Angeles: Atlantic Records, 1967.

Frazier, E. Franklin. *Black Bourgeoisie*. New York: Free Press, 1954.

———. *The Negro Family in Chicago*. University of Chicago Press, 1932.

Freedia, Big. *God Save the Queen Diva*. With Nicole Balin. New York: Gallery Books, 2015.

Freeman, Lance. *There Goes the Hood: Views of Gentrification from the Ground Up*. Philadelphia: Temple University Press, 2011.

Frey, William H. "Race and Ethnicity." In *The State of Metropolitan America*, edited by Alan Berube, William H. Frey, Alec Friedhoff, Emily Garr, Emilia Istrate, Elizabeth Kneebone, Robert Puentes, Audrey Singer, Adie Tomer, and Howard Wial, 51–63. Washington, DC: Brookings Institution, 2008.

Gan, Jessi. "'Still at the Back of the Bus': Sylvia Rivera's Struggle." *CENTRO: Journal of the Center for Puerto Rican Studies* 19, no. 1 (2007): 124–40.

Gans, Herbert. *The Levittowners: Ways of Life and Politics in a New Suburban Community*. 1967. Reprint, New York: Columbia University Press, 1982.

———. *The Urban Villagers: Group and Class in the Life of Italian-Americans*. New York: Free Press, 1962.

Gates, Henry Louis, Jr. "The Chitlin Circuit." *New Yorker* 3 (1997): 44–55.

Gaunt, Kyra D. "YouTube, Twerking and You: Context Collapse and the Handheld Co-presence of Black Girls and Miley Cyrus." *Journal of Popular Music Studies* 27, no. 3 (2015): 244–73.

George, Nelson. *The Death of Rhythm and Blues*. New York: Penguin, 2003.

———. *Hip Hop America*. New York: Penguin, 2005.

———. *Where Did Our Love Go? The Rise and Fall of the Motown Sound.* Urbana: University of Illinois Press, 2007.

Gibson, Chris. "Recording Studios: Relational Spaces of Creativity in the City." *Built Environment* 31, no. 3 (2005): 192–207.

Gilmore, Glenda, and Thomas Sugrue. *These United States: A Nation in the Making, 1890 to the Present* New York: Norton, 2015.

Gilroy, Paul. *The Black Atlantic: Modernity and Double Consciousness.* Cambridge, MA: Harvard University Press, 1993.

———. *Black Britain: A Photographic History.* London: Al Saqi, 2007.

———. *Darker Than Blue: On the Moral Economies of Black Atlantic Culture.* Cambridge, MA: Harvard University Press, 2010.

Gittleman, Maury, and Edward N. Wolff. "Racial Differences in Patterns of Wealth Accumulation." *Journal of Human Resources* 39, no. 1 (2004): 193–227.

Gmelch, George. "Return Migration." *Annual Review of Anthropology* 9 (1980): 135–59.

Goffman, Alice. *On the Run: Fugitive Life in an American City.* Chicago: University of Chicago Press, 2014.

Goffman, Erving. *The Presentation of Self in Everyday Life.* New York: Doubleday, 1959.

Goldfield, David. *Black, White and Southern: Race Relations and Southern Culture, 1940 to the Present.* Baton Rouge: Louisiana State University Press, 1991.

Goldscheider, Frances K., and Calvin Goldscheider. "The Intergenerational Flow of Income: Family Structure and the Status of Black Americans." *Journal of Marriage and Family* 23, no. 2 (1991): 499–508.

Gomez, Michael Angelo. *Exchanging Our Country Marks: The Transformation of African Identities in the Colonial and Antebellum South.* Chapel Hill: University of North Carolina Press, 1998.

Gordon, Robert. *Respect Yourself: Stax Records and the Soul Explosion.* New York: Bloomsbury, 2013.

Gordy, Berry. *To Be Loved: The Music, the Magic, the Memories of Motown.* New York: Warner Books, 2013.

Gossett, Reina, and Sasha Wortzel. *Happy Birthday Marsha.* Official trailer. Accessed September 20, 2016. www.happybirthdaymarsha.com/.

Gotham, Kevin Fox. *Race, Real Estate, and Uneven Development: The Kansas City Experience, 1900–2000.* Albany: State University of New York Press, 2002.

Gotham, Kevin Fox, and Krista Brumley. "Using Space: Agency and Identity in a Public-Housing Development." *City and Community* 1, no. 3 (2002): 267–89.

Gottdiener, Mark, and Chris G. Pickvance. *Urban Life in Transition.* Newbury, CA: Sage, 1991.

Gottschalk, Marie. *The Prison and the Gallows: The Politics of Mass Incarceration in America*. New York: Cambridge University Press, 2006.

Gramsci, Antonio, and Joseph A. Buttigieg. *Prison Notebooks*. Vol. 2. New York: Columbia University Press, 1992.

Grant, Japhy. "Duanna Johnson Murdered 'Execution Style' in Memphis." *Queerty*. November 11, 2008. www.queerty.com/duanna-johnson-murdered-execution-style-in-memphis-20081111.

Green, Victor H. *The Negro-Motorist Green Book*. New York, 1949.

Greenberg, Cheryl. "Black and Jewish Responses to Japanese Internment." *Journal of American Ethnic History* 14, no, 2 (1995): 3–37.

Greene, Theodore. "Gay Neighborhoods and the Rights of the Vicarious Citizen." *City and Community* 13, no. 2 (2014): 99–118.

Greer, Christina. *Black Ethnics: Race, Immigration and the Pursuit of the American Dream*. New York: Oxford University Press, 2013.

Gregory, Steven. *Black Corona: Race and the Politics of Place in an Urban Community*. Princeton: Princeton University Press, 1998.

Griffin, Farah Jasmine. "Children of Omar Resistance and Reliance in the Expressive Cultures of Black New Orleans Cultures." *Journal of Urban History* 35, no. 5 (2009): 656–67.

———. *"Who Set You Flowin'?": The African-American Migration Narrative*. New York: Oxford University Press, 1995.

Griffin, Larry J. "The Promise of a Sociology of the South." *Southern Cultures* 7, no. 1 (2001): 50–75.

Gros, Jean-Germain. "Towards a Taxonomy of Failed States in the New World Order: Decaying Somalia, Liberia, Rwanda and Haiti." *Third World Quarterly* 17, no. 3 (1996): 455–72.

Gross, Kali N. *Colored Amazons: Crime, Violence, and Black Women in the City of Brotherly Love, 1880–1910*. Durham: Duke University Press, 2006.

Grossman, James R. *Land of Hope: Chicago, Black Southerners, and the Great Migration*. Chicago: University of Chicago Press, 1991.

Guy-Sheftall, Beverly. *Words of Fire: An Anthology of African-American Feminist Thought*. New York: New Press, 1995.

Habermas, Jürgen. *The Theory of Communicative Action*. Vol. 2, *A Critique of Functional Reason*, translated by Thomas A. McCarthy. Boston: Beacon, 1987.

Hagan, John. *Who Are the Criminals? The Politics of Crime Policy from the Age of Roosevelt to the Age of Reagan*. Princeton: Princeton University Press, 2012.

Hall, Jacquelyn Dowd. "The Long Civil Rights Movement and the Political Uses of the Past." *Journal of American History* 91 no. 4 (2005): 1233–63.

Hall, Stuart. "What Is This 'Black' in Black Popular Culture?" *Social Justice* 20, no. 1 (1993): 104–114.

Halle, David. *New York and Los Angeles: Politics, Society, and Culture—A Comparative View*. Chicago: University of Chicago Press, 2003.

Hanchard, Michael George. *Orpheus and Power: The "Movimento Negro" of Rio de Janeiro and São Paulo, Brazil, 1945–1988*. Princeton: Princeton University Press, 1998.

Hancock, Ange-Marie. "W. E. B. Du Bois: Intellectual Forefather of Intersectionality? *Souls* 7, nos. 3–4 (2005): 74–84.

Hannerz, Ulf. *Soulside: Inquiries into Ghetto Culture and Community*. New York: Columbia University Press, 1969.

Harding, David. "Cultural Context, Sexual Behavior, and Romantic Relationships in Disadvantaged Neighborhoods." *American Sociological Review* 72, no. 3 (2007): 341–64.

———. *Living the Drama: Community, Conflict, and Culture among Inner-City Boys*. Chicago: University of Chicago Press, 2010.

Harris-Lacewell, Melissa V. *Barbershops, Bibles, and BET: Everyday Talk and Black Political Thought*. Princeton: Princeton University Press, 2006.

Harrison, Alferdteen, ed. *Black Exodus: The Great Migration of from the American South*. Jackson: University Press of Mississippi, 2012.

Harrison, Bennett. *Deindustrialization in America*. New York: Basic Books, 1982.

Hartman, Chester W. *There Is No Such Thing as a Natural Disaster: Race, Class, and Hurricane Katrina*. New York: Taylor and Francis, 2006.

Hartman, Saidiya V. *Scenes of Subjection: Terror, Slavery, and Self-Making in Nineteenth-Century America*. New York: Oxford University Press, 1997.

Harvey, David. "Government Policies, Financial Institutions and Neighborhood Change in United States Cities." In *Captive Cities*, edited by Michael Harloe, 123–40. London: Wiley, 1977.

———. "On the History and Present Condition of Geography: An Historical Materialist Manifesto." *Professional Geographer* 36, no. 1 (1984): 1–11.

———. *Spaces of Capital: Towards a Critical Geography*. New York: Routledge, 2001.

———. *The Urban Experience*. Baltimore: Johns Hopkins University Press, 1989.

———. "What Kind of Geography for What Kind of Public Policy?" *Transactions of the Institute of British Geographers*, no. 63 (1974): 18–24.

Harvey, David, and Bruce Braun. *Justice, Nature and the Geography of Difference*. Cambridge, MA: Blackwell, 1996.

Hawkeswood, William G. *One of the Children: Gay Black Men in Harlem*. Berkeley: University of California Press, 1992.

Haynes, Bruce D. *Red Lines, Black Spaces: The Politics of Race and Space in a Black Middle-Class Suburb*. New Haven: Yale University Press, 2008.

Hayward, Eva. "Lessons from a Starfish." In *Queering the Non/Human*, edited by Myra Hird, 249–63. New York: Routledge, 2008.

Hemenway, Robert E. *Zora Neale Hurston: A Literary Biography.* Urbana: University of Illinois Press, 1977.

Henry, Charles P. *Culture and African American Politics.* Bloomington: Indiana University Press, 1990.

Higashida, Cheryl. "Aunt Sue's Children: Re-viewing the Gender(ed) Politics of Richard Wright's Radicalism." *American Literature* 75, no. 2 (2003): 395–425.

Higginbotham, Evelyn Brooks. *Righteous Discontent: The Women's Movement in the Black Baptist Church, 1880–1920.* Cambridge, MA: Harvard University Press, 1993.

Hill, Daniel G. *The Freedom-Seekers: Blacks in Early Canada.* 1981. Reprint, Toronto: Stoddard, 1992.

Hill, Lauryn. "Every Ghetto, Every City." *The Miseducation of Lauryn Hill.* New York: Columbia Records, 1998.

Hine, Darlene Clark. *Hine Sight: Black Women and the Re-construction of American History.* Bloomington: Indiana University Press, 1994.

———. "Rape and the Inner Lives of Black Women in the Middle West." *Signs* 14, no. 4 (1989): 912–20.

Hirsch, Arnold R. *Making the Second Ghetto: Race and Housing in Chicago, 1940–1960.* Chicago: University of Chicago Press, 1983.

Hirsch, Arnold, and Raymond Mohl, eds. *Urban Policy in Twentieth-Century America.* New Brunswick: Rutgers University Press, 1993.

Hirschman, Albert O. *Exit, Voice and Loyalty: Responses to Decline in Firms, Organizations, and States.* Cambridge, MA: Harvard University Press, 1970.

Hobbs, Holly. "'I Used That Katrina Water to Master My Flow': Rap Performance, Disaster, and Recovery in New Orleans." *Southern Spaces.* May 6, 2015. https://southernspaces.org/2015/i-used-katrina-water-master-my-flow-rap-performance-disaster-and-recovery-new-orleans.

Hochschild, Arlie. *The Managed Heart: The Commercialization of Human Feeling.* 2nd ed. Berkeley: University of California Press, 2003.

Holloway, Jonathan Scott. *Confronting the Veil: Abram Harris Jr., E. Franklin Frazier, and Ralph Bunche, 1919–1941.* Chapel Hill: University of North Carolina Press, 2003.

———. *Jim Crow Wisdom: Memory and Identity in Black America since 1940.* Chapel Hill: University of North Carolina Press, 2013.

hooks, bell. *Talking Back: Thinking Feminist, Thinking Black.* Boston: South End, 1989.

Hopkinson, Natalie. *Go-Go Live: The Musical Life and Death of a Chocolate City.* Durham: Duke University Press, 2012.

Howard, Lillie P. *Zora Neale Hurston.* Boston: Twayne, 1980.

Humphreys, Margaret. *Yellow Fever and the South*. Baltimore: Johns Hopkins University Press, 1999.

Hunt, Darnell M. *Screening the Los Angeles "Riots": Race, Seeing, and Resistance*. New York: Cambridge University Press, 1997.

Hunt, Darnell, and Ana-Christina Ramón. *Black Los Angeles: American Dreams and Realities*. New York: New York University Press, 2010.

Hunt, Larry L., Matthew O. Hunt, and William W. Falk. "Who Is Headed South? Return Migration in Black and White, 1970–2000." *Social Forces* 87 (2008): 95–119.

Hunter, Floyd. *Community Power Structure: A Study of Decisions Makers*. Chapel Hill: University of North Carolina Press, 1953.

Hunter, Floyd, Ruth Connor Schaffer, and Cecil G. Sheps. *Community Organization: Action and Inaction*. Chapel Hill: University of North Carolina Press, 1956.

Hunter, Marcus Anthony. *Black Citymakers: How "The Philadelphia Negro" Changed Urban America*. New York: Oxford University Press, 2013.

———. "A Bridge over Troubled Urban Waters: W. E. B. Du Bois's *The Philadelphia Negro* and the Ecological Conundrum." *Du Bois Review: Social Science Research on Race* 10, no. 1 (2013): 7–27.

———. "The Nightly Round: Space, Social Capital, and Urban Black Nightlife." *City and Community* 9, no. 2 (2010): 165–86.

———. "W. E. B. Du Bois and Black Heterogeneity: How *The Philadelphia Negro* Shaped American Sociology." *American Sociologist* 46, no. 2 (2015): 219–23.

Hunter, Marcus Anthony, Mary Pattillo, Zandria Felice Robinson, and Keeanga-Yamahtta Taylor. "Black Placemaking: Celebration, Play, and Poetry." *Theory, Culture and Society*. 33, no. 7–8 (2016): 31–56.

Hunter, Marcus Anthony and Zandria F. Robinson. "The Sociology of Urban Black America," Annual Review of Sociology 42 (2016): 385–405.

Hunter, Tera. *To 'Joy My Freedom: Southern Black Women's Lives and Labors after the Civil War*. Cambridge, MA: Harvard University Press, 1997.

Hurston, Zora Neale. *Dust Tracks on a Road: An Autobiography*. 1942, Reprint, New York: Harper Perennial, 1991.

———. *Mules and Men*. 1935. Reprint, New York: Harper Perennial Modern Classics, 2008.

Hurt, Byron. *Soul Food Junkies*. New York: PBS Films, 2012.

Hyra, Derek S. *The New Urban Renewal: The Economic Transformation of Harlem and Bronzeville*. Chicago: University of Chicago Press, 2008.

———. *Race, Class, and Politics in the Cappuccino City*. Chicago: University of Chicago Press, 2016.

"Initiatives: #SayHerName." African American Policy Forum. Accessed September 20, 2016. www.aapf.org/sayhername/.

Iton, Richard. *In Search of the Black Fantastic: Politics and Popular Culture in the Post–Civil Rights Era.* New York: Oxford University Press, 2008.

Jackson, John A. *A House on Fire: The Rise and Fall of Philadelphia Soul.* New York: Oxford University Press, 2004.

Jackson, John L. *Harlemworld: Doing Race and Class in Contemporary Black America.* Chicago: University of Chicago Press, 2001.

———. *Real Black: Adventures in Racial Sincerity.* Chicago: University of Chicago, 2005.

Jacobs, Jane. *The Death and Life of Great American Cities.* New York: Random House, 1981.

Jahoda, Gloria. *The Trail of Tears.* New York: Holt, 1975.

James, C. L. R. *The Black Jacobins: Toussaint L'Ouverture and the San Domingo Revolution.* New York: Random House, 1963.

Jaynes, Gerald David. *Branches without Roots: Genesis of the Black Working Class in the American South, 1862–1882.* New York: Oxford University Press, 1986.

Joas, Hans. *The Creativity of Action.* Chicago: University of Chicago Press, 1996.

Johnson, Allen. "The Constitutionality of the Fugitive Slave Acts." *Yale Law Journal* 31, no. 2 (1921): 161–82.

Johnson, Charles S. *Growing Up in the Black Belt: Negro Youth in the Rural South.* Washington, DC: American Council on Education, 1941.

———. *Shadow of the Plantation.* Chicago: University of Chicago Press, 1934.

Johnson, Gaye Theresa. *Spaces of Conflict, Sounds of Solidarity: Music, Race, and Spatial Entitlement in Los Angeles.* Berkeley: University of California Press, 2013.

Johnson, Hans. "Just the Facts: California's Population." *Public Policy Institute of California.* Accessed September 20, 2016. www.ppic.org/main/publication_show.asp?i=259.

Johnson, James Weldon. *Black Manhattan.* New York: Atheneum, 1968.

Jones, Charles Earl. *The Black Panther Party (Reconsidered).* Baltimore: Black Classic Press, 1998.

Jones, Nikki. *Between Good and Ghetto: African American Girls and Inner-City Violence.* Piscataway: Rutgers University Press, 2009.

"Judge Orders Aretha Franklin's Childhood Home in Tennessee to Be Torn Down." *Fox 8.* Accessed September 20, 2016. http://myfox8.com/2016/06/15/judge-orders-aretha-franklins-childhood-home-in-tenessee-to-be-torn-down/.

Karnig, Albert. "Black Economic, Political, and Cultural Development: Does City Size Make a Difference?" *Social Forces* 57, no. 4 (1979): 1194–211.

Karnig, Albert K., and Susan Welch. *Black Representation and Urban Policy.* Chicago: University of Chicago Press, 1980.

Kasarda, John. "Industrial Restructuring and the Changing Location of Jobs." In *State of the Union: America in the 1990s.* Vol. 1, *Economic Trends,* edited by Reynolds Farley, 215–67. New York: Sage Foundation, 1995.

Kasino, Michael, dir. *Pay It No Mind: The Life and Times of Marsha P. Johnson.* New York: Redux Pictures, 2012. YouTube video, 55:30. Posted by Michael Kasino. October 15, 2012. www.youtube.com/watch?v=rjN9W2KstqE.

Kates, Robert William, Craig E. Colten, Shirley Laska, and Stephen P. Leatherman. "Reconstruction of New Orleans after Hurricane Katrina: A Research Perspective." *Proceedings of the National Academy of Sciences* 103, no. 40 (2006): 14653–60.

Katz, Michael B., ed. *The "Underclass" Debate: Views from History.* Princeton: Princeton University Press, 1993.

Keller, Cyrus S. "African Americans in California and Our Pioneer Churches." *Age* 4 (1902): 194–97.

Kelley, Robin D. G. *Freedom Dreams: The Black Radical Imagination.* Boston: Beacon, 2002.

———. *Race Rebels: Culture, Politics, and the Black Working Class.* New York: Simon and Schuster, 1996.

———. *Yo' Mama's Disfunktional! Fighting the Culture Wars in Urban America.* Boston: Beacon, 2001.

Kelling, George L., and James Q. Wilson. "Broken Windows: The Police and Neighborhood Safety." *Atlantic* 249, no. 3 (1982): 29–38.

Kent v. Dulles. 357 U.S. 116 (1958). *Legal Information Institute.* Accessed September 20, 2016. www.law.cornell.edu/supremecourt/text/357/116.

———. *Justia.* Accessed September 20, 2016. https://supreme.justia.com/cases/federal/us/357/116/case.html.

Kerner Commission. *Report of the National Advisory Commission on Civil Disorders.* Washington, DC: U.S. Government Printing Office, 1968.

Kerr, Audrey Elisa. *The Paper Bag Principle: Class, Colorism, and Rumor and the Case of Black Washington.* Knoxville: University of Tennessee Press, 2006.

Khanna, Parag. *Connectography: Mapping the Future of Global Civilization.* New York: Random House, 2016.

King, Deborah K. "Multiple Jeopardy, Multiple Consciousness: The Context of a Black Feminist Ideology." *Signs* 14, no. 1 (1988): 42–72.

King, Russell. "Return Migration: A Neglected Aspect of Population Geography." *Area* 10, no. 3 (1978): 175–82.

Kinkead, Mik. "Remembering Duanna Johnson." *GLAAD.* November 14, 2008. www.glaad.org/2008/11/14/remembering-duanna-johnson.

Krivo, Lauren J., and Ruth D. Peterson. "Extremely Disadvantaged Neighborhoods and Urban Crime." *Social Forces* 75, no. 2 (1996): 619–48.

———. "Macrostructural Analyses of Race, Ethnicity, and Violent Crime: Recent Lessons and New Directions for Research." *Annual Review of Sociology* 31 (2005): 331–56.

Kruse, Kevin M. *White Flight: Atlanta and the Making of Modern Conservatism.* Princeton: Princeton University Press, 2005.

Kurashige, Scott. *The Shifting Grounds of Race: Black and Japanese Americans in the Making of Multiethnic Los Angeles*. Princeton: Princeton University Press, 2010.

Kyriakoudes, Louis M. *The Social Origins of the Urban South: Race, Gender, and Migration in Nashville and Middle Tennessee, 1890–1930*. Chapel Hill: University of North Carolina Press, 2003.

Lacy, Karyn R. "Black Spaces, Black Places: Strategic Assimilation and Identity Construction in Middle-Class Suburbia." *Ethnic and Racial Studies* 27, no. 6 (2004): 908–30.

———. *Blue-Chip Black: Race, Class, and Status in the New Black Middle Class*. Chicago: University of Chicago Press, 2007.

Ladner, Joyce A., ed. *The Death of White Sociology: Essays on Race and Culture*. Baltimore: Black Classic Press, 1973.

———. *Tomorrow's Tomorrow: The Black Woman*. Garden City, NY: Doubleday, 1971.

Ladson-Billings, Gloria, and William Tate IV. "Toward a Critical Race Theory of Education." *Teachers College Record* 97, no. 1 (1995): 47–68.

LaGrange, Teresa C., and Robert A. Silverman. "Low Self-Control and Opportunity: Testing the General Theory of Crime as an Explanation for Gender Differences in Delinquency." *Criminology* 37, no. 1 (1999): 41–72.

Landon, Fred. "The Negro Migration to Canada after the Passing of the Fugitive Slave Act." *Journal of Negro History* 5, no. 1 (1920): 22–36.

Lamar, Kendrick. "Mortal Man." *To Pimp a Butterfly*. Los Angeles: Top Dawg Entertainment/Santa Monica: Aftermath Entertainment; Interscope Records, 2015.

Laymon, Kiese. *Long Division*. Chicago: Agate, 2013.

Lazin, Lauren, dir. *Tupac: Resurrection*. Los Angeles: Paramount Pictures, 2003.

Lee, Malcolm D., dir. *Welcome Home, Roscoe Jenkins*. Universal City, CA: Universal Studios, 2008.

Lefebvre, Henri. *The Production of Space*. Vol. 142. Oxford: Blackwell, 1991.

Lehman, Nicolas. *The Promised Land: The Great Black Migration and How It Changed America*. New York: Vintage Books, 1992.

Lerman, Amy E., and Vesla M. Weaver. *Arresting Citizenship: The Democratic Consequences of American Crime Control*. Chicago: University of Chicago Press, 2014.

Leslie, Camilo Arturo. "Territoriality, Map-Mindedness, and the Politics of Place. *Theory and Society* 45, no. 2 (2016): 169–201.

Levering-Lewis, David, ed. *W.E.B. Du Bois: A Reader*. New York: Holt, 1995.

Lewis, Oscar. *Five Families: Mexican Case Studies in the Culture of Poverty*. New York: Basic Books, 1975.

Liebenow, J. Gus. *Liberia: The Quest for Democracy*. Bloomington: Indiana University Press, 1987.

Liebow, Elliot. *Tally's Corner.* Boston: Little, Brown, 1967.

Light, Ivan. "Gambling among Blacks: A Financial Institution." *American Sociological Review* 42, no. 6 (1977): 892–904.

Lipsitz, George. *The Possessive Investment in Whiteness: How White People Profit from Identity Politics.* Philadelphia: Temple University Press, 2006.

Lloyd, Richard. "Cities in the American South." *Annual Review of Sociology* 38 (2012): 483–506.

Locke, Alain L. *The New Negro: An Interpretation.* New York: Boni, 1925.

Logan, John, and Harvey Molotch. *Urban Fortunes: The Political Economy of Place.* Berkeley: University of California Press, 2007.

Long, Larry H., and Kristin A. Hansen. "Trends in Return Migration to the South." *Demography* 12, no. 4 (1975): 601–14.

Lukes, Steven. *Power.* New York: New York University Press, 1986.

MacLeod, Jay. *Ain't No Makin' It: Aspirations and Attainment in a Low-Income Neighborhood.* Boulder, CO: Westview, 1995.

Majors, Richard, and Janet Mancini Billson. *Cool Pose: The Dilemmas of Black Manhood in America.* New York: Lexington Books, 1993.

Marable, Manning. *Beyond Black and White: Transforming African-American Politics.* New York: Verso, 1995.

———. *Black Leadership.* New York: Columbia University Press, 2013.

———. *How Capitalism Underdeveloped Black America: Problems in Race, Political Economy, and Society.* Chicago: Haymarket Books, 2015.

———. *Malcolm X: A Life of Reinvention.* New York: Penguin, 2011.

———. *W.E.B. Du Bois: Black Radical Democrat.* New York: Routledge, 2015.

Marks, Carole. *Farewell—We're Good and Gone: The Great Black Migration.* Bloomington: Indiana University Press, 1989.

———. "The Urban Underclass." *Annual Review of Sociology* 17 (1991): 445–66.

Marsh, Kris, William A. Darity Jr., Philip N. Cohen, Lynne M. Casper, and Danielle Salters. "The Emerging Black Middle Class: Single and Living Alone." *Social Forces* 86, no. 2 (2007): 735–62.

Marx, Anthony. *Making Race and Nation: A Comparison of the United States, South Africa and Brazil.* New York: Cambridge University Press, 1998.

Massey, Douglas S. "American Apartheid: Segregation and the Making of the Underclass." *American Journal of Sociology* 96, no. 2 (1990): 329–57.

Massey, Douglas S., Len Albright, Rebecca Casciano, Elizabeth Derickson, and David N. Kinsey. *Climbing Mount Laurel: The Struggle for Affordable Housing and Social Mobility in an American Suburb.* Princeton: Princeton University Press, 2013.

Massey, Douglas S., and Nancy A. Denton. *American Apartheid: Segregation and the Making of the Underclass.* Cambridge, MA: Harvard University Press, 1993.

———. "The Dimensions of Residential Segregation." *Social Forces* 67, no. 2 (1988): 281–315.

———. "Trends in the Residential Segregation of Blacks, Hispanics, and Asians: 1970–1980." *American Sociological Review* 52, no. 6 (1987): 802–25.

May, Reuben A. Buford. *Talking at Trena's: Everyday Conversations at an African American Tavern.* New York: New York University Press, 2001.

May, Reuben A. Buford, and Mary Pattillo-McCoy. "Do You See What I See? Examining a Collaborative Ethnography." *Qualitative Inquiry* 6, no. 1 (2000): 65–87.

McAdam, Doug. *Political Process and the Development of Black Insurgency, 1930–1970.* Chicago: University of Chicago Press, 1999.

McCall, Leslie. "The Complexity of Intersectionality." *Signs* 30, no. 3 (2005): 1771–800.

McKee, James B. *Sociology and the Race Problem: The Failure of a Perspective.* Urbana: University of Illinois Press, 1993.

McKittrick, Katherine. "'Black and 'Cause I'm Black I'm Blue: Transverse Racial Geographies in Toni Morrison's *The Bluest Eye*." *Gender, Place and Culture: A Journal of Feminist Geography* 7, no. 2 (2000): 125–42.

———. *Demonic Grounds: Black Women and the Cartographies of Struggle.* Minneapolis: University of Minnesota Press, 2006.

———. "Freedom Is a Secret." In McKittrick and Woods, *Black Geographies,* 97–114.

———, ed. *Sylvia Wynter: On Being Human as Praxis.* Durham: Duke University Press, 2014.

———. "'Who Do You Talk to, When a Body's in Trouble?': M. Nourbese Philip's (Un)silencing of Black Bodies in the Diaspora." *Social and Cultural Geography* 1, no. 2 (2000): 223–36.

McKittrick, Katherine, and Clyde Adrian Woods, eds. *Black Geographies and the Politics of Place.* Toronto: Between the Lines, 2007.

McLoughlin, William G. *After the Trail of Tears: The Cherokees' Struggle for Sovereignty, 1839–1880.* Chapel Hill: University of North Carolina Press, 2014.

McRoberts, Omar. *Streets of Glory: Church and Community in a Black Urban Neighborhood.* Chicago: University of Chicago, 2000.

Mele, Christopher. *Selling the Lower East Side: Culture, Real Estate and Resistance in New York City.* Minneapolis: University of Minnesota Press, 2000.

Menjívar, Cecilia. *Fragmented Ties: Salvadoran Immigrant Networks in America.* Berkeley: University of California Press, 2000.

Miller, Matt. *Bounce: Rap Music and Local Identity in New Orleans.* Amherst: University of Massachusetts Press, 2012.

Mintz, Steven. "A Historical Ethnography of Black Washington, D.C." *Records of the Columbia Historical Society, Washington, DC* 52 (1989): 235–53.

Mohl, Raymond A. "Making the Second Ghetto in Metropolitan Miami, 1940–1960." *Journal of Urban History* 21 (1995): 395–427.

Mollenkopf, John. *The Contested City.* Princeton: Princeton University Press, 1983.

———. *Power, Culture, and Place: Essays on New York City.* New York: Russell Sage Foundation, 1988.

Molotch, Harvey, William Freudenberg, and Krista E. Paulsen. "History Repeats Itself, but Wow? City Character, Urban Tradition, and the Accomplishment of Place." *American Sociological Review* 65, no. 6 (2000): 791–823.

Moore, Mignon R. *Invisible Families: Gay Identities, Relationships and Motherhood among Black Women.* Berkeley: University of California Press, 2011.

———. "Lipstick or Timberlands? Meanings of Gender Presentation in Black Lesbian Communities." *Signs: Journal of Women in Culture and Society* 32, no. 1 (2006): 113–39.

Morenoff, Jeffrey D., and David J. Harding. "Incarceration, Prisoner Reentry, and Communities." *Annual Review of Sociology* 40 (2014): 411–29.

Morenoff, Jeffrey D., Robert J. Sampson, and Stephen W. Raudenbush. "Neighborhood Inequality, Collective Efficacy, and the Spatial Dynamics of Urban Violence." *Criminology* 39, no. 3 (2006): 517–58.

Morris, Aldon D. *The Origins of the Civil Rights Movement.* New York: Simon and Schuster, 1986.

———. "Political Consciousness and Collective Action." *Frontiers in Social Movement Theory*, ed. Carol McClurg Mueller and Aldon D. Morris, 351–73. New Haven: Yale University Press, 1992.

———. *The Scholar Denied: W. E. B. Du Bois and the Birth of American Sociology.* Berkeley: University of California Press, 2015.

Morrison, Toni. *Sula.* New York: Vintage Books, 1973.

Morse, David. *Motown and the Arrival of Black Music.* New York: Macmillan, 1971.

"Mos Def on Why He Left the U.S.: 'America's a Very Challenging Place for Me.'" *Radio.com. May 4, 2015.* http://radio.com/2015/05/04/mos-def-leaving-america-interview/.

Mouw, Ted. "Estimating the Causal Effect of Social Capital: A Review of Recent Research." *Annual Review of Sociology* 32 (2006): 79–102.

Moynihan, Daniel P. *The Negro Family: The Case for National Action.* Washington, DC: U.S. Government Printing Office, 1965.

Muhammad, Khalil Gibran. *The Condemnation of Blackness: Race, Crime, and the Making of Modern Urban America.* Cambridge, MA: Harvard University Press, 2011.

Murphy, Alexandra K. 2012. "'Litterers': How Objects of Physical Disorder Are Used to Construct Subjects of Social Disorder in a Suburb." *Annals of the American Academy of Political and Social Science* 642, no. 1 (1965): 210–27.

Mydral, Gunnar. *An American Dilemma*. New York: Harper and Brothers, 1944.

Nager, Larry. *Memphis Beat: The Lives and Times of America's Musical Crossroads*. New York: St. Martin's Press, 1998.

Neal, Mark Anthony. "Sold Out on Soul: The Corporate Annexation of Black Popular Music." *Popular Music and Society* 21, no. 3 (1997): 117–35.

———. *Songs in the Key of Black Life: A Rhythm and Blues Nation*. New York: Routledge, 2014.

———. *Soul Babies: Black Popular Culture and the Post-soul Aesthetic*. New York: Routledge, 2002.

Newman, Katherine. *No Shame in My Game: The Working Poor In the Inner City*. New York: Vintage Books, 1999.

———. "No Shame: The View from the Left Bank." *American Journal of Sociology* 107, no. 6 (2002): 1577–99.

Nixon, Makani Themba, and Nan Rubin. "Speaking for Ourselves: A Movement Led by People of Color Seeks Media Justice Not Just Media Reform." *Nation* 277, no. 16 (2003): 17–19.

Northup, Solomon. *Twelve Years a Slave*. New York: Norton, 2016.

"The Notorious B I G ft Puff Daddy and Lil Kim Live at Source Awards, 1995." YouTube video, 4:59. Posted by Pablo Granja. July 8, 2011. www.youtube .com/watch?v=zvA56qWhMME&list=RDzvA56qWhMME

Odum, Howard W. *Southern Regions of the United States*. Chapel Hill: University of North Carolina Press, 1936.

Oliver, Melvin L., and Thomas M. Shapiro. *Black Wealth/White Wealth: A New Perspective on Racial Inequality*. New York: Routledge, 1997.

Olney, James. "'I Was Born': Slave Narratives, Their Status as Autobiography and as Literature." *Callaloo* 20 (1984): 46–73.

Omi, Michael, and Howard Winant. *Racial Formation in the United States*. New York: Routledge, 2014.

"Outkast Winning Best New Rap Group at the Source Awards, 1995." YouTube video, 5:36. Posted by TheMaxTrailers. October 12, 2014, www.youtube.com /watch?v=vwLG7aSYM3w.

Pager, Devah. *Marked: Race, Crime, and Finding Work in an Era of Mass Incarceration*. Chicago: University of Chicago Press, 2008.

Papachristos, Andrew V., Tracey L. Meares, and Jeffrey Fagan. "Attention Felons: Evaluating Project Safe Neighborhoods in Chicago." *Journal of Empirical Legal Studies* 4, no. 2 (2007): 223–72.

Park, Robert E. "The City: Suggestions for the Investigation of Human Behavior in the City Environment." *American Journal of Sociology* 20, no. 5 (1915): 577–612.

Park, Robert, Ernest Burgess, and Roderick D. McKenzie, eds. *The City*. 2nd ed. Chicago: University of Chicago Press, 1924.

Parsons, Talcott. *The Structure of Social Action: A Study in Social Theory with Special Reference to a Group of Recent European Writers*. Vol. 1. New York: Free Press, 1968.

Patterson, David K. "Yellow Fever Epidemics and Mortality in the United States, 1693–1905." *Social Science and Medicine* 34, no. 8 (1992): 855–65.

Patterson, Orlando. *Rituals of Blood: Consequences of Slavery in Two American Centuries*. New York: Basic Civitas Books, 1998.

Pattillo, Mary. "Black Middle-Class Neighborhoods." *Annual Review of Sociology* 31 (2005): 305–29.

———. *Black on the Block: The Politics of Race and Class in the City*. Chicago: University of Chicago Press, 2007.

Pattillo, Mary, Bruce Western, and David Weiman, eds. *Imprisoning America: The Social Effects of Mass Incarceration*. New York: Sage Foundation, 2004.

Pattillo-McCoy, Mary. *Black Picket Fences: Privilege and Peril among the Black Middle Class*. Chicago: University of Chicago Press, 1999.

Pendergrass, Sabrina. "Perceptions of Race and Region in the Black Reverse Migration to the South." *Du Bois Review: Social Science Research on Race* 10, no. 1 (2013): 155–78.

Perkins, Douglas D., and Ralph B. Taylor. "Ecological Assessments of Community Disorder: Their Relationship to Fear of Crime and Theoretical Implications." *American Journal of Community Psychology* 24, no. 1 (1996): 63–107.

Perry, Imani. *Prophets of the Hood: Politics and Poetics in Hip Hop*. Durham: Duke University Press, 2004.

Peterson, Ruth D., and Lauren J. Krivo. *Divergent Social Worlds: Neighborhood Crime and the Racial-Spatial Divide*. New York: Sage Foundation, 2010.

———. "Racial Segregation and Black Urban Homicide." *Social Forces* 71, no. 4 (1993): 1001–26.

Peterson, Ruth D., Lauren J. Krivo, and Mark A. Harris. "Disadvantage and Neighborhood Violent Crime: Do Local Institutions Matter?" *Journal of Research in Crime and Delinquency* 37, no. 1 (2000): 31–63.

Pettit, Becky. *Invisible Men: Mass Incarceration and the Myth of Black Progress*. New York: Sage Foundation, 2012.

Piven, Frances Fox, and Richard A. Cloward. *Poor People's Movements: Why They Succeed, How They Fail*. New York: Pantheon Books, 1977.

"Police Beating a Trans Woman Who Was Later Murdered." YouTube video, 8:26. Posted by ehipassiko. November 24, 2008. www.youtube.com/watch?v=-IAPTk69XPo.

Powdermaker, Hortense. *After Freedom: A Cultural Study of the Deep South*. New York: Viking, 1939.

Preston, Michael B., Lenneal J. Henderson Jr., and Paul L. Puryear, eds. *The New Black Politics: The Search for Political Power.* 2nd ed. New York: Longman, 1987.

Price-Spratlen, Townsand. "Urban Destination Selection among African Americans during the 1950s Great Migration." *Social Science History,* 32 no. 3 (2008): 437–69.

Pulido, Laura. *Black, Brown, Yellow, and Left: Radical Activism in Los Angeles.* Berkeley: University of California Press, 2006.

Purifoy, Danielle. "Finding Independence in Mebane." *Scalawag,* August 15, 2016. www.scalawagmagazine.org/in-conditions-of-fresh-water/finding-black-independence-in-mebane.

Purifoy, Danielle, and Torkwase Johnson. "A Place Called Mebane." *Scalawag,* August 8, 2016. www.scalawagmagazine.org/in-conditions-of-fresh-water/a-place-called-mebane.

Raboteau, Albert J. *Slave Religion: The "Invisible Institution" in the Antebellum South.* New York: Oxford University Press, 1980.

Rainwater, Lee. *Behind Ghetto Walls: Black Families in a Federal Slum.* Chicago: Aldine, 1970.

Rakow, Lana F., ed. *Women Making Meaning: New Feminist Directions in Communication.* New York: Routledge, 2015.

Redmond, Shana. *Anthem: Social Movements and the Sound of Solidarity in the African Diaspora.* New York: New York University Press, 2013.

Reed, Adolph. *Race, Politics, and Culture.* New York: Greenwood, 1986.

———. "Romancing Jim Crow: Black Nostalgia for a Segregated Past." *Village Voice,* April 16, 1996.

———. *W.E.B. Du Bois and American Political Thought: Fabianism and the Color Line.* New York: Oxford University Press, 1997.

Reed, John S. *The Enduring South: Subcultural Persistence in Mass Society.* Chapel Hill: University of North Carolina Press, 1986.

———. *One South: An Ethnic Approach to Regional Culture.* Baton Rouge: Louisiana State University Press, 1982.

Rhodes, Jane. *Mary Ann Shadd Cary: The Black Press and Protest in the Nineteenth Century.* Urbana: University of Illinois Press, 1998.

Rhomberg, Chris. *The Broken Table: The Detroit Newspaper Strike and the State of American Labor.* New York: Sage Foundation, 2012.

———. *No There There: Race, Class and Political Community in Oakland.* Berkeley: University of California Press, 2004.

Richie, Beth. *Arrested Justice: Black Women, Violence, and America's Prison Nation.* New York: New York University Press, 2012.

Rios, Victor M. *Punished: Policing the Lives of Black and Latino Boys.* New York: New York University Press, 2011.

Roberts, Dorothy E. "The Social and Moral Cost of Mass Incarceration in African American Communities." *Stanford Law Review* 56, no. 5 (2004): 1271–305.

Robinson, Zandria Felice. "Beyonce's Black Southern Formation." *Rolling Stone,* February 8, 2016.

———. "How Beyonce's 'Lemonade' Exposes the Inner Lives of Black Women," *Rolling Stone,* April 28, 2016.

———. "Intersectionality." In *Handbook of Contemporary Sociological Theory,* edited by Seth Abrutyn, 477–99. New York: Springer International, 2016.

———. *This Ain't Chicago: Race, Class, and Regional Identity in the Post-soul South.* Chapel Hill: University of North Carolina Press, 2014.

Robnett, Belinda. *How Long? How Long? African-American Women in the Struggle for Civil Rights.* New York: Oxford University Press, 1997.

Rodney, Walter. *How Europe Underdeveloped Africa.* London: Bogle-L'Ouverture, 1972.

Rose, Tricia. *Black Noise: Rap Music and Black Culture in Contemporary America.* Middletown, CT: Wesleyan University Press, 1994.

Royster, Jacqueline Jones, ed. *Southern Horrors and Other Writings: The Anti-lynching Campaign of Ida B. Wells, 1892–1900.* Boston: Bedford Books, 1997.

———. "To Call a Thing by Its True Name: The Rhetoric of Ida B. Wells." *Reclaiming Rhetorica: Women in the Rhetorical Tradition,* no. 1 (1995): 167–84.

Ruble, Blair. *Washington's U-Street.* Baltimore: Johns Hopkins University Press, 2010.

Rushing, Wanda. *Memphis and the Paradox of Place: Globalization and the American South.* Chapel Hill: University of North Carolina Press, 2009.

Sampson, Robert J. *Great American City: Chicago and the Enduring Neighborhood Effect.* Chicago: University of Chicago Press, 2013.

Sampson, Robert J., Jeffrey D. Morenoff, and T. Gannon-Rowley. "Assessing 'Neighborhood Effects': Social Processes and New Directions in Research." *Annual Review of Sociology* 28 (2002): 443–78.

Sampson, Robert J., Stephen W. Raudenbush, and Felton Earls. "Neighborhoods and Violent Crime: A Multilevel Study of Collective Efficacy." *Science* 277 (1997): 918–24.

Santa Clara County Public Health Department. *2008–12 Death Database.* Accessed August 11, 2013. https://chhs.data.ca.gov/.

———. *Behavioral Risk Factor Survey.* San Jose, CA: Santa Clara County Public Health Department, 2009.

———. *Behavioral Risk Factor Survey.* San Jose, CA: Santa Clara County Public Health Department, 2013.

Sassen, Saskia. *Cities in a World Economy.* 2nd ed. New York: Pine Forge, 2000.

Schein, Richard H., ed. *Landscape and Race in the United States*. New York: Routledge, 2006.

Schnittker, Jason, and Andrea John, "Enduring Stigma: The Long-Term Effects of Incarceration on Health." *Journal of Health and Social Behavior* 48, no. 2 (2007): 115–30.

Scott, Allen J., and Edward W. Soja. *The City: Los Angeles and Urban Theory at the End of the Twentieth Century*. Berkeley: University of California Press, 1996.

Scott, James C. *Seeing Like a State: How Certain Schemes to Improve the Human Condition Have Failed*. New Haven, CT: Yale University Press, 1998.

———. *Weapons of the Weak: Everyday Forms of Peasant Resistance*. New Haven, CT: Yale University Press, 2008.

Scribner, Richard A., Deborah A. Cohen, and Thomas A. Farley. "A Geographic Relation between Alcohol Availability and Gonorrhea Rates." *Sexual Transmitted Disease* 25, no. 10 (1998): 544–48.

Select Bipartisan Committee to Investigate the Preparation for and Response to Hurricane Katrina. *A Failure of Initiative: Final Report of the Select Bipartisan Committee to Investigate the Preparation for and Response to Hurricane Katrina*. Vol. 109. No. 377. Washington, DC: U.S. Government Printing Office, 2006.

Seligman, Amanda. *Block by Block: Neighborhoods and Public Policy on Chicago's West Side*. Chicago: University of Chicago Press, 2005.

Shadd, Mary Ann. *A Plea for Emigration; or, Notes of Canada West, in Its Moral, Social, and Political Aspect: With Suggestions respecting Mexico, W. Indies and Vancouver's Island, for the Information of Colored Emigrants*. No. 47542. Detroit: Pattison, 1852.

Shakur, Afeni. "Lecture: Afeni Shakur Delivers Keynote Address of Vanderbilt University's Black History Month Commemoration." *Discover Archive*. February 9, 2007. http://discoverarchive.vanderbilt.edu/handle/1803/878.

———. "Tupac Amaru Shakur Foundation Mission Statement." Unpublished papers. Stone Mountain, CA, 2000.

Shakur, Tupac. *The Rose That Grew from Concrete*. New York: Simon and Schuster, 2009.

Shakur, Tupac, Afeni Shakur, Jacob Hoye, Karolyn Ali, and Walter Einenkel. *Tupac: Resurrection, 1971–1996*. New York: Simon and Schuster, 2003.

Shapiro, Susan P. "Agency Theory." *Annual Review of Sociology* 31 (2005): 263–84.

Sharkey, Patrick. *Stuck in Place: Urban Neighborhoods and the End of Progress toward Racial Equality*. Chicago: University of Chicago Press, 2013.

Sharkey, Patrick, and J. Farber. "Where, When, Why, and for Whom Do Residential Contexts Matter? Moving Away from the Dichotomous

Understanding of Neighborhood Effects." *Annual Review of Sociology* 40 (2014): 559–79.

Shaw, Rashida Z. "Insert [Chitlin Circuit] Here: Teaching an Inclusive African American Theatre Course." *Theatre Topics* 19, no. 1 (2009): 67–76.

Shedd, Carla. *Unequal City: Race, Schools, and Perceptions of Injustice.* New York: Sage Foundation, 2015.

Silver, Christopher, and John V. Moeser. *The Separate City: Black Communities in the Urban South, 1940–1968.* Lexington: University Press of Kentucky, 1995.

Singh, Nikhil. *Black Is a Country.* Cambridge, MA: Harvard University Press, 2004.

Sitkoff, Harvard, and Eric Foner. *The Struggle for Black Equality, 1954–1992.* New York: Macmillan, 1993.

Sledge, Matt "Bounce Star Big Freedia Pleads Guilty to Theft of Nearly $35k in Section 8 Housing Vouchers." *Advocate,* March 18, 2016.

Small, Mario Luis. "Is There Such a Thing as 'The Ghetto'? The Perils of Assuming That the South Side of Chicago Represents Poor Black Neighborhoods." *City* 11, no. 3 (2007): 413–21.

———. *Unanticipated Gains: Origins of Network Inequality in Everyday Life.* New York: Oxford University Press, 2009.

Small, Mario Luis, David J. Harding, and Michèle Lamont. "Introduction: Reconsidering Culture and Poverty." *Annals of the American Academy of Political and Social Science* 629 (2010): 6–27.

Small, Mario Luis, and Katherine Newman. "Urban Poverty after *The Truly Disadvantaged:* The Rediscovery of the Family, the Neighborhood, and Culture." *Annual Review of Sociology* 27 (2001): 23–45.

Smith, A. Wade, and Joan V. Moore, "East-West Differences in Black Economic Development." *Journal of Black Studies* 16, no. 2 (1985): 131–54.

Smith, Dorothy E. *The Everyday World as Problematic: A Feminist Sociology.* Toronto: University of Toronto Press, 1987.

Smith, Neil. "Neo-critical Geography; or, The Flat Pluralist World of Business Class." *Antipode* 37, no. 5 (2005): 887–99.

Smith, Suzanne E. *Dancing in the Street: Motown and the Cultural Politics of Detroit.* Cambridge, MA: Harvard University Press, 2009.

Soja, E. *Postmetropolis: Critical Studies of Cities and Regions.* Malden, MA: Blackwell, 2000.

Sonenshein, Raphael. *Politics in Black and White: Race and Power in Los Angeles.* Princeton: Princeton University Press, 1993.

Spear, Alan H. *Black Chicago: The Making of a Negro Ghetto, 1890–1920.* Chicago: University of Chicago Press, 1967.

Spillers, Hortense J. *Black, White, and in Color: Essays on American Literature and Culture.* Chicago: University of Chicago Press, 2003.

———. "Mama's Baby, Papa's Maybe: An American Grammar Book." *Diacritics* 17, no. 2 (1987): 65–81.

Squires, Gregory D., and Charis E. Kubrin. *Privileged Places: Race, Residence, and the Structure of Opportunity.* Boulder, CO: Rienner, 2006.

Stack, Carol B. *All Our Kin: Strategies for Survival in a Black Community.* New York: Harper and Row, 1974.

———. *Call to Home: African Americans Reclaim the Rural South.* New York: Basic Books, 1996.

Stanley, Jerry. *I Am an American: A True Story of Japanese Internment.* New York: Crown, 1994.

Staples, Robert, ed. *The Black Family: Essays and Studies.* Boston: Cengage Learning, 1999.

State of California Department of Finance. *State and County Population Projection, 2010–60.* Sacramento, CA: State of California Department of Finance, 2013.

State of California Department of Justice. *Crime Statistics and Demographics.* Sacramento, CA: Criminal Justice Statistics Center, 2012.

Stepto, Robert B. *From behind the Veil: A Study of Afro-American Narrative.* Urbana: University of Illinois Press, 1991.

Steptoe, Andrew, and Pamela J. Feldman. "Neighborhood Problems as Sources of Chronic Stress: Development of a Measure of Neighborhood Problems, and Associations with Socioeconomic Status and Health." *Annals of Behavioral Medicine* 23, no. 3 (2001): 177–85.

"Suge Knight Disses Puff Daddy." *Source Awards.* YouTube video, 1:04. Posted by Felix Montana. August 3, 1995. www.youtube.com/watch?v= mv2OMXngkEs.

Sugrue, Thomas J. "Affirmative Action from Below: Civil Rights, the Building Trades, and the Politics of Racial Equality in the Urban North, 1945–1969." *Journal of American History* 91, no. 1 (2004): 145–73.

———. *The Origins of the Urban Crisis: Race and Inequality in Postwar Detroit.* Princeton: Princeton University Press, 1996.

———. *Sweet Land of Liberty: The Forgotten Struggle for Civil Rights in the North.* New York: Random House, 2008.

Sullivan, Mercer L. *Getting Paid: Youth Crime and Work in the Inner City.* Ithaca: Cornell University Press, 1989.

Suttles, Gerald D. *The Social Order of the Slum: Ethnicity and Territory in the Inner City.* Chicago: University of Chicago Press, 1968.

Swain, Carol M. *Black Faces, Black Interests: The Representation of African Americans in Congress.* Cambridge, MA: Harvard University Press, 1995.

Tabb, William K., and Larry Sanders, eds. *Marxism and the Metropolis: New Perspectives in Urban Political Economy.* New York: Oxford University Press, 1984.

Tate, Katherine. *From Protest to Politics: The New Black Voters in American Elections*. New York: Sage Foundation, 1993.

Taylor, Charles. *Human Agency and Language: Philosophical Papers I*. New York: Cambridge University Press, 1985.

Telles, Edward M., and Vilma Ortiz. *Generations of Exclusion: Mexican-Americans, Assimilation, and Race*. New York: Sage Foundation, 2008.

Thomas, June Manning, and Marsha Ritzdorf, eds. *Urban Planning and the African American Community*. Thousand Oaks, CA: Sage, 1996.

Thomas, Lynnell L. *Desire and Disaster: Tourism, Race, and Historical Memory*. Durham: Duke University Press, 2014.

Thompson, J. Phillip, III. *Double Trouble: Black Mayors, Black Communities, and the Call for a Deep Democracy*. New York: Oxford University Press, 2006.

Tolnay, Stewart E. "The African American 'Great Migration' and Beyond." *Annual Review of Sociology* 29 (2003): 209–32.

———. "Black Competition and White Vengeance: Legal Execution of Blacks as Social Control in the Cotton South, 1890 to 1929." *Social Science Quarterly* 73, no. 3 (1992): 627–44.

———. "Educational Selection in the Migration of Southern Blacks, 1880–1990." *Social Forces* 77, no. 2 (1998): 487–514.

Tolnay, Stewart E., and E. M. Beck. "Black Flight: Lethal Violence and the Great Migration, 1900–1930." *Social Science History* 14, no. 3 (1990): 347–70.

———. "Racial Violence and Black Migration in the American South, 1910 to 1930." *American Sociological Review* 57, no. 1 (1992): 103–16.

Trotter, Joe William. *Black Milwaukee: The Making of an Industrial Proletariat, 1915–45*. Urbana: University of Illinois Press, 1985.

———. *The Great Migration in Historical Perspective: New Dimensions of Race, Class, and Gender*. Bloomington: Indiana University Press, 1991.

Tuch, Steven, and Jack K. Martin. "Regional Differences in Whites' Racial Policy Attitudes." In *Racial Attitudes in the 1990s: Continuity and Change*, edited by Steven Tuch and Jack K. Martin, 165–74. Westport, CT: Greenwood, 1997.

"Tupac: The Lost Interview." *Vibe*. YouTube video, 24:17. Posted by TheDarkAssassins1511. October 14, 2013. www.youtube.com/watch?v=NPP3Up4pdVE.

Turner, Patricia A. *I Heard It through the Grapevine: Rumor in African-American Culture*. Berkeley: University of California Press, 1993.

U.S. Census Bureau. *American Community Survey: 1-Year Estimates*. Washington, DC: U.S. Government Printing Office, 2012.

Van Cleve, Nicole Gonzalez. *Crook County: Racism and Injustice in America's Largest Criminal Court*. Palo Alto: Stanford University Press, 2016.

Vaz, Kim Marie. *The "Baby Dolls": Breaking the Race and Gender Barriers of the New Orleans Mardi Gras Tradition.* Baton Rouge: Louisiana State University Press, 2013.

Venkatesh, Sudhir Alladi. *American Project: The Rise and Fall of a Modern Ghetto.* Cambridge, MA: Harvard University Press, 2000.

———. *Off the Books: The Underground Economy of the Urban Poor.* Cambridge, MA: Harvard University Press, 2006.

Virginia Legislature. *Hathi Trust Digital Library.* Accessed September 20, 2016. https://babel.hathitrust.org/cgi/pt?id=njp.32101073363291;view=1up; seq=252.

"VLOG: Throw Back Thursday //Twerking in the Supermarket." YouTube video, 8:32. Posted by GrowWithNiki Gaga. December 3, 2015. www.youtube.com /watch?v=T7DHSzLGCgY.

Wacquant, Loïc. "The Curious Eclipse of Prison Ethnography in the Age of Mass Incarceration." *Ethnography* 3, no. 4 (2002): 371–97.

———. "Deadly Symbiosis When Ghetto and Prison Meet and Mesh." *Punishment and Society* 3, no. 1 (2001): 95–133.

———. "The Penalisation of Poverty and the Rise of Neo-liberalism." *European Journal on Criminal Policy and Research* 9, no. 4 (2001): 401–12.

———. "Scrutinizing the Street: Poverty, Morality, and the Pitfalls of Urban Ethnography." *American Journal of Sociology* 107, no. 6 (2002): 1468–532.

Wailoo, Keith. *Drawing Blood: Technology and Disease Identity in Twentieth-Century America.* Baltimore: Johns Hopkins University Press, 1999.

———. *Dying in the City of the Blues: Sickle Cell Anemia and the Politics of Race and Health.* Chapel Hill: University of North Carolina Press, 2014.

Wakefield, Sara, and Christopher Wildeman. *Children of the Prison Boom: Mass Incarceration and the Future of American Inequality.* New York: Oxford University Press, 2014.

Walcott, Rinaldo. *Black Like Who? Writing Black Canada.* Toronto: Insomniac, 2003.

———. "Caribbean Pop Culture in Canada; or, The Impossibility of Belonging to the Nation." *Small Axe* 5, no. 1 (2001): 123–39.

———. "Homopoetics: Queer Space and the Black Queer Diaspora." In McKittrick and Woods, *Black Geographies,* 233–45.

———. "Lament for a Nation: The Racial Geography of the Oh! Canada Project." *Fuse Magazine* 19 (1996): 15–23.

———. *Performing the Postmodern: Black Atlantic Rap and Identity in North America.* Toronto: University of Toronto, 1996.

———. "'A Tough Geography': Towards a Poetics of Black Space(s) in Canada." In *Unhomely States: Theorizing English-Canadian Postcolonialism,* edited by Cynthia Sugars, 277–88. Peterborough, Ontario: Broadview, 2004.

————. "'Who Is She and What Is She to You?' Mary Ann Shadd Cary and the (Im)possibility of Black/Canadian Studies." *Atlantis: Critical Studies in Gender, Culture and Social Justice* 24, no. 2 (2000): 137–46.

Walker, Lewis. *Black Eden: The Idlewild Community.* Jackson: Mississippi State University Press, 2002.

Walton, John. "Urban Sociology: Contributions and Limits of Political Economy." *Annual Review of Sociology* 19 (1993): 301–20.

Warwick, Dionne. "Do You Know the Way to San Jose." *Dionne Warwick in Valley of the Dolls.* New York: Scepter Records, 1968.

Waters, Mary. *Black Identities.* New York: Sage Foundation, 1999.

Weber, Max. *Economy and Society: An Outline of Interpretive Sociology.* Berkeley: University of California Press, 1978.

————. *The Protestant Ethic and the Spirit of Capitalism.* New York: Routledge, 2002.

————. *The Theory of Social and Economic Organization.* New York: Free Press, 1964.

Welch, Michael Patrick, Brian Boyles, Zack Smith, and Jonathan Traviesa. *New Orleans: The Underground Guide.* Baton Rouge: Louisiana State University Press, 2014.

Wellman, Barry. "The Community Question: Intimate Networks of East New Yorkers." *American Journal of Sociology* 84, no. 5 (1979): 1201–21.

————, ed. *Networks in the Global Village: Life in Contemporary Communities.* Boulder, CO: Westview, 1999.

Wellman, Barry, and Barry Leighton. "Networks, Neighborhoods, and Communities: Approaches to the Study of the Community Question." *Urban Affairs Quarterly* 14, no. 3 (1979): 363–90.

Wells, Ida B. *Crusade for Justice: The Autobiography of Ida B. Wells.* Chicago: University of Chicago Press, 2013.

Wells-Barnett, Ida B. *Southern Horrors: Lynch Law in All Its Phases.* New York: New York Age Print, 1892–94.

Western, Bruce, and Christopher Wildeman. "The Black Family and Mass Incarceration." *Annals of the American Academy of Political and Social Science* 621, no. 1 (2009): 221–42.

Wheatle, Alex. *The Dirty South.* London: Serpent's Tale Books, 2008.

White, Deborah Gray. *Ar'n't I a Woman? Female Slaves in the Plantation South.* New York: Norton, 1999.

Whyte, William Foote. *Street Corner Society.* Chicago: University of Chicago Press, 1955.

Wiese, Andrew. *Places of Their Own: African American Suburbanization in the Twentieth Century.* Chicago: University of Chicago Press, 2005.

Wildeman, Christopher. "Parental Incarceration, Child Homelessness, and the Invisible Consequences of Mass Imprisonment." *Annals of the American Academy of Political and Social Science* 651, no. 1 (2014): 74–96.

Wilkerson, Isabel. *The Warmth of Other Suns: The Epic Story of America's Great Migration.* New York: Vintage Books, 2011.

Wilson, William Julius. *The Declining Significance of Race.* Chicago: University of Chicago Press, 1978.

———. *Power, Racism and Privilege Race Relations in Theoretical and Sociohistorical Perspectives.* New York: Macmillan, 1973.

———. "Studying Inner-City Social Dislocations: The Challenge of Public Agenda Research: 1990 Presidential Address." *American Sociological Review* 56, no. 1 (1991): 1–14.

———. *The Truly Disadvantaged: The Inner City, the Underclass, and Public Policy.* Chicago: University of Chicago Press, 1987.

———. *When Work Disappears: The World of the New Urban Poor.* New York: Knopf, 1996.

———. "Why Both Social Structure and Culture Matter in a Holistic Analysis of Inner-City Poverty." *Annals of the American Academy of Political and Social Science* 629 (2010): 200–219.

Wilson, William Julius, and Robert Aponte. "Urban Poverty." *Annual Review of Sociology* 11 (1985): 231–58.

Wilson, William Julius, and Richard P. Taub. *There Goes the Neighborhood.* New York: Vintage, 2006.

Wirth, Louis. "Urbanism as a Way of Life." *American Journal of Sociology* 44, no. 1 (1938): 1–24.

Woldoff, Rachael A. *White Flight/Black Flight: The Dynamics of Racial Change in an American Neighborhood.* Ithaca: Cornell University Press, 2011.

Wood, Marcus. *Blind Memory: Visual Representations of Slavery in England and America, 1780–1865.* Manchester: Manchester University Press, 2000.

Woods, Clyde. *Development Arrested: Race, Power and the Blues in the Mississippi Delta.* New York: Verso, 1998.

"'The World Is My Country': Shows Origin of Yasiin Bey's World Passport." Vimeo video, 8:37. Posted by Arthur Kanegis. Accessed September 20, 2016. https://vimeo.com/153306229.

Wright, Richard. *Black Boy: A Record of Childhood and Youth.* New York: Random House, 2000.

———. *Native Son.* New York: Random House, 2000.

Yanuck, Julius. "The Garner Fugitive Slave Case." *Mississippi Valley Historical Review* (1953): 47–66.

Yee, Shirley J. *Black Women Abolitionists: A Study in Activism, 1828–1860.* Knoxville: University of Tennessee Press, 1992.

———. "Finding a Place: Mary Ann Shadd Cary and the Dilemmas of Black Migration to Canada, 1850–1870." *Frontiers: A Journal of Women Studies* 18, no. 3 (1997): 1–16.

X, Malcolm. *The Autobiography of Malcolm X*. With Alex Haley. New York: Ballantine Books, 1989.

———. "The Ballot or the Bullet." *All Time Greatest Speeches*. Vol. 2. New York: Master Classics Records, Sony Music Entertainment, 2009.

Zerilli, Linda M. G. *Feminism and the Abyss of Freedom*. Chicago: University of Chicago Press, 2005.

Zuberi, Tukufu, and Eduardo Bonilla-Silva, eds. *White Logic, White Methods: Racism and Methodology*. New York: Rowman and Littlefield, 2008.

Index